WILLIAM BLAKE ON SELF AND SOUL

WILLIAM BLAKE
ON SELF AND SOUL

LAURA QUINNEY

HARVARD UNIVERSITY PRESS
Cambridge, Massachusetts, and London, England 2009

Printed in the United States of America

Library of Congress Cataloging-in-Publication Data

Quinney, Laura.
William Blake on self and soul / Laura Quinney.
p.   cm.
Includes bibliographical references and index.
ISBN 978-0-674-03524-9
1. Blake, William, 1757–1827—Knowledge—Psychology. 2. Self in literature.
3. Identity (Psychology) in literature. 4. Subjectivity in literature. I. Title.
PR4148.P8Q85 2009
821′.7—dc22   2009011507

For Billy, Daniel, and Julian

The axis of reality runs through the egotistic places.
—William James, *The Varieties of Religious Experience*

For a Tear is an Intellectual thing.
—William Blake, *Jerusalem*

Contents

Preface   *xi*

Acknowledgments   *xv*

A Note on Citation   *xvii*

Introduction: The Impossible Self   1

1. Empiricism and Despair   27

2. Wordsworth, Plato, and Blake   66

3. *The Four Zoas:* Transcendental Remorse   90

4. *Milton:* The Guarded Gates   125

5. *Jerusalem:* The Will to Solitude   155

Notes   *179*

Bibliography   *183*

Index   *189*

Preface

It has always been clear that William Blake was both a political radical and a radical psychologist. The most illuminating interpretations of Blake—by Northrop Frye, Harold Bloom, Brian Wilkie, and Mary Lynn Johnson, to name a few—emphasize his subtlety and innovation in the understanding of human psychology. This book addresses what Blake said about a specific aspect of psychology—a reflexive aspect, deeper and stranger in itself than thought and feeling—the subject's experience of its own interiority. What is the self's relation to itself? Blake thought that under certain conditions, it was bound to be anxious and lonely. That is, he thought that if the self is identified with the main consciousness or "I," especially the "I" as a center of rationality, it will feel solitary and insecure. The greater its insecurity, the more it tries to swell into a false but mighty "Selfhood." And the larger the Selfhood bulks, the lonelier it grows. As Peter Otto rightly characterizes it, "Fallen existence is a world in which one isolated self is pitted against another" (19). But why is that so? How does the illusion of Selfhood arise? What damage does it do? Why does the subject cling to it? How can one break its hold? This fundamental inquiry spurs Blake's development and leads him to some of his most original thinking.

In this book I attempt to show that Blake's psychology of subjectivity is astute, innovative, and complex, to demonstrate that it was a pivotal inquiry he pursued and evolved over the whole course of his writing career, and to suggest that he was prompted in part by self-examination, analyzing and endeavoring to overcome his own loneliness and despair. In his study of the self's struggle with itself lies the deeper motive of Blake's polemic against the thinking of his contemporaries, namely, empiricism, the philosophy of the Enlightenment and the New Science. Blake's hostility to these movements represents not merely a poet's defense of "Imagination" and "Vision" but also a penetrating psychological critique: Blake sees these ideas as affecting the subject's self-description. They promote passivity and despair by belittling the subject, and exacerbate the subject's self-division by denying its immortal longings. In Blake's epic psychomachia *The Four Zoas,* he has one of his characters voice the anguished self-confusion of Lockean man: "I am like an atom / A Nothing left in darkness yet I am an identity." This character, Tharmas, understands that as a *merely* natural being, he is *merely* a node of solitary consciousness, yet from within the intuition presses on him that he is something grander and more significant, a special being, an "identity." The demystifying science of empiricism deepens the self's incoherence to itself. Blake responds by formulating a therapy for the bewilderment of the self. But as he goes on he perceives greater and greater obstacles—in its very nature—to the remaking of subjectivity.

Blake believed one could behold the traumatic nature of empiricist selfhood in the earlier poems of William Wordsworth. The uneasy self of Wordsworth's poetry exemplifies the sorrows of Natural Man. Blake and Wordsworth had emerged out of an intellectual culture dominated by John Locke, but whereas Blake reacted by rejecting received opinion, Wordsworth molded empiricism to his own ends. In Wordsworth's poetry of the 1790s, he adapted the terms of empiricism creatively in order to elaborate his intuitions about the hauntedness of the interior life. Later, Wordsworth borrowed an antithetical model of the mind from Plato and Immanuel Kant without ever giving up his sense that the interior is divided and self-puzzling. Wordsworth's legacy shows what Blake was up against. In the high Romantic tradition, Wordsworth, with his theme of the atomic self and its depressive anxieties, prevailed: Samuel Taylor Coleridge, in essence, shared Wordsworth's views and the younger Romantics take after them. The troubled lyric "I" of Romantic and post-Romantic poetry owes a great deal to the empiricist representation of the self—or so Blake would argue. He wrote an incisive critique of this tradition before it got fully underway.

In his effort to counter baleful empiricist notions, Blake became interested in the alternative offered by Platonic transcendentalism, particularly as it metamorphosed into the heterodox religions of Gnosticism and Neoplatonism. Both characterize the soul as an "acosmic" entity, not belonging to this world, but having a true home in a transcendental realm. The transcendental realm is anonymous or unknowable, yet it is present in the innermost soul, here and now. These ancient religious philosophies accept the soul's loneliness but offer remedies, and their remedies do not depend, as orthodox Christianity does, on subjecting the soul to an ambiguous anthropomorphized God, with his system of deferred rewards and punishments. This approach appeals to Blake who collapses all spiritual hierarchy, finding godliness in the "Great Humanity Devine," in which the soul participates and by which it gains access to "the Eternal Now." Blake has faults to find with both Neoplatonism and Gnosticism (and he tends to ignore their differences), but he approves of their argument that the cure for the soul's loneliness is to be found within itself—in the recognition and assertion of its transcendental provenance, that is to say, its integrity and freedom, and its share in Eternity.

Of course Blake is not content to reprise another man's system. He probes all of these philosophies and subjects them to an original psychological analysis. Many books and articles have been written about Blake's use of Gnosticism and Neoplatonism. Some have focused on showing a straightforward pattern of influence and have, therefore, limited themselves to tracing out what they present as Blake's more or less wholesale "borrowings" from earlier tradition. This is particularly true of pioneering works such as those of Kathleen Raine and George Mills Harper, written in the middle of the twentieth century. Only a handful of more recent works on Blake and Gnosticism have taken a similar tack (e.g., Peter J. Sorenson). Other studies touch in passing on Blake's relationship with Gnosticism or Neoplatonism, often noting that he has adapted rather than simply borrowed from these sources (e.g., Mary Hall, Morton D. Paley, and Thomas Altizer). I seek to investigate why Blake was interested in such ideas to begin with, and why he felt compelled to revise them. In every case, it is the representation of subjectivity to which he is alert. Blake analyzes the psychology implicit in the philosophical doctrine and evaluates it, perceiving that under the names of empiricism and Platonism, Gnosticism and Neoplatonism, certain experiences of selfhood have been codified, and that those codes have a self-ratifying effect. Eventually

Blake tries out his own therapeutic formulations. This project draws him into deeper and deeper, more and more detailed study of the psychology of what he calls "Natural Man," or, as I shall term it, "the empiricist subject." Yet none of Blake's solutions is as plain as his decisive rhetoric might lead us to suppose. Over time, he perceived ever larger obstacles to the psychological salvation he was at work devising.

The book discusses Blake's works in chronological order in order to follow the growth of his ideas about subjectivity. Chapters 1 and 2 explore Blake's basic paradigm, beginning with a general introduction to his critique of empiricism, focusing on the study of his major long poems of the 1780s and 1790s, then offering a contrast of his views with those of Wordsworth. Chapters 3, 4, and 5 take up the epic prophecies, the poems in which Blake is vitally amplifying and transforming his first ideas. For Blake seems to have inquired into the experience of interiority most intently during the time when he was writing the Urizen books *Milton* and *The Four Zoas*. It was a decade of rapid and exciting discovery. I strive to capture the momentum of Blake's unfolding speculation.

My argument treats as synonymous a number of terms that are distinguished within and between different disciplines: ego, self, inner life, phenomenal self, empirical self, central consciousness. Blake did not use any of these terms nor do the words that he did use overlap with these exactly. Yet one must employ them in order to translate his ideas out of his idiosyncratic vocabulary. I use the word that seems best to render his meaning in a given context. This book is sympathetically and passionately written, not because I share all of Blake's ideas, but because I think that their forcefulness is part of their meaning, and to convey their meaning I had to muster as much of their force as I could.

Acknowledgments

It took a long time to write this book. Along the way many people gave me help and encouragement for which I gladly thank them here: Harold Bloom, Thomas Brennan, Marshall Brown, John Burt, Stanley Cavell, Lorna Clymer, Leopold Damrosch, Erin Erhart, Frances Ferguson, Melissa Franklin, Paul Fry, Marilyn Gaull, Hannah Ginsborg, Deborah Gordon, Dr. Stacey Gore, Moshe Halbertal, Nicholas Halpern, Geoffrey Hartman, Neil Hertz, Ann Hochschild, Emily Bernard Jackson, Yoon Lee, Robin Miller, Jeff Nunokawa, Leah Price, Christopher Pye, Marc Redfield, Thomas Reinert, James Schwartz, Paul Solman, Karen Swann, and Daniel Warren. I am grateful for all their kindness to my parents-in-law, Alma and Stephen Flesch, and to my father, Richard, and my sister, Anne. Those who endured the most while I was writing the manuscript are my husband and sons, to whom the book is dedicated.

The earliest writing I did for this project was published as "Escape from Repetition: Blake versus Locke and Wordsworth," in *Ritual, Routine, and Regime: Repetition in Early Modern British and European Cultures* (Toronto: Univ. of Toronto Press, 2006). A portion of my chapter on "Wordsworth, Plato, and Blake" appeared originally under the title "Wordsworth's Ghosts and the Model of the Mind," in *European Romantic Review*, 9:2 (Spring 1998), 293-300. Another portion appeared as "Swerving Neoplatonists" in *The Wordsworth Circle* 37:1 (Winter 2006), 31-38. That portion is published here in a revised form. I thank both journals for permission to reprint material from my articles.

A Note on Citation

All citations of Blake's poetry refer to *The Complete Poetry and Prose of William Blake*, 2nd edition, edited by David Erdman, with commentary by Harold Bloom (Berkeley: Univ. of California Press, 1982). Citations are provided in parentheses after the quotation. Short poems, annotations, and prose are cited by page number in the Erdman edition, abbreviated as "E." Poems with plates are cited by plate and line number, followed by the Erdman page number. Quotations from *The Four Zoas,* which has pages instead of plates, are cited by page and line number. Blake's titles are abbreviated as follows:

Amer	*America*
BA	*The Book of Ahania*
BL	*The Book of Los*
BU	*The [First] Book of Urizen*
Eur	*Europe*
FZ	*The Four Zoas*
J	*Jerusalem*
M	*Milton*
MHH	*The Marriage of Heaven and Hell*
Thel	*The Book of Thel*
Tir	*Tiriel*
TNNR b	*"There Is No Natural Religion b"*
VDA	*Visions of the Daughters of Albion*

WILLIAM BLAKE ON SELF AND SOUL

Introduction:
The Impossible Self

In one sense the self is thriving. Magisterial works such as Charles Taylor's *The Sources of the Self* and Jerrold Siegel's *The Idea of the Self,* as well as the plethora of other recent titles on the self testify to the current fascination of the topic. Yet it is a widespread assumption among contemporary philosophers and literary theorists that the concept of "the self" is obsolete. At the end of their recent book, *The Rise and Fall of Self and Soul,* Raymond Martin and John Barresi conclude that the notion of the self as a "unified entity" has been permanently debunked by modern science and philosophy: "Analysis has been the self's undoing. As a fragmented, explained, and illusory phenomenon, the self [can] no longer retain its elevated status. And it is hard to see how it might ever again regain that status. It is as if all of Western civilization has been on a prolonged ego trip that reality has finally forced it to abandon" (304–5).

Seventeenth- and eighteenth-century science did away with the concept of the "soul," and the eighteenth century replaced it with the concept of "self," but the march of progress liquidated that notion too, along with the related idea of the universal "subject." Thus much contemporary thought dismisses the discourses of soul, self, and subject as anachronisms. This common view is, I believe, malformed because it entails dismissing the actual *experience* of subjectivity, that is, the subject's experience of itself *as a subject*. The self supposed to be obsolete is the unitary subject, the integral, transcendent self linked to the traditional religious idea of the immortal soul. I state categorically that the actual subject has never mistaken itself for a Subject of this kind. Modern skeptical thought congratulates itself for a work of demystification that the subject by virtue of its subjectivity performs every day.

Martin and Barresi concede that this "ego trip" is likely to go on despite our putative enlightenment: the idea of a unified self is not dispensable because many everyday practices depend on it. More deeply, the individual has an intuition of selfhood so strong that it cannot be summarily dispelled: "each of us seems to have a kind of direct, experiential access to him- or herself [a Cartesian intuition] that makes the development of theories of the self and personal identity, however interesting, seem somewhat beside the point" (302). The intuition of selfhood is tenacious; it rides roughshod over the rational truth. As is often the case, we are enlightened in theory but benighted in practice: "For many central and persistent purposes of everyday life, theory and practice are likely to remain autonomous, at least when it comes to theories of the self" (303). But does the everyday self really live with itself so naively and happily? Here Martin and Barresi make a mistake characteristic of those who treat the concepts of self and soul in the abstract: they fail to inquire further into the self's own relationship to the idea of selfhood. For whereas the intuition of selfhood persists within the self, it also is already embattled within the self.

If the intuition of selfhood attends Western subjectivity, then so does its frustration. Subject-life entails interior struggle and disappointment because the actual "self" fails to coincide with its own self-definition. Even to speak of "the self" or "subject" here is a misnomer: we must say that an elusive and as-yet-ununified "self" feels an imperative to find in itself a "Self" worthy of the name and that the imperative never desists, although such a Self cannot be found. The self does not possess its intuition of selfhood in comfort—it does not fall back on a reassuring confidence in its integrity, but rather seeks for such confidence in vain; it seeks wholeness, but encounters self-division and self-doubt. Disillusionment with "the self" that contemporary thinkers attribute to modernity actually *defines* the experience of selfhood. When Jacques Lacan deconstructs the Cartesian cogito and demonstrates that "I" is not self-coincident, he may scandalize the theorist, but the subject is likely to assent because Lacan's claim captures the felt insecurity of selfhood. The "error" of René Descartes's philosophical idealism cannot be sustained, Lacan says, for "There is no subject without, somewhere, *aphanisis* [fading, disappearance] of the subject, and it is in this alienation, in this fundamental division, that the dialectic of the subject is established" (221). The rhetorical power of Lacan's argument lies in its appeal to the experience of subjectivity. Whatever the ontological truth of the matter, to be a subject is to feel that such a description of subjectivity is true. The *language* of "self" and "subject" may have been rendered atavistic, but the *concepts* can never lose their hold on the individual subject, because subjectivity is constituted in its balked relation to them.

In fact, the intuition of selfhood has always been perplexed in theory as well as in practice. Western philosophy and literature have borne witness since the time of Greek mythology to the fragmentation of the self. This sense of fragmentation has given rise to the many fascinating paradigms of self-division: everything from Plato's tripartite division of the soul to Gnosticism's evocation of the "incrusted" transcendental spirit, Augustine's description of the "darkness hidden within" him, Descartes's dualism, and Kant's faculty psychology, to Sigmund Freud's map of the psyche and Melanie Klein's kaleidoscopic "inner chaos." Radically dissimilar as these paradigms of self-division and their provenances are, they all emphasize the confusion of the self in relation to its own selfhood. They begin by treating the self's embattled experience of itself as a central fact that cries out for explanation. And the fact is sufficiently central that its explanation opens a window on expansive metaphysical views. It becomes the pivot of far-reaching claims. The self's experience of itself as fragmented testifies to larger truths about human nature and sometimes divine nature and the nature of reality. Each theory offers up this feature of subjective experience as a validation of particular ontological truths. Why must reason struggle with emotion and appetite? Because reason is the highest faculty of the soul; it is confirmation of the soul's origin in the intelligible world. Why is the transcendental soul benighted in the world? Because it fell from heaven, and was waylaid here by an evil god. Why is there darkness hidden within? Because of the human soul's inherent perversity. Why is the ego beleaguered? It is menaced by insubordinate repressed energies.

The beauty of these claims is that evidence of their truth becomes available to everyone through the simplest act of introspection. Common experience of selfhood is the proof, as Socrates shows in the *Phaedo* when he disputes the definition of the soul as a "harmony." The soul is a harmony neither in our experience of the inner life nor in the literary representation of it. (The tripartite division of the soul appears in the *Phaedrus;* in this passage, "soul" is a unitary faculty but selfhood is divided.)

> We previously agreed that if the soul were a harmony, it would never be out of tune with the stress and relaxation and the striking of the strings or anything else done to its composing elements, but that it would follow and never direct them?
>
> We did so agree, of course.
>
> Well, does it now appear to do quite the opposite, ruling over all the elements of which one says it is composed, opposing nearly all of them throughout life, directing all their ways, inflicting harsh and painful punishments on them, at times in physical culture and medicine, at other times more gently by threats and exhortations, holding converse with desires and passions and fears as if it were one thing talking to a different one, as Homer wrote somewhere in the *Odyssey* where he says that Odysseus "struck his breast and rebuked his heart saying, 'Endure, my heart, you have endured worse than this.'"
>
> (94 c–d, *Complete Works* 82)

The soul must discipline the wayward passions and appetites, and the result is frequent internal conflict. This internal conflict, a basic fact of psychological experience, is offered as evidence for the soul's sovereignty and then, in a leap, of its divinity and immortality. Strikingly, it is not the soul's conviction of its own transcendence but rather the persistence and strength of inner conflict that proves it is transcendent. The self's fraught experience of itself testifies to major metaphysical realities. It is a surety that, like Platonic recollection, lies in every heart as intimate and indubitable truth.

From the point of view of science, the authoritative discourse of our own time, the self's experience of itself has lost its hold on truth-value. Since the eighteenth century, the evidentiary value of introspection has come under grave suspicion. The story of how and why this change occurred is incisively told by E. S. Reed in his book *From Soul to Mind: The Emergence of Psychology from Erasmus Darwin to William James*. Developments in eighteenth-century thought cast doubt on the significance of the subject's testimony as to its own state. The tradition of British empiricism in particular taught investigators to treat the witness of consciousness with suspicion: Humean skepticism introduced the idea that consciousness may be self-deceiving, and Hartleian associationism argued that it is shaped by unconscious processes of which, by definition, it has no knowledge. The subject's experience of itself was thus radically demoted in testamentary status and the study of it banished to "unscientific" discourses: philosophy (primarily phenomenology), religion, literature, and "humanistic" psychology. In Reed's view, the chief casualty of this disciplinary divide is respect for "concrete, lived experience" (220), now treated by science as an amorphous and incidental phenomenon unavailable to analysis. Reed concludes severely that scientific psychology has thus rendered itself irrelevant: "Once the science of psychology arrogates the right to reject out of hand the content of a person's experience—because it is too inchoate, mystical, or whatever—it can no longer pronounce on the meaning of that experience. Psychology in its present divided state applies at best intermittently and incompletely to the lives most of us lead." Reed warns that as a consequence, a void appears where authoritative response to ordinary inner struggle should be. Scientific psychology abandons "the important territory connecting everyday experience with meaningful self-understanding" to the seductive manipulation of demagogues and fanatics (220).

According to Reed, the last scientific psychologist to try to bridge the gap was William James, who in his view resisted the subdivision of disciplines and maintained the value of investigating "a wider realm of experience" (220) than his contemporaries. James insisted not only on taking the experience of consciousness seriously but also on treating it as a subject about which science ought to find something useful to say. James wrote a deft argumentative sally that Reed does not cite but that clearly supports his view of James. It occurs in *The Varieties of Religious Experience*, at a moment when James is questioning the scientific ideal of objectivity.

> It is absurd for science to say that the egotistic elements of experience should be suppressed. The axis of reality runs solely through

the egotistic places,—they are strung upon it like so many beads. To describe the world with all the various feelings of the individual pinch of destiny, all the various spiritual attitudes, left out from the description—they being describable as anything else— would be something like offering a printed bill of fare as the equivalent for a solid meal. Religion makes no such blunder. The individual's religion may be egotistic, and those private realities which it keeps in touch with may be narrow enough; but at any rate it always remains infinitely less hollow and abstract, as far as it goes, than a science which prides itself on taking no account of anything private at all. (499–500)

Much as I delight in James's polemical vigor, I cannot pretend I know enough to evaluate his comments on the limitations of scientific psychology. But neither do I think it is his aim to endorse "religion." James points out that, when it comes to addressing "private" experience, there is a very strict division of labor between "scientific" and "unscientific" discourses. His polemicism enters in when he adds that supercilious disregard of subjective experience leads to a certain irrelevance. I quote this passage because I wish to draw an analogy between what James and Reed see as the neglect of lived psychological experience in scientific psychology and the suspicion of "the self" in much current literary discussion. Martin and Barresi in "Paradise Lost," their chapter on twentieth-century challenges to the discourse of the self, name as demystification's major figures Ferdinand de Saussure, Jacques Lacan, Michel Foucault, and Jacques Derrida, the thinkers most influential for current literary study. In fact, neither Lacan nor Derrida scotched the topic of the self; they adduce the bafflements of the self's desire for masterful selfhood with some degree of sympathy. More clearly influential for this particular species of demystification is the received Foucault, the poststructuralist sloganeer who coined the catch phrase "the subject is dead." (I will return further on to a subtler, deeper Foucault.) The dogmatic reception of these thinkers has promoted wholesale disdain for psychological discourse. This disdain sometimes reaches the level of unthinking caricature. The trend is so common that I hardly know where to begin citing instances of it. Consider this example, chosen at random from an undergraduate textbook on literary criticism. Catherine Belsey opens her essay "Literature, History, Politics" with a mocking portrait of the literary psychological subject: "The sole inhabitant of the universe of literature is Eternal Man (and the masculine form is appropriate), whose brooding, feeling presence precedes, determines and transcends history" (428). Belsey reflexively, and symptomatically, conflates attention to subject-life with sexism, ahistoricism, and gross metaphysical illusion. (The strangely, unintentionally Blakean phrase "Eternal Man" gives one pause because it would have so radically different a resonance in his poetry.) The assumption seems to be that analyzing the experience of selfhood automatically means endorsing a bogus concept of Self. But that is the very concept perpetually under siege in ordinary psychological experience. The Self is always with us, already undermined, but there can be no progress in understanding its problematic relation to the actual experience of selfhood if the very discourse is declared taboo. Both James and Reed describe with admirable clarity the distortion that results from fixed inattention to subjective experience. It is ironic that literary study should have come to join in this neglect because subjective experience has since the Enlightenment increasingly become the province of literature and of other discourses dismissed as "merely" literary (such as psychoanalysis). Many literary texts have devoted themselves to dramatizing the experience of interior schism and struggle that science, the most authoritative discourse of our day, refuses to address. Yet a good deal of literary criticism now also refuses to address it.

As Socrates's citation from the *Odyssey* suggests, Western literature has always paid attention to the self's experience of itself and, particularly, to its experience of its own disunity. Yet literary treatment of these topics seems to accelerate from the late eighteenth century onward, and any number of compelling examples could be adduced from Romantic, Victorian, and Modernist novels and poetry. To give a smattering, consider the representation of the subject divided against itself or puzzled by its own nature in such canonical works as Samuel Taylor Coleridge's "Dejection," George Eliot's *The Mill on the Floss*, Alfred Lord Tennyson's *In Memoriam*, Virginia Woolf's *Mrs. Dalloway*, and T. S. Eliot's "The Love Song of J. Alfred Prufrock." The popularity of these topics is no accident. As Reed shows, the later eighteenth through early twentieth centuries witness the official splitting of the subject between conscious and unconscious, with the result that the testimony of consciousness is demoted. Literary focus on the experience of subjectivity occurs simultaneously with the bracketing of subjectivity in scientific discourse, and it

can be interpreted as a response. Literature picks up where some other con-
temporary discourses leave off, drawing on the fascinating new anatomies of
the subject formulated in contemporary science and philosophy but seeking
to explore them as they are experienced in psychological life.

The major philosophical debates in eighteenth- and nineteenth-century
Britain revolve around the clash between religion and the New Science. For
our purposes, the important form of this clash is the dramatic challenge sci-
entific materialism and a newly naturalistic psychology pose to traditional
ideas of self and soul. Can the old theological discourse of the "soul" serve
any function in a scientific environment? Can it be replaced with a naturalis-
tic concept of "self," which emphasizes the preservative instincts of the or-
ganism? Should that concept, too, be superceded by theories of mind and
brain functioning founded on sensory atomism? Essentially there is a show-
down between scientific materialism and subjective intuition. The important
intervention of literature is this: it shows that the questions raised by scien-
tists and philosophers *already* influence the self's experience of itself. The
self carries on these debates and feels the force of these questions in the form
of anxiety and self-bafflement. To give an example: the exploration of self-
division might be said to climax in the period's emblematic text on the sub-
ject, Robert Louis Stevenson's *Dr. Jekyll and Mr. Hyde*. In Jekyll's last testimony,
he reflects with repugnance on his "other" half.

> [Jekyll] had now seen the full deformity of that creature that
> shared with him some of the phenomena of consciousness, and
> was co-heir with him to death: and beyond these links of com-
> munity, which in themselves made the most poignant part of his
> distress, he thought of Hyde, for all his energy of life, as of some-
> thing not only hellish but inorganic. This was the shocking thing;
> that the slime of the pit seemed to utter cries and voices; that the
> amorphous dust gesticulated and sinned; that what was dead and
> had no shape, should usurp the office of life.   (319)

Reed discusses *Dr. Jekyll and Mr. Hyde* in the context of contemporary
speculation about the existence of a rational "unconscious" (164–66). To my
mind, it more obviously dramatizes the contemporary discussion of "soul" in
its relation to matter. Does matter think? Does mere neural activity create

the "illusion" of consciousness and the intuition of soul? Regardless of whether Stevenson takes a position on the controversy, he makes a claim that the contemporary science does not: namely, that the intellectual debate is experienced *as conflict* by and within an individual psyche. For a tear is an intellectual thing. Jekyll is tormented by the gulf between subjectivity and material being; his horror at the errant vitality of Hyde reflects the subject's alienation from the body and its autonomy. Consciousness balks but cannot extract itself from its entanglement with the body. The body is neither inert nor, by contrast with Plato and Descartes, is it merely a source of deception and temptation; it has its own ways and will from which consciousness or reason can by no means detach themselves. Clearly Jekyll's experience is not universal. Yet the novel does what horror stories commonly do: it raises everyday conflicts to the register of the supernatural. The literary text takes up the philosophical issues, translating them into psychological crisis: the center of consciousness, or "I," reacts to material being with dread and uncertainty.

But the quandary from which Jekyll suffers is not necessarily substance dualism, for the "I" in him that quarrels with material being does not identify itself as a different order of being (an intelligible substance, something divine). Instead his anxiety seems topical; it reflects the pressure that scientific materialism exerts over the sense of self. (Not that materialism was invented in eighteenth-century Britain, but then and there it established a major cultural empire it had never had before.) It was the Romantic poets, two generations before Stevenson, who first began to explore the impact of materialism on self *within* the experience of the subject. The isolation of consciousness in the material world is a topic uniquely associated with Romanticism. The contemporary prestige of materialism made the isolation of consciousness a more acute problem because, stripped of its transcendent provenance, consciousness must struggle to make sense of its existence. Why must one labor under the burden of subjectivity if there is no intelligible world to which the soul belongs, or if mind itself reduces to the firing of neurons? One Romantic reaction is to reinstate the transcendent provenance of the spirit, although usually with considerable new refinements. In *Biographia Literaria*, Coleridge borrows from German Idealism to oppose the living Subject and the "dead" object world. Instead of arguing the issue in the abstract, the Romantic crisis lyric—Coleridge's "Frost at Midnight," Percy Shelley's "Mont Blanc," Keats's "Ode to a Nightingale"—dramatizes the plight of a subject struggling to understand its relation to the object world. Such dramatization can reach impressive heights of complexity: Wordsworth's Intimations Ode presents the traumatic experience of consciousness awakening to its alienation from actuality and seeking, with all deliberate if uncertain will, to create for itself a faith in its transcendent provenance. No dramatization of this plight is starker than the anguished soliloquy of Shelley's *Alastor* Poet, who addresses his urgent questions about the purpose of consciousness to a swan who cannot understand him.

> And what am I that I should linger here,
> With voice far sweeter than thy dying notes,
> Spirit more vast than thine, frame more attuned
> To beauty, wasting these surpassing powers
> In the deaf air, to the blind earth, and heaven
> That echoes not my thoughts?
>
> ("Alastor," ll. 285–90, *Shelley's Poetry and Prose* 81)

Shelley presents as psychologically tormenting the experience of the subject marooned in a no-man's-land between lost transcendence and reductive materialism. With his intellectual sophistication and keen historical sense, Shelley might have thought the *Alastor* Poet's anguish premature or primitive. But the whole body of his work, right down to the Neoplatonic poignancy of *Adonais,* with its fierce claim that "Life . . . Stains the white radiance of Eternity" (l. 463, *Shelley's Poetry and Prose* 426), manifests his respect for the aspirations of the subject and his insistence that pat formulas are insufficient to cure its unease.

This is where Blake comes in. Of all the Romantics, Blake was keenest and most systematic in his critique of materialism; more to the point, he was the one who insisted in the most explicit terms that the intuition of selfhood does not dissipate just because it has been renounced. For Blake the intuition of selfhood includes the intuition of its transcendence—its superiority to the material world—and he maintained that if this intuition is simply discounted as an illusion, it will not die down but rather rankle and torment. Martin and Barresi rather complacently say that it is progress to "shed illusions" and that it shows how important the repudiation of the concept of self is that "it may be psychologically impossible to embrace [it] wholeheartedly" (302).

But what happens when we are unable to embrace it? We become avatars of Hegel's unhappy consciousness; we find ourselves living at odds with our own subjectivity. Blake satirized the proponents of such dead-end unbelief in the person of the Idiot Questioner, "who publishes doubt & calls it knowledge, whose Science is Despair" (M 41:15, E142). His target was equally the empiricists and the *philosophes*—"[Francis] Bacon, [Isaac] Newton & Locke," "Voltaire Rousseau Gibbon Hume" (M 41:5, E142; J 52, E201)—all to his mind reductive skeptics who superciliously disregard the torment of subjectivity.

But Blake thought Lockean empiricism especially guilty of imposing cruel strictures on the subject, requiring it to regard its experiences as irreal, shadowy epiphenomena of a "real" physical world. This theory outraged Blake— he thought it entailed forcible suppression of the subject's need and its nature; its just and unavoidable need to esteem subjectivity and its natural intuition of transcendence. Blake claimed that the subject laboring under the injunctions of empiricism will suffer from a kind of schizophrenia in which it has to treat as phantasmal (the inner life) what at the same time presses upon it with the utmost urgency. In short, he found empiricist psychology simplistic and grossly inadequate. Blake thought of himself as providing what his philosophical contemporaries had abjured: an account of inner realities from the subject's point of view. For he perceived that the science and philosophy of his own day had become increasingly committed to discounting the value of perception and introspection, and that they were thereby simply abandoning the subject to its vexed experience of itself. The subject's bewildering intuition of transcendence, in particular, was definitively discharged, which left it with no choice but to go seek a home in False Religion.

Blake's essential topic is the unhappiness of the subject within its own subjectivity, or to use a more plangent idiom, the loneliness of the soul. This unhappiness is very often expressed in dualism, either of mind-body or of subject-object; both imply that subjectivity is anomalous in a material world and that each subject is isolated from others. Blake seeks to repair this deep ontological wound. He starts from the premise that consciousness intrinsically experiences the intuition of soul and its loneliness in the world (its failure to fit in), or at least consciousness in what he would have called the "six thousand years" of Western history. The major religions and philosophical movements of the West have built on this intuition and also strengthened it. Sacrificial religion, Judaism, orthodox Christianity, Aristotle, and the Stoics all conspire to diminish the ontological status of the human being in its own eyes by representing the soul as "an atom in darkness," a mere spot of consciousness engulfed by all-powerful external forces. The most recent avatars of this error can be found in empiricism and the New Science.

Blake's critique of empiricism is usually described in philosophical terms as an objection to its ontology, its treatment of Nature and natural man as final realities. But Blake's more profound objection to empiricism is psychological: the New Science is "a Science [of] Despair" (M 41:15, E142). It encourages the center of consciousness, or "I," to regard itself as passive and helpless. The "I" has been thrust into a material world whose power and influence over it are disproportionate; it is invisible and intangible where the world is solid and real. The world was there before it, and so its "life" is largely reactive. It floats about, an immaterial node, embedded in its disturbing private experience. It can master neither the stimuli to which it is exposed nor the effects of stimuli in its interior. The "I" finds the self to be dark and strange, occupied by things it does not acknowledge as its own—hidden processes and extrinsic "impressions" the world has forced upon it.

In empiricist psychology, personal identity, or the unique "I," is stranded. Because it is immaterial, it is isolated in the material world, and because it is an atomic or unique existence, it is isolated in itself. Blake summarizes this plight in *The Four Zoas* in the opening lament of Tharmas, who complains of having a troubling and contradictory sense of self:

> I am like an atom
> A Nothing left in darkness yet I am an identity
> I wish & feel & weep & groan Ah terrible terrible
>
> (FZ 4:43–45, E302)

Tharmas says he feels like an "atom" because he is experiencing his subject-life in the terms that empirical science suggests. He must figure the "I" as a thing because the spiritual terms have been debarred. So he describes the "I" as a little node of consciousness adrift in a dark and alien world of matter. It is a like an atom: single, essential, small, opaque. And yet it is not material after all. Consciousness is not comparable to matter, but once matter is stipulated as the prevailing reality, consciousness loses definition. What place in a material world can that have which is immaterial, and hence wispy and spectral? So Tharmas pessimistically revises his formulation; his "I" is even less than an atom, it is "A Nothing left in darkness." But that description does not seem quite accurate to him either, and he has to revise again. "I am . . . A Nothing left in darkness yet I am an identity."

Dwarfed by the dominance of matter, the "I" feels that it is nothing, and yet it also has the opposite intuition: it knows itself as the one reality it is sure of (as Descartes would say), the one true being, an "identity." How to explain this contradiction? The word "identity" takes over here from the word "atom": it is still reductive, it still suggests thing-ness. Blake no doubt alludes to the chapter of Locke's *Essay* in which he defines "personal identity," or continuity of the self, in minimal terms as present consciousness plus its continuous memories of itself. This is a narrow definition, befitting a materialist psychology, and to Blake's mind it deserves parody. Blake counters the empiricist definition in this passage by using the word "identity" in a subtly ironic sense, intimating its perverse inadequacy. Tharmas clearly feels no better once he has defined consciousness as "identity" because he right away dissolves into incoherent emotional protest: "Ah terrible terrible." Thus he characterizes himself as an "identity" *insofar as* he "wish[es] & feel[s] & weep[s] & groan[s]" in vain. Tharmas finds that selfhood seems on the one hand insignificant, and on the other, absolutely central. Even in an empiricist, the interior life reasserts its urgency, but it cannot assign a meaning or purpose to either its tumults or their bearing on anything without. "A Nothing left in darkness" ought not to be burdened with a vain but engulfing internal life, and that is what seems so "terrible."

Empiricism's reductive accounts of identity fail to address the urgency of the inner life. Blake's point is not that philosophy remains irrelevant to our daily practice, but rather something much deeper. He perceives that the subject cannot possibly conform to the proscription on selfhood implicit in empiricism; it cannot live peacefully with the contradiction between the conclusions of naturalism and the intuition of selfhood. The place of the subject in a material world has become a vital issue with the rise of the New Science, and the New Science, Blake says, has imposed on the subject an untenable view of itself. One cannot *live* with the bracketing of subjectivity; it creates a form of psychological division too agitating to be ignored. The transcendent intuition pursues you even if you disavow it. It must be owned, but possibly the worst way to own it is through orthodox cosmology, theology, or eschatology in which the divinity of the soul is referred to the noblesse oblige of a tyrannical creator-god and to fulfillment in another life. Blake recommends instead identifying it with a creative power that is your own possession in the here and now. Above all, he says, how the self thinks and feels about itself must be taken into account. A descriptive psychology like his own, he asserts, speaks directly to the self's intuitions and fictions about itself.

When Tharmas adopts the empiricist view of the subject—when he defines himself as Natural Man—he falls into a revealing state of confusion. His bafflement reminds us that although empiricism and the scientific materialism to which it is related claim to present an objective or "neutral" view, they are themselves ideological, forcefully "interpellating a subject," as we would say now, rather than leaving the domain blank, as it purports to do. Peter Otto forcefully remarks: "Blake is *not* suggesting that Locke, Bacon, and Newton are wrong in their descriptions of fallen humanity. In fact they are correct" (19). That *is* how we live now. Any body of knowledge that gives an account of human nature automatically "interpellates a subject," and it perpetrates bad faith when it claims that it does not. Blake makes this argument in his address "To the Deists," where he insists "Man must & will have Some Religion; if he has not the Religion of Jesus, he will have the Religion of Satan" (J 52, E201). Consciously or not, everyone holds some concept of the human and the divine and their interrelation. There is such a view hidden in empiricism, precisely insofar as it denies that anything meaningful can be said about the divine and the relation of the human to the divine. For embedded in this notion is an assertion of the subject's helplessness. If we must have a view, says Blake, let us have a more constructive one. Let us have Blake's own, in which there is neither a distant nor a punitive God and the human subject does not have to look upon itself as a poor thing abandoned to darkness.

In fact, the subject would come to this pass even if Bacon and Newton and Locke had never existed. In his early poems, Blake lays the blame squarely on empiricism, but later he recognizes that empiricism is not solely to blame: the temptation to consider oneself a merely Natural Man is inevitable, although the empiricists encourage submission to it. Blake came to believe that the subject experiences its own intuition of transcendence as embattled, under siege by home-grown doubts and imposed ideologies. Orthodox Christianity has mishandled this intuition, but perhaps some other of the lost religions handled it more tactfully. In Blake's antipathy to orthodox Christianity, he turned back to Gnosticism and Neoplatonism, contemporary religious developments that also followed in the wake of Platonic dualism but that rejected the worship of a vengeful anthropomorphized God. In this book, I will show that Blake adapted and altered some of the language of Gnosticism and Neoplatonism, but my aim is not to provide source criticism. It is more important to see why he was interested in these ideas in the first place, and that reason can be simply put: Blake saw that these two religions of personal salvation, with their novel definitions of the nature of God and the soul, addressed the persistence of the transcendental intuition. Both descend from the essential Platonic claim that the body belongs to the base material world and the soul to a higher immaterial plane; more pertinent to Blake's purposes, both follow Plato's lead in arguing that the soul feels, and thus comes to know, its discomfiture in the material world through the anguishing emotion of "homesickness."

At the end of Book IX of the *Republic*, Glaucon, Socrates's interlocutor, catches on to the visionary character of the perfect city they have been founding in imagination: it "can't be accommodated anywhere in the world, and therefore rests at the level of ideas" (592b, *Republic* 343). Striking a note that is new in the dialogue, Socrates replies: "It may be, however, that it is retained in heaven as a paradigm for those who desire to see it and, through seeing it, to return from exile" (592b, *Republic* 343). The new note—pathos—is introduced by the idea that in beholding the visionary world, the soul beholds the world from which it is exiled, and momentarily returns to it. With this reply, Socrates answers the implicit question: What is the value of this ideal, "the perfect city," or of any purely imaginary, idealistic projection? It satisfies the soul's deepest desire: to rejoin what shares its nature. The Greek word is *katoikein*—to go home—and the *Phaedo* promises that with death the soul will finally have its homecoming. This promise might be gratifying did it not entail a painful implication: the soul is in the meantime not at home; it is alone, wandering, adrift, ill at ease. These are the affecting implications of Plato's metaphor. It manifestly complements the other famous metaphor of the body as a "prison house" for the soul, which Plato adopted from the Orphics and

Pythagoreans, earlier inventers of the religion of personal salvation to which the Gnostics and Neoplatonists (as well as the Christians) revert.

The Gnostics carry the theme of the prison house to its extreme in their vision of the soul exiled from heaven, pining for it, trapped in an alien world made by a vicious lesser God. Much Gnostic literature addresses this deep sense of estrangement, or "lostness," in the self, as, for example, this poignant Mandaean hymn from *The Gnostic Bible*:

> I am a poor man from the fruit.
> They took me from far away. I am far.
> I am a poor man whom life spoke to.
> I am far. The light beings took me away.
> They carried me here from the good
> to where the wicked live.
> They installed me in the world of the wicked
> where all is malice and fire.
>
> I didn't ask for it. I didn't want to come
> to this awful place.
> By my strength and light I suffer through
> This misery. By illumination and praise.
> I remain a stranger in their world.
> I stand among the wicked like a child without a father.
> Like a fatherless child, an untended fruit.
>
> (Barnstone and Myer 562)

Hans Jonas, profound scholar of the psychology of Gnosticism, uses the affective terms *dread* and *anxiety* to characterize this Gnostic evocation of homesickness. More pointedly, he calls it "existential alienation."[1]

In fact, I began work on this book some time ago with the study of existential alienation in the Romantic crisis lyric, more precisely, in a preoccupation with the Intimations Ode, which shares the Gnostic view that Nature is a dubious foster mother who aims to make her child forget the glories it has known and that imperial palace whence it came. Wordsworth is divided against the world and also against himself in the Intimations Ode: this leads to anxiety and self-estrangement and to a series of questions—What is this state? Where does it come from? What can I do about it?—that remain unresolved at the end of the poem. Although the critical tradition usually treats Blake as an anomaly in terms of Romantic psychology—as the one major poet of Romanticism both plainly religious and optimistic—I believe he deals with the same central Romantic affect as Wordsworth: the anxiety of existential alienation. As I will argue, he disapproves of Wordsworth for resigning himself to dualism and the permanent alienation of the soul, but he criticizes Wordsworth precisely because he shares Wordsworth's sense of the urgency of the problem: it is the solution about which they disagree. The true basis of Blake's critique of empiricism is that it exacerbates existential alienation. The basis of his interest in Gnosticism and Neoplatonism is that they recognize it and address it. They honor the "transcendent intuition," that is, the self's sense of isolation and alienation—from within and from without—and its sense that because it does not fit in here, it must have a home elsewhere; it must have that within that transcends this world. Blake liked Gnosticism and Neoplatonism for recognizing that (at least initially) transcendent intuition *pains;* it is a source of anxiety and trouble rather than of confidence or peace. Any number of Blake's mythic figures suffer like Tharmas from existential alienation and transcendent intuition that no degree of rational philosophy can put to rest. Blake firmly believes that the solution is to honor the affect and answer it, not to dismiss, suppress, or attempt to explain it away.

Existential alienation is linked to an experience of self-alienation, or conflict within between what thinks itself the "real" part of the self and what it identifies as false or accrued. A long series of works that cross the boundaries among philosophy, psychology, and religion address this fundamental experience of self-alienation: to those we have already named (Plato, Augustine, the Romantics, Freud, Lacan), we may add Martin Heidegger, who contributes useful terms I shall quote in just a moment. The subject's experience of itself is constitutively an experience of anxiety for a number of different reasons, some of which are traced out above. To this number may be added a contradictory relation to agency: a fierce determination to activity in one aspect of the self, and a sense of passivity and helplessness in the other. Helplessness prompts anxiety in itself, and confusion exacerbates it. Often the passivity abides in that aspect that seems to have been given by the world, or co-opted by it. Perhaps it would even be better to call this an anxiety of "self-ownership." David Farrell Krell gives a succinct paraphrase of Heidegger on the "ineradicable insecurity" or "groundlessness" of human existence.

This insecurity is due to the fact that our existential trajectories—
our life projects, roles, and identities—have "always already" been
shaped by a past that we can never get behind and they head off
into a future in which they will always be incomplete, cut short
by a death we can neither avoid nor control. We exist as a "thrown
project." We have no choice but to project our life projects to-
ward the impenetrable horizon of our impending deaths. This
gives rise to the "uncanny" feeling that we are not at home in our
lives.   (235)

Here is the well-known *Geworfenheit*, or "throwness," a term which Hei-
degger evolves in giving a naturalistic explanation of what, as we saw earlier,
the Gnostics call spiritual "exile." Jonas argues, in fact, that throwness is an
"originally Gnostic" term (*Gnostic Religion* 344). He cites Valentinus, who
wrote of this world "wherein we have been thrown" and, Jonas adds, "in
Mandaean literature it is a standing phrase: life has been thrown into the
world, light into darkness, the soul into the body" (*Gnostic Religion* 35).
According to Jonas, the word serves the same psychological purpose in Hei-
degger as in Gnosticism, where "it expresses the original violence done to me
in making me be where I am and what I am, the passivity of my choiceless
emergence into an existing world I did not make and whose law is not mine"
(*Gnostic Religion* 335). Gnosticism emphasizes the bewilderment of the sub-
ject, not only belated by its ontological nature but also internally divided be-
tween the intentional and the automatic. The internal "violence" remains the
most shocking and the most anxiety provoking: "For the power of the star
spirits, or of the cosmos in general, is not merely the external one of physical
compulsion, but even more the internal one of self-estrangement. Becoming
aware of itself, the self also discovers that it is not really its own, but is rather
the involuntary executor of cosmic designs" (*Gnostic Religion* 329).

Self-recognition entails recognition of otherness within the self. This
recognition can be related, although with a manifest loss of nuance, to Au-
gustine's dread of the darkness within, or the ego's apprehension of the id, or
to the subduction of identity under Lacan's Symbolic Order. All are forms of
the self's alienated experience of itself in which it reacts with dread to an in-
voluntary portion, which seems to have been obtruded into it by the outside
world. For all of these thinkers, anxiety characterizes the experience of sub-

jectivity and yet—this is all-important—it does not exact passive endurance. It can be put to work. As Jonas nicely points out, "the image of the throw imparts a dynamic character to the whole of the existence thus initiated" (*Gnostic Religion* 335). One embarks on a quest to understand, to address, to heal, if possible, or at least to turn the anxiety to a constructive use (e.g., to turn it into hope). Blake is clearly one of the therapeutic number, persuaded that the subject does not have to dwell at odds with its own subjectivity (and appalled by materialism because it abandons one to existential anxiety without redress). He is bent on a radical solution. His solution, it turns out, is more radical than any but that of the Gnostics and the Neoplatonists, who like him went so far as to refashion both the human and divine.

Blake's solution is more original than has perhaps been recognized. Received opinion tends to characterize him as fighting a rearguard action against the eighteenth-century "naturalization of the soul,"[2] that is, to think of him as pleading for a return to the old, now debunked, assumption that within each person is an individual immortal soul. In fact, he does not regress to such traditional views. In 1513 the Lateran Council codified the personal immortality of the soul as official church doctrine. It anathematized Averroës's argument that the intellectual soul is impersonal—universal, shared, and identical in everyone. Blake's idea of the soul is much closer to Averroës's heresy than to orthodox doctrine, although, as we shall see, his view even so has startlingly unique features. Blake does not counter by saying that the personal immortal soul is the real thing, as the Lateran Council instructed; just the opposite. He attacks the traditional valorization of the personal immortal soul, which he regards as an erroneous notion founded on egotism. Blake thinks too much respect is accorded to the empirical ego both by his culture and by individual psyches within his culture. He calls this empirical ego, which is grasping, desperate, and defensive, "the Selfhood" (somewhat confusingly for us, who have been using the term *selfhood* in a more neutral sense). In Blake's poem *Milton*, the poet John Milton, who has returned from the afterlife to correct his errors, realizes that he actually has to annihilate this Selfhood before he can see the truth, or live properly, or fulfill his vocation as a prophet. He accuses Satan, the avatar of False Religion, of sponsoring selfishness by promoting the idea of personal immortality and the goal of personal salvation.

Blake does not call for the recovery of a "true self," which is to him another form of egotism traveling in an idealistic disguise. He emphatically subverts the

so-called Romantic valorization of the "real individual" behind the accultur-
ated self.[3] Blake classes Jean-Jacques Rousseau among the villains of his mi-
lieu, numbering him (wrongly) among the Deists. But perhaps he objected
to Rousseau and thought him a Deistic egotist because of his Urizenic com-
mitment to his unique self, which Rousseau claims to have preserved at least
in part from the distortions of socialization. According to Rousseau, my true
self is one to which I alone have access, and that is bound to be compromised
in its encounters with otherness. So Rousseau's *Confessions* declares on its open-
ing page: "I know my own heart . . . I am made unlike anyone I have ever
met" (6). Blake would bridle at this proud insistence on first-person authority
and singularity (as opposed to the intellectual originality on which he prided
himself). He would say: indeed, the ego tries many ruses to persuade us that
it is our "real self." It may masquerade as something original, authentic, and
pure. But that too is just another veil, another false self. The real part of us is
impersonal.

For the simple substance of the soul, Blake substitutes a divided interior
life in which a Selfhood or empirical ego occludes an impersonal transcen-
dence. Thus there is something left after the Selfhood is annihilated. But what
it means for transcendence to be impersonal is somewhat hard to formulate.
That Blake was trying to work it out explains, again, why he went back to
Plotinus, who held that the transcendent part of one's being descends from
the impersonal Oversoul, and to the Gnostics, who held similarly that the
soul is *not* the unique individual but rather a floating spark of the divine. In a
characteristically compressed formulation, Blake explains that the node of
identity presents itself as the focal point, or center, of the self, but what lies at
our hearts is divinity, wide and deep, by which we participate in a sense of
larger being: "What is Above is Within, for every-thing in Eternity is translu-
cent: / The Circumference is Within: Without, is formed the Selfish Center"
(J 71:6–7). Note the spatial metaphor: the node of singularity, the point, atom,
or "Center," which informs the concepts not only of ego but also of self and
soul, is dispersed into its antithesis, an embracing "Circumference." So far
Blake's ideas coincide well enough with Neoplatonism, but at this juncture
Blake makes a difficult, original turn. He redefines this impersonal transcen-
dence as intellectual creativity, and then asserts that although the Circum-
ference, or ontological reality behind the veil of Selfhood, is impersonal, it
remains intellectually individuated. His own task, he says, is

> To open the Eternal Worlds, to open the immortal Eyes
> Of Man inwards into the Worlds of Thought: into Eternity
> Ever expanding in the Bosom of God, the Human Imagination
>
> (J 5:16–18, E147)

One feels Blake's delight in upending spatial metaphors (what? We open our eyes inward?) and attendant theological clichés (the Human Imagination is Bosom of God?). The "Worlds of Thought" *are* the Eternal Worlds; there are none other. Note the plural: although "the Human Imagination" is one, and there is no unique being, there are unique visions. This glorious variation evidently does not result from egotism, nor inevitably resolve into it, which means that prophetic self-assertion is not to be confused with individual pride. Blake will encounter some problems in maintaining this idea, but at any rate, it seems to inform his image of Paradise: Eden as a place of "Mental Fight," intellectual debate in sterling form. Although Eden has no place for selfishness, it does for the individual mind and for intellectual passion. And lest the reader become entangled trying to visualize Paradise as a senate hall, I hasten to add that because Blake gives little sign of believing in an afterlife, his Eden has to be construed as a virtual Heaven, not a mode of life in the afterworld but a purely mental reality available to us now.

This brings us to the last, and perhaps most significant, of Blake's soteriological innovations: in Blake the "transcendence" of the soul does not have its traditional sense. For him "transcendent" does not mean that the soul has a divine origin, or that it will after death return to a divine sphere. The soul is divine now, and all that is there is of the divine. "What is Above is Within." For the soul to be "transcendent" means that it can recognize its divinity, and it can embrace it by entering immediately into a conviction of its greatness and an enjoyment of its creativity. This is "the Eternal Now" that Blake implores us to ascend. In Blake's vocabulary the opposite of the Eternal Now is not the vanquished past or the dubious future but "Eternal Death," the great object of the ego or personal soul's fear as it pleads for immortality. No mind can reach the power or dignity of which it is capable until free of this fear. In Lavater's *Aphorisms on Man,* Blake found what he called "a vision of the Eternal Now," detaching the proper vocation of humanity from linear temporality: "Whatever is visible is the vessel or veil of the invisible past, present, future—as man penetrates to this more, or perceives it less, he raises or depresses his dignity of being" (E592). The prophetic mind feels that it participates in all times; it dwells in "the Eternal Spheres of Visionary Life" (M 34.51), and let the death of the body be damned. Thus Blake's "transcendence" is paradoxically immanent: it is a new way of living in the world now.

At this point it becomes clear why Blake believes he offers a cure for existential alienation: his immanent transcendence reconciles the self to actuality. It allows us to fulfill our vocation as transcendent beings in the present and to reclaim this world as ours. Early on, Blake is programmatically anti-dualistic, criticizing the separation of body and soul, subject and object. He makes the astute "Devil" of *The Marriage of Heaven and Hell* declare, "If the doors of perception were cleansed every thing would appear to man as it is: infinite" (MHH 14). Later he wavers, sometimes falling back into dualism (Nature is the enemy: "Natural Objects always did & now do Weaken, deaden & obliterate Imagination in Me" [E665]), but at other times he is exuberantly inclusive:

> For Cities
> Are Men, fathers of multitudes, and Rivers & Mountains
> Are also Men; every thing is Human, mighty! sublime!
> In every bosom a Universe at expands.
>
> (J 33:47–49, E180)

Visionary power brings the world alive, healing the rift between subject and object. But the mind has to work its way through to the paradox of such immanent transcendence. It does not come to us automatically or instinctively; it is not a property of youth or innocence. (The speakers of the *Songs of Innocence* have a pastoral relation to Nature, not a visionary one.) Visionary power is an achievement of the mature soul, a product of thought and experience. Here again Blake disputes Rousseau. It is not a question of returning to an earlier stage in one's development, of reverting to a purer self as yet undeformed by adulthood or socialization. Instead, you discover something you did not know about your nature and your capabilities. But discovery alone is not enough: you must recast yourself so that you can fulfill the newfound vocation. The Seven Angels of the Presence command Milton to extirpate his ego; they say it is a matter first of self-examination and then of major self-surgery: "Judge then of thy Own Self: thy Eternal Lineaments explore / What is Eternal & Changeable? & What Annihilable? . . . All that can be Annihilated must be Annihilated!" (M 32, 30–31). This call for change is more radical than

Rousseaustic, Christian, or even Gnostic psychologies propose, for self-purification in itself is inadequate. It is not a question of returning to, or recalling, a lost self. You must altogether remake yourself or, more pointedly, remake your self. Despite Blake's quarrel with Stoicism, his prescription resembles the Stoic injunction to self-transformation, as Foucault analyzes it in *The Hermeneutics of the Subject:* the goal is to "become again what we should have been but never were" (95).

I bring in Foucault's argument here because it helps us to understand Blake's meaning and place him within a religio-philosophical tradition. *The Hermeneutics of the Subject* makes up some of the lectures that led up to the writing of *The Care of the Self,* the third volume in *The History of Sexuality.* In these lectures, Foucault goes back to ancient philosophy to uncover a distinction between two models of knowledge: an older ethic in which the search for truth necessitates a transformation of the seeking subject, and the modern scientific approach to "objective" knowledge, which leaves the subject untouched. Foucault calls the epoch of the changeover "the Cartesian moment," after which knowledge in itself is thought to give access to truth. The older ethic requires also "care of the self"; the subject has to return to itself and remake itself so that it can gain access to truth, and respond adequately to the truth it has discovered. The phrase "care of the self" translates Plato's *epimeleia heautou,* and Foucault argues that this form of "spirituality" informs almost all the important movements in ancient philosophy: "throughout Antiquity (in the Pythagoreans, Plato, the Stoics, the Cynics, Epicureans and Neo-Platonists), the philosophical theme (how to have access to the truth?) and the question of spirituality (what transformations in the being of the subject are necessary for access to the truth?) were never separate" (*Hermeneutics of the Subject* 17). The subject will be abjured to go to "work on himself" (*Hermeneutics of the Subject* 26); care of the self requires undertaking a deliberate labor of self-transformation.

Foucault defines this "spirituality" in terms readily applicable to Blake, who has been called "the last great religious poet in England" (Ackroyd 18) despite espousing heterodoxies that border on irreligion.

> For spirituality, the truth is not just what is given to the subject, as
> reward for the act of knowledge as it were, and to fulfill the act of
> knowledge. The truth enlightens the subject; the truth gives beat-
> itude to the subject; the truth gives the subject tranquility of the

soul. In short, in the truth and in access to the truth, there is something that fulfills the subject himself, which fulfills or trans-figures his very being. In short, I think we can say that in and of itself an act of knowledge could never give access to the truth, unless it was prepared, accompanied, doubled, and completed by a certain transformation of the subject, not of the individual, but of the subject himself in his being as a subject.

(Foucault, Hermeneutics of the Subject 16)

I repeat this for emphasis: the subject has to change *his being as a subject.* That is, the subject has to change more than the way he or she thinks about a given topic, however large the topic, even if it be the order of reality or the nature of the human and the divine. As soon as he or she begins to discover these larger truths, there should occur what Foucault calls "rebound" effects *(de retour)* or "effects of the truth on the subject" (*Hermeneutics of the Subject* 16). Subjectivity is illuminated; the subject begins to experience his or her own subjectivity differently, sees the possibility of a new way of existing as a subject, and strives for it. Blake thought the kind of truths he proposed ought to have this looping end, although even he would not have put it as ecstatically as Foucault does in his paraphrase above. In fact, as I will demonstrate, Blake thinks the first effects of awakening will be painful.

The transformation of the self necessitates a mapping of the self. Care of the self has from the beginning produced such anatomies. The wide, deep, and diverse tradition of anatomizing the self has persisted not because of some common general interest in psychology, or from a more mechanical inheritance of metaphors, but because many bodies of thought (orthodox religion, mysticism and cult, philosophical ethics and psychoanalysis) share the premise that something is wrong in the self insofar as it is self-vexing. Something is awry; something needs to be fixed. But what needs fixing, and how? The common conclusion is that the soul is somehow at war with itself. Foucault quotes Epictetus: "He says that when one does wrong, in reality there is a *makhe:* a battle, a conflict in the person who commits the sin" (*Hermeneutics of the Subject* 139). How can such self-thwarting come about? The soul must be in pieces that compete with each other. These parts of the self have to be named, and from thence come the anatomies, usually in the form of schema or maps—the technical term is *psychotopography.* This focus on the entities and their names can lead to a static tableau (Reason faces off against the Imagination and the Understanding, or the Ego against the Id and the Superego), and yet the point is to account for the dynamics of inner conflict. What is fighting what, and what makes one or the other side prevail? Can they be reconciled? Must one part prevail? What does the perfected or "saved" soul look like? Paradigms of self-division chart the sources of inner conflict in such a way as to image a suspension of hostilities—if not an end to the war, at least a truce.

Blake can usefully be classed among the thinkers who foster care of the self. It is in this sense that he is a throwback, and for this reason that he felt a kinship with the ancient philosophy-religions. He bears a prophecy that means to change the relation of the self to itself—because he perceives the self to be unhappy in itself. Like the ancient philosophers Foucault lists above, Blake believes that the subject left to its own devices will encounter its subjectivity as a source of anxiety and bafflement. Like the others he offers a diagnosis of what is awry, then proceeds to invent a model of the self that explains the problem and allows one to imagine how it may be fixed, how the "Circumference" may be "opened" behind the "Center." Blake participates in this long tradition by creating his own psychotopography, or better, psychotopographies (because he changes and recreates them over time). In specific historical terms—in terms of his reaction to the empirical and philosophical psychology of own time—his goal was to provide a rigorous analysis that did not (as they did) reductively focus on self-interest or sensory atomism.

Many students of Blake have made specific connections between Blake's psychology and psychoanalysis—and I will draw some such connections too—but the real affinity lies deeper than any overlap in ideas. We can discern points of contact among Blake's ideas and Gnosticism, Neoplatonism, Heidegger, and psychoanalysis because all work on a particular form of the care of the self, that is, on providing an account of why the subject lives at odds with its own subjectivity. Such projects did not come to a halt, says Foucault, with the "Cartesian moment," but since then the discourses that share this aim have been separated out from science and dismissed as literature or religion. Because Marxism and psychoanalysis demand a transformation in the subject, they have been regarded as unscientific and linked to secular religion. I think that Blake's "religion" is of the same kind: he understood his therapeutic ambition to remake the subject as a direct antithesis to the spiritual abstinence of contemporary science. He flaunted his secular religiousness deliberately by constantly writing of God and Christ even though he was an atheist and an unbeliever.

All representations of the inner life are catachresis, that is, metaphors without a literal term. Earlier I cited the *Republic*'s image of the soul longing to return from its exile in the material world, to go home. The *Phaedrus* introduces the image of the self as a chariot with Reason as charioteer and emotion and appetite as the white steeds that draw it. The Gnostics and Neoplatonists adopt the metaphor of the prison house and the lost child. The Stoics represent the self as a pivot in what Foucault calls "the great image of turning around toward oneself" (*epistrephein pros heauton*, or *convertere ad se*). Locke's metaphor is the famous dark closet; James counters with the stream of consciousness. Although nothing could be closer to the self than its own experience, it has nothing but figures of speech with which to describe it. Blake boldly invents his own metaphors to analyze the different parts of the self: the "veil" of Selfhood, the "broken heart gates," the baleful giants who guard them. Why should anyone doubt the suggestiveness of these figures (or of Plato's or Freud's) because they are merely metaphors? Let us take our cue from Søren Kierkegaard who, in *Concluding Unscientific Postscript,* dauntlessly affirms, "If anyone says that this is only an exercise in elocution, that I have only a bit of irony, a bit of pathos, a bit of dialectic with which to work, I shall answer: what else should a person have who wants to present the ethical?" (153). Yes, we only have metaphors: what else should we have who wish to fathom subjective experience?

I

Empiricism and Despair

A Worm of Sixty Winters

And why [are] men bound beneath the heavens in a reptile form
A worm of sixty winters creeping on the dusky ground.

(Tir 8:10–11, E285)

In his first prophetic book, the unengraved *Tiriel* (1789), Blake portrays the
unhappiness of the subject who has internalized the empiricist view of hu-
man nature and its subordination to material reality. As Mary Hall[1] observes,
Tiriel is "a prototype of 'the Human Illusion,' . . . the largest view of man
permitted by the natural and mechanical philosophers" (74). Blake will later
call this illusion "Natural Man." He had not yet evolved this term when he
wrote *Tiriel*, but he passionately apprehended the target of his critique; the
tragic subject-life of the empiricist. Tiriel is a patriarchal tyrant, a proto-
Urizen who curses and fears his children; like Thel, he tries to regress from
the impasse of his paranoia to the "vales of Har," but flight is impossible, and
he comes back to the dead end of his emotions. The poem closes with an
aria of existential disgust in which Tiriel laments the soul's incarceration in a
"reptile form." He says disdainfully that he has been "Compelld to pray

repugnant & to humble the immortal spirit" (8:22, E285), showing that he rejects the prayer and the humbling in which he nonetheless acquiesces. Tiriel may call the spirit "immortal," but he thinks of it as powerless to counteract the pressures of materiality and socialization. He is divided and depressed. "Over the weary hills the blind man took his lonely way / To him the day & night alike was dark & desolate" (Tir 4:1, E280). His thoughts and feelings do not have his own endorsement. They even seem pointless to him. In the manner of Hegel's "unhappy consciousness," Tiriel is living at odds with his own subject life.

Tiriel has been brought to this pass of self-contempt and self-estrangement because he accepts the materialist ontology of empiricism. He believes he is nothing but "a worm of sixty winters." Blake will repeat this phrase throughout his poetry; it becomes his icon for the belittling self-definition of Natural Man. How is it that the subject comes to experience itself in this way, and to think this way about itself? What are the consequences—psychological, social, and intellectual—of this experience of self? Can the subject be taught to think differently? In his early critiques of empiricism (1788–1791), Blake is beginning to reflect on these questions. From *Thel* and the treatises to *Visions of the Daughters of Albion*, Blake's early work dramatizes his understanding of how empiricism gives rise to despair.

Blake's early satire of salon culture, "An Island in the Moon," slips in a reference to "An Easy of Huming Understanding by John Lookye Gent" (E456). Despite its subversive humor—exemplified by this delightful paronomasia—the work has a certain melancholy. As Hall writes, it illustrates the "selfishness and general lack of communication" and the "cacophony" of "a mechanical society" (30). Blake interprets the narcissism, envy, and competition of the London salons as arising in some way from the cultural domination of Enlightenment values. He portrays this literary circle as hostile to enthusiasm and prophecy; certainly it was hostile to him, and in the end he ceased to be welcome on account of his vehemence. Thus his rejection of empiricism is bound up from the beginning with his own loneliness and cultural alienation.[2] In Blake's first works, he is more intent on diagnosing the malady than on suggesting a cure. But already his sense of the issues goes much deeper than the topic—the criticism of Lockean epistemology—might imply. Blake's dispute with empiricism is not properly philosophical but psychological.

In "There is No Natural Religion b," Blake contemns Lockean empiricism for providing a reductive account of subjective experience. It slights, or even represses, the imaginative component of perception—what Blake calls "the Poetic or Prophetic character," or, more plainly, "Inspiration and Revelation." According to empiricism, we have for our original stimulus only the elements of material reality: the pitiful circle of things, the routines of clock time and nature. If we truly are confined to natural reality, then our subjective experience must be increasingly homogenous. The subject as empiricism conceives it is condemned to monotony and hence to stultification—known in Blake's poetry as the sleep of Urizen, or, "Forgetfulness, dumbness, necessity!" (BU 10:24, E75). Of such a subject Blake says rightly, "despair must be his eternal lot" (TNNR b, E2). And so it would be for everyone if the empiricists had it right: "If it were not for the Poetic or Prophetic character the Philosophic & Experimental would soon be at the ratio of all things, & stand still unable to do other than repeat the same dull round over again" (TNNR b, E3). But, Blake asserts axiomatically, we are *not* confined to natural reality. He means to show, by reductio, that Locke's account is mistaken. Yet an ironic subtext cuts across this assurance: as Blake knows, many people do find experience a "dull round," overwhelmed as they are by the temptations of philosophical materialism—and thus despair is their lot. Anyone who believes in merely Natural Man must eventually regard himself as a worm of sixty winters, or as a later prophecy puts it, "a poor mortal vegetation / Beneath the moon of Ulro" (M 24[26]:24–25, E120). Nature will emerge as an omnipotent reality, possessed of the force of necessity, and will consequently come to seem tyrannical and malicious.

Why should empiricism have such dark psychological consequences? In *Fearful Symmetry* Northrop Frye paraphrased, with unsurpassable lucidity, what we might call the first order of Blake's critique. "Empiricism," "Natural Religion," and "Deism" exalt into an authoritative philosophical position what is actually a terrible fear haunting humankind: the fear that the natural world is the real world. Natural Religion and Deism frame this notion in religious terms by proposing that the natural world is part of the Creation, and that it therefore expresses something about the essence of God. Empirical science says more simply that material reality is the *only* certain, solid, and knowable reality. In Blake's argument, these claims come to the same thing and have the same dire implications. The natural world is a world of death; it contains either objects that are merely inert or subjects that are merely short-lived phantoms. It is the world of linear time, or inexorable clock-time that brings forth living things only in order to extinguish them and replace them with others in endless, vain cycles of mortality. Saturn devours his children, as Frye points out. From the laws of nature spring necessity, and surrendering to necessity spells helplessness and despair. How dreadful for us if this is *the* "reality" because then we must believe that we dwell in a fundamentally hostile world, and that from it the soul will be dismissed to "Non-Entity" or "Eternal Death."

Christianity ought to give us some relief from this terror insofar as it imagines that God made both this world and a better one: but Blake suggests that nobody who believes in the divine origin of natural reality can believe without doubt in the afterlife. For if God made this world, if it is a reality expressing his being, then he is a monster from whom we have every reason to dread the worst. From this dark suspicion arises the concept of a punitive God whom we need to appease by means of sacrifice, for if he is a death-loving God only blood can please him. All the deep crimes humanity commits against itself—all the nightmares of "War & Religion"—follow this sacrificial logic, by which an incurable despair frantically spends itself in idle violence. Nature worship, although it seems benign, actually conceals submission to the truth of Eternal Death, and a submission of this kind, however tacit, leads to self-centered anxiety and desperation. It also leads to a philosophical and psychological quandary: What is the purpose of consciousness in a world where only matter is real?

The Book of Thel dramatizes the experience of consciousness finding itself to be an anomaly in the material world, and attempting to rationalize its predicament in purely naturalistic terms. These turn out to be quite inadequate. The poem demonstrates, in other words, that the empiricist subject is bound to be an unhappy subject, unable to reconcile itself to "reality" as it is represented in an empiricist framework. Thel begins by departing from the unselfconscious life of the other "daughters of Mne Seraphim." She separates herself out in solitude, as Urizen withdraws from the Eternals, and the Gnostic Sophia disengages herself from the Aeons. Like theirs, her act equates self-consciousness with consciousness itself; she individuates herself by going apart to think, "in paleness [seeking] the secret air," finding identity in solitary contemplation (Thel 1:2, E3). But consciousness precipitated out as a singularity will discover itself to be isolated. Thel feels uneasy right away, plunged into the philosophical problem of consciousness—namely the question of how it can be naturalized or recast as an integral feature of the material world. In the first three sections of the poem, various natural phenomena offer their solutions to the problem, but none of them proves satisfactory.

With her first utterance Thel laments her transience, classing herself with other short-lived natural phenomena: "Ah Thel is like a watry bow, and like a parting cloud / Like a reflection in a glass, like shadows in the water" (1:8-9, E3). She does not explicitly distinguish herself as a mind—in fact, she compares herself to phenomena that are distinctly unaware—but her sense that she is different emerges in the last lines of her speech, where she wishfully imagines an easy dissolution of consciousness.

> Ah gentle may I lay me down, and gentle rest my head.
> And gentle sleep the sleep of death. and gentle hear the voice
> Of him that walketh in the garden in the evening time.
>
> (Thel 1:12–14, E3)

Awareness of transience would seem to be an unnecessary burden, and her first thought is to subdue it. With her anastrophe "gentle . . . gentle . . . gentle . . . gentle," Thel is humming herself a lullaby, dreaming that mind can fade painlessly away. Such is the power of fantasy that she rather surprisingly transforms the interrogating God of Genesis into a murmurer of lullabies, too. She is crossing the God of the Hebrew Bible with the tenderhearted providential Jesus of popular Christianity, lovingly invoked by many of the speakers in the *Songs of Innocence*. Other characters in *The Book of Thel* also attempt to solve the problem of consciousness through an appeal to conventional religion, and the effort is a failure every time. In this case, Thel's jump to a death wish is precipitate—the philosophical process has been short-circuited—and moreover, sheer fantasy cannot dispel her serious concerns.

How can a thinking being be integrated into a world that apparently has no use for thought? The natural phenomena who offer Thel their consolation—the Lilly, the Cloud, the Worm, and the matron Clod of Clay—are not able to set her mind at rest because they never quite address themselves to this question, and how could they? Thel at first resists the spurious identification. As Sheila Spector observes, "To Thel, being like a 'watry bow,' 'a parting cloud,' or 'a smile upon an infants face' is quite literally 'the sleep of death' " (1;13, E 3) (65). Thel first uses the phrase "sleep of death," wishfully, yet, Spector implies, the reader comes to see that the words echo the Gnostic notion that a *human* life steeped in its own materiality becomes a spiritual "sleep," a sinking into catatonic ignorance. What is good enough for a lily or a cloud is not good enough for a human being.

The Lilly points out that, although she is merely "a watery weed," yet she is "visited from heaven and he that smiles on all. / Walks in the valley and each morn over me spreads his hand" (Thel 1:19–20, E4). If such as she is blessed, why should "the mistress of the vales of Har" complain? Thel answers that she is not in fact in the same chain of being as the Lilly: as a natural phenomenon, the Lilly plays a role in the natural world—nourishing the lamb, purifying the honey, scenting the air—while Thel has to live her life to herself and leaves no trace. The Lilly summons the Cloud, which vanishes rapidly without a trace, and Thel confesses the similarity between herself and him but also points out the difference: the Cloud does not complain, "yet I complain, and no one hears my voice" (Thel 3:4, E4). The Cloud assures Thel that his being continues. He is "link'd in a golden band" to the dew, and they "walk united, bearing food to all our tender flowers" (Thel 3:15–16, E5). When he passes away, "It is to tenfold life, to love, to peace, and raptures holy" (Thel 3:11, E5). Thel takes this, perhaps too literally, to demonstrate that the Cloud, like the Lilly, has significance insofar as it participates in the cycle of nature. She answers that she does not participate in the natural cycle in the way they do: "I fear I am not like thee . . . all shall say, without a use this shining woman liv'd, / Or did she only live to be at death the food of worms" (Thel 3:19, 22–24, E5). Blake's satirical intelligence flares at this, as the Cloud seizes on Thel's plaint, replying:

> Then if thou art the food of worms. O virgin of the skies,
> How great thy use, how great thy blessing.
>
> (Thel 3:25–26, E5)

It would be a mistake to think that Blake endorses this idea. The Cloud goes on to explain, "everything that lives, / Lives not alone, nor for itself" (Thel 3:26–27, E5), but this assertion is not to be confused with Blake's "Everything that lives is *Holy*" (MHH 25, E45; my italics). In the Cloud's absurd suggestion, Blake is mocking the attempt to redeem strictly natural existence. Consciousness cannot be content with its fate because the body nurtures worms.

But Thel is impressed with the Worm—"I see thee like an infant wrapped in the Lillys leaf" (4:3, E5)—and even more, with the maternal Clod of Clay, who delivers the first true Song of Innocence in the poem, that is, the first utterance in which contentment is matched by spiritual depth:

> O beauty of the vales of Har. we live not for ourselves,
> Thou seest me the meanest thing, and so I am indeed;
> My bosom of itself is cold. and of itself is dark,
> But he that loves the lowly, pours his oil upon my head.
> And kisses me, and binds his nuptial bands around my breast.
>
> (Thel 4:10–12, 5:1–2, E5)

Unlike the Cloud and the Lilly, the Clod of Clay does not presume to correct Thel. Moreover, she admits that she does not know herself how it is that she has been blessed. She remains in a state of thoughtful uncertainty, but is not thereby rendered incapable of life and love (as Thel is). "I ponder, and I cannot ponder, yet I live and love" (5:6, E6). In her fruitless pondering, or questioning, she is the closest to Thel of the three natural phenomena, and at the same time, she offers Thel an example of happiness achieved without a spurious theory. Thel is satisfied with this response; the Clod's tender love for the Worm persuades Thel that God has indeed "cherish'd it / With milk and oil," in other words, that nature is good (Thel 5:10–11, E6).

Thel is on her way to becoming reconciled to the order of nature. But precisely because she has been lulled into acceptance, she is due for a cruel shock. However benevolent and appealing the maternal Clod of Clay, she is nonetheless a natural being whose philosophy of existence will not work for Thel. The Clod of Clay invites her to "enter my house," that is, the sod or essence of matter, and also the clay of which the body is made. The scene immediately reverses from pastoral to infernal. Thel finds herself in a dark catacomb of human suffering, where the "dead" instead of resting are tormented.

> Thel enter'd in & saw the secrets of the land unknown;
> She saw the couches of the dead, & where the fibrous roots
> Of every heart on earth infixes deep its restless twists:
> A land of sorrows & tears where never smile was seen.
>
> (Thel 6:2–5, E6)

Blake sets the template here for a pattern of imagery that will recur in many later poems. The dim subterranean land where the dead are infixed, twisting and turning in their anguish, reappears at crucial moments in *The Four Zoas* and *Jerusalem* (among other works), where it figures the suffering of the empiricist subject or Natural Man, buried alive by materiality. That is what Thel is witnessing here: the despair to which the empiricist subject— anyone who believes that he or she is the creature of a merely natural order— will ultimately fall prey. Thel has made a temporary peace with nature, but she will not be able to sustain it. Human consciousness cannot live happily without conviction of its transcendental provenance (says Blake) and the persecuting grave into which the Clod insidiously invites Thel stands for the collapse of morale that will ensue when Thel outlives her episode of senti- mentality. She will see nature for what it is—*not* benevolent—and will feel again the oppressions of materiality and the anxiety of Eternal Death that moved her to philosophical musings at the outset. But now she will not be musing. What had had the character of inquiry and self-pleasing meditation becomes harrowing or "infixed" dread, once the finality of nature is con- firmed. The play of thought subsides, repressed by the stultification of ex- perience. Thel travels through the psychological underworld, observing the strange community of Natural Man in which everyone undergoes the same suffering in isolation from everyone else: "She wanderd in the land of clouds thro' the valleys dark, listning / Dolours & lamentations . . . Till to her own grave plot she came" (Thel 6:6–7, E6). Now Thel rejoins her own experience, as one of the myriad suffocating "subjects" of empiricism, compelled to live at odds with their own subjectivity—longing for transcendence but per- suaded to disown their longing. The voice that speaks to Thel from her grave expresses a terror of the senses that is easy to interpret in a Freudian vein as reflecting Thel's dread of sexual incarnation. She flees shrieking back to the vales of Har rather than cross the threshold of sexual experience. I propose instead that her terror of the senses stems from the psychological dualism na- tive to the empiricist subject.

The complaint from the grave carries to a hysterical extreme the Lockean claim that knowledge comes to us through the senses. Blake plays on what Nancy Yousef nicely terms "the metaphor of internment" in Lockean episte- mology. As she argues, "The tabula rasa remains the most well-known (albeit misattributed) figure for the mind associated with the *Essay* but its most compelling representation—and the one that, in its ambiguity, would exercise a powerful hold on scientific and literary imagination—is the dark room" (32). This is a metaphor Locke himself uses in a famous and frequently cited passage: "External and internal Sensation . . . alone, as far as I can discover, are the Windows by which light is let into this *dark room*. For, methinks, the *Understanding* is not so much unlike a Closet wholly shut from light, with only some little openings left, to let in external visible Resemblances, or *Ideas* of things without" (2.11.17). This passage has long been recognized as the object of Blake's satirical remark in *The Marriage of Heaven and Hell*: "For man has closed himself up, till he sees all things thro' the narrow chinks of his cavern" (MHH 14, E39). The metaphor of the dark room suggests that the subject is isolated, mystified, and embattled.

Blake incisively parodies this paranoid view in the monologue from the grave. The passivity of the mind and the automatic activity of the senses lead to an awful vulnerability in the experiencing subject.

> Why cannot the Ear be closed to its own destruction?
> Or the glistning Eye to the poison of a smile!
> Why are the Eyelids stord with arrows ready drawn,
> Where a thousand fighting men in ambush lie?
> Or an Eye of gifts & graces, show'ring fruits & coined gold!
> Why a Tongue impress'd with honey from every wind?
> Why an Ear, a whirlpool fierce to draw creations in?
> Why a Nostril wide inhaling terror trembling & affright.
> Why a tender curb upon the youthful burning boy!
> Why a little curtain of flesh on the bed of our desire?
>
> (Thel 6:11–12, E6)

The senses are represented as uncontrollable apertures through which external stimuli come flooding in. They are personified as independent entities because the empiricist subject feels estranged from his or her own body. This is ironic insofar as materialism espouses the view that no ontological distinction separates mind and body. But the philosophical argument reverses into its opposite when it enters into psychological life. The consciousness that regards itself as a merely empirical phenomenon (a firing of neurons) will feel *less,* not more, connected to the body despite, or rather because of, being reduced to the same substance: now the subject subsides into a chaos of atomic properties, with the mind as the common register but not the agent of experience. Consciousness intuits itself as unique and yet cedes reality to the life of the body, which consequently seems alien and autonomous. It was resistance to psychological disassociation of this kind, in which mind is separated from and subordinated to body, that led Blake to repudiate dualism in *The Marriage of Heaven and Hell,* and to make his celebrated claim that the perception of the creation as infinite "will come to pass by an improvement of sensual enjoyment" (MHH 14, E39). Sexual liberation is not all Blake is aiming for. More generally, he promotes the restoration of the mind to its properly active—and thus, joyous—relation to the body. Sex comes up in this passage from *Thel,* "the tender curb . . . the little curtain of flesh," because consciousness estranged from the senses will experience the sexual body as a frustrating imposition and impediment.

Thel ends with this dramatization of embattled consciousness because Blake thinks the ultimate fate and worst outcome of empiricist subjectivity lies in internal disassociation, and the disintegration of agency that follows from it (more on this in the next section). Thence come inertia and despair. It is a dead end. No wonder Thel turns around and flies back to her inexperienced state. Blake thereby indicates that materialism offers *no* solution to the existential problem of consciousness. Thel attempts to find meaning for humanity within a purely natural order, and her attempt fails. She may arrive at a comforting theory, but in actual experience the theory breaks down, and consciousness deprived of agency frets itself away into psychological miasma. What is at stake is happiness, and Blake means to demonstrate that Natural Man cannot be happy. Sooner or later the disappointment of agency, and the paranoia of nature, will come home to him, and for these troubles the empiricist framework offers no therapy.

Blake's exhilaration with the depth of his argument as an intellectual and spiritual paradigm can be felt in *The Marriage of Heaven and Hell* (begun in 1790), and it is in this poem that he first presents a worthy alternative to the despair of empiricism. The *Songs of Innocence* (1789) imagine interior lives susceptible of happiness, but it is happiness achieved at the cost of naivete. By contrast, the narrator of the *Marriage*—along with its "Devil"—have transcended both wishfulness and cultural indoctrination. They assert their own assured Nietzschean countervalues, evincing their freedom from received idea and cultural myth along with the sheer joy of their iconoclasm.

The narrator repudiates the contraction of the human being in Christianity as well as empiricism. The human being is neither a besieged subject, peering out "thro' the narrow chinks of his cavern," nor a "good Soul" endangered by vicious "Energies" of the body, which tempt one to sin and eternal torment (MHH 4, E34). Both of these constructions turn on a mind–body dualism that stimulates paranoia in the subject, fear of the power "out there"—in the external world, in the body, and even "within" the self, in the murky interior life that escapes the control of the "good soul," Reason, or consciousness. The unhappiness of the subject begins in this dualism. Error must be attacked at the root: "first the notion that man has a body extinct from his soul is to be expunged" (MHH 14, E39).

In the *Marriage,* Blake satirically conflates the dualism of Christianity and its self-appointed antagonist, the empiricism and materialism of the Enlightenment. But he is perfectly aware of the distinction between mind–body and soul–body dualism. Elsewhere he critiques each independently. *Thel* illustrates the dilemma of the mind–body dualist who cannot believe in the immortality of mere "consciousness." "To Tirzah," a Song of Experience, demonstrates the rage and paralysis of the ascetic estranged from the body by soul–body dualism. It is a temptation to assume that the poem expresses Blake's own views, but that would be a mistake, just as it is a mistake to imagine that any of the *Songs of Experience* do. The personae of Experience may perceive some truths aright, but they are throttled by their own cynicism and hopelessness. The Experienced Nurse seethes with frustration, certain that she is wasting her life, where the skittish lover of "The Angel" feels it is already too late. Even "London," the poem whose speaker readers (and scholars)[3] are most likely to conflate with Blake, shows the crippling effect of the pessimism Blake attributes to "Experience," which is, after all, not to be confused with wisdom. The speaker of "London" is an incisive social critic—the "Chimney-sweepers cry" *does* incriminate the hypocrisy of "Every blackning Church"—but he or she cannot get beyond the emphatic iteration of scandal ("In every cry . . . In every voice . . . in every ban . . . I hear"). Meanwhile, the ascetic of "To Tirzah" dwells in a barely tolerable state of hatred toward "Mother Nature," which created the world and the body in which the soul is imprisoned.

> Thou Mother of my Mortal part.
> With cruelty didst mould my Heart.

[37]

And with false self-decieving tears,
Didst bind my Nostrils Eyes & Ears.

Didst close my Tongue in senseless clay
And me to Mortal Life betray:
The Death of Jesus set me free,
Then what have I to do with thee?

(E30)

In truth, the speaker is imprisoned less by the body he loathes than by the "mind-forg'd manacles" of his harsh Pauline spirituality. The illustration shows a fainting man attended by a bearded elder whose robe is inscribed with the Pauline formula of resurrection: "It is raised a Spiritual Body" (Blake, *Songs* pl. 52). In other contexts, Blake quotes this phrase approvingly, but he was not averse to ironic treatment of scripture or to criticism of Paul, and here the quotation seems to be used enigmatically.[4] The speaker of "To Tirzah" remains in sore need of spiritual refreshment. Perhaps he is fainting under the psychological burden created by Paul's dread of the physical body. The speaker's hatred toward the Creation, and impatience to be released from it, recall the doctrines of some Gnostics, including Marcion, who said the world was made up of "beggarly elements." "Particularly repulsive to him was the 'uncleanliness' of sex and of childbirth, none of which could have anything to do with the salvation of man" (Pelikan 73).

Blake himself militates against the rejection of the Creation by praising sex and espousing "the improvement of sensual enjoyment" as an avenue to truth (MHH 14, E39). But such a rejection was surely tempting to him as a thinker opposed to the franchise of nature, one who could pronounce programmatically, contra Wordsworth: "This World is too poor to produce one seed" (E656). In the rest of his work, Blake will labor to balance the repudiation of nature against the idea of its visionary transformation. Leopold Damrosch argued that Blake was a dualist who wanted to be a monist, that is, he was philosophically committed to a certain view that he could not always believe.[5] Blake's position seems fairly consistent in theory, but his attitudes waver; certainly he is sometimes Gnostic in his antagonism to nature. The *Marriage* represents the high-water mark of Blake's sensual polemic, and also the last time he portrays intellectual freedom as spontaneous and unproblematic.

In the Continental Prophecies, Blake broadens his argument out into a hermeneutic of history. In these works he first begins to mythologize history and psychology, and their relation to one another, through the dramatic interaction of his basic cast: Urizen, Los, Enitharmon, and Orc. In one thematic strain, he pursues the subject of "To Tirzah": the psychological distortion caused when alien nature is personified as Nature. He focuses on two interlinked psychological issues embodied in the characters of Enitharmon and Orc (mother and son), respectively: In one of her aspects, Enitharmon represents the distortion of human experience and sexuality caused by belief in a (sadistic) "Mother Nature," while Orc expresses the desperate resistance to her Necessity that periodically bestirs individuals and societies. Orc can be seen as a descendent of the speaker in "To Tirzah." Both *America* and *Europe* begin with mythological Preludia in which Blake ponders the relationship between Orc and "the shadowy female," a daughter of Enitharmon who stands for his erroneous projection of nature.

Contemporary revolutionary movements represent the awakening from centuries of Christianity and materialism. All this time humanity has been—to borrow a phrase from Wallace Stevens—asleep in its own life: "Eighteen hundred years: Man was a Dream!" (a "Human Illusion"; Eur 9:2, E63). But now that Newton has blown the "Trump" of doom, error comes to a head and the delusion implodes. Orc arises and contests with Urizen, the spirit of tyranny and reaction, the false God, whose punitive character parallels the frightfulness of the nature he is supposed to have created. It is specifically Enitharmon who has dreamt the "dream-Man" of the last eighteen-hundred years: that is to say, the false concept of "Mother Nature" fosters a false concept of humanity. What is wrong and damaging about this conception of nature? In the materialist paradigm, nature has wholly made us, and she is all that sustains and nourishes us—she is "mother" in this sense—but she is a devious and capricious mother, capable of causing undeserved harm at any moment; and in an act of supreme treachery, she made us mortal. How are we to regard this strange mother? With fear and trembling.

In *Europe* Enitharmon is shown exulting in her power; this exultation reflects at once the cruelty that has to be attributed to the fictitious Mother Nature and the truly malign triumph of the delusion itself. Later, in *Milton*, Blake will write the definitive version of the "shadowy female's" malicious monologue. Her sadism movingly illustrates the panic of Natural Man.

[39   ]

I will lament over Milton in the lamentations of the afflicted
My Garments shall be woven of sighs & heart broken lamentations
The misery of unhappy Families shall be drawn out into its border
Wrought with the needle with dire sufferings poverty pain & woe
Along the rocky Island & thence throughout the whole Earth
There shall be the sick Father & his starving Family! there
The Prisoner in the stone Dungeon & the Slave at the Mill
I will have Writings written all over it in Human Words
That every Infant that is born upon the Earth shall read
And get by rote as a hard task of a life of sixty years.

(M 18:5–14, E111)

In this view, natural reality is seen as essentially malign. Nature intends not only to crush human beings but also to make them see themselves as crushed—to defeat human agency and "teach" the "worm of sixty winters" his helplessness. She will prove that life is an inescapable round of miseries, demonstrating it over and over until he learns the terrible lesson "by rote." Every "poor mortal vegetation" shall be broken on this same wheel, "the Circle of Destiny," or conviction of one's entrapment. This is the some paranoid thought to which Thel was led: if nature is reality, then we are destined for humiliation.

In *Europe* Blake combines this psychological critique with a social one. He thinks that the sinister "mystery" of Mother Nature is assigned to—and exploited by—women themselves in a society that prescribes radically asymmetrical gender roles. In intervolving sexuality with sin and judgment, and imposing a cult of chastity on women in particular, Christian culture in the West has skewered the relations between men and women, reducing female sexuality to a mode of manipulation and forcing women into devious exertions of agency. The perverse power-pleasure that results Blake will eventually term (infelicitously) "the Female Will."[6] Enitharmon's speech of triumph links the malformation of the Female Will with the humiliation of the human being in materialism and in Christian doctrine.

Arise O Rintrah thee I call! & Palamabron thee!
Go! Tell the human race that Womans love is Sin!
That an Eternal Life awaits the worms of sixty winters
In an allegorical abode where existence hath never come:

> Forbid all Joy, & from her childhood shall the little female
> Spread nets in every secret path.   (Eur 5:4–9, E62)

Setting Enitharmon's malignity aside, in this speech we see Blake's asser-
tion that a certain set of religious and social formations are dialectically re-
lated: the displacement of divinity out of humanity (into the God beyond);
the consequent reduction in the status of the human being; the subjection to
sin, judgment, and punishment; the deferral of Eternal Life; the association
of sex with sin; the rise of the cult of chastity; the pathologizing of sex and
gender relations. He had adumbrated some of these connections in the *Songs
of Experience,* but here he is able to sum them up as elements of one consis-
tent program. The triumph of Enitharmon, or the Female Will, represents
the role that the concept of Mother Nature plays in encouraging people to
cooperate in their own degradation.

This degradation promotes fatalism: Nature arrogates to herself the
power of Necessity, and human beings, in their ontological diminishment,
lack any counterforce. Fatalism of this kind then invades the social sphere,
motivating conservatism and passivity. But from time to time the frustration
of helplessness grows too great to be borne. Resistance and rebellion burst
out, either within one heart or within an oppressed nation: this reckless defi-
ance is Orc, the adolescent terror. Blake admires Orc in some respects, but he
shows the impetuous resistance of Orc to be short lived. As Frye pointed out
in his analysis of the "Orc cycle," Orc flares up and all too soon subsides. The
reason is that he has launched a superficial insurgency. He may wish to re-
verse the power dynamic, but his conception of humanity and its relation to
power remains unchanged. Opposition born of despair retains despair and re-
verts to it. Fatalism still undergirds Orc's thinking: he throws himself against
the window like a little bird. His actions are intertwined with a crippled self-
conception; thus he is called "the Human Shadow" in *Urizen* (BU 19:43, E79),
another version of the "Human Illusion." He is a son of Los not only because
he represents some inkling of transcendence, although compromised be-
yond efficacy, but also because he represents an error, that is, an (unfortu-
nate) product of imagination. His birth to Enitharmon, in *Urizen,* precipi-
tates a crisis for his parents; a "tight'ning girdle" (BU 20:9, E80) spontaneously
encloses Los's chest, creating the "Chain of Jealousy" with which mother
and father bind their Promethean son to a rock. The meaning of this event is

presumably that in our world transcendental consciousness issues in self-defeating forms.

Orc rebels against a Necessity he knows no way of transcending. He kicks against the pricks. But the force by which he feels himself to be entrammeled is illusory: it is the classic example of a "mind-forg'd manacle" whose chains are "Brittle perhaps as straw" (Shelley's phrase, l. 182 from "Julian and Maddalo," *Shelley's Poetry and Prose*, 125). The natural world certainly has power over the human being, but only in some respects, and Blake takes the Kantian view that the sublime human "vocation" is to discover the soul's freedom from the domination of nature. In a multilayered irony, Orc represents despairing resistance to a self-generated concept of necessity. This is why, in the Preludia to *America* and *Europe,* he and the "shadowy female" are shown to be locked in a sadomasochistic symbiosis. In *America,* the "nameless female" brings food to Orc while he gestates for fourteen years in a "dark abode." She cannot speak until he rapes her, after which she exults in her possessive power: "I know thee, I have found thee, & I will not let thee go" (Amer 2:7, E52). Dark, violent gods and "struggling afflictions" for humanity are born. The shadowy daughter rightly perceives that the two of them, she and Orc, combine to extinguish humanity's hope for itself: "thy fire and my frost / Mingle in howling pains, in furrows by thy lightnings rent; / This is eternal death; and this the torment long foretold" (Amer 2:15–17, E52). Orc does not represent true opposition to the fatalism of material power; he is, rather, its partner, sustained by it in his despair as he bestows on it its voice and identity. In *Europe,* Blake shows more plainly that the shadowy female is Orc's projection, stipulating in the opening line of the Preludium that "The nameless shadowy female arose from out the breast of Orc" (Eur 1:1, E60). The rest of the Preludium consists of her anguished monologue; she is speaking not as gleeful mean mother (or wife or sister—she is all three in *America*), but as a Nature that shares in the existential dismay she creates, regarding herself too as a fount of futile being.

> My roots are brandish'd in the heavens, my fruits in earth beneath
> Surge, foam, and labour into life, first born & first consum'd
> Consumed and consuming!   (Eur 1:8–10, E60)

Like Thel, she quarrels with the vanity of own Creation, reproaching her mother Enitharmon for "caus[ing] my name to vanish, that my place may not be found." And she rejects existence on these terms: "Then why shouldst thou accursed mother bring me into life?" She takes this nihilistic view because she speaks for a concept of nature that identifies it strictly with linear temporality. She beholds infinity itself pass her by: "I see it smile & I roll inward & my voice is past" (Eur 2:16, E61). In the untitled proem to *Europe*, Blake asks a Fairy who has been mocking empiricism, "tell me, what is the material world, and is it dead?" (Eur iii:13, E60). The Fairy laughs and offers to "shew you all alive / The world, when every particle of dust breathes forth its joy" (Eur iii:16–17, E60). The grieving shadowy female is the "dead" nature of the empiricists—nature cut off from its own share in Eternity. Orc and the shadowy female, the humiliation of the soul and the death of nature, go hand in hand.

Debasement and Self-Division

In the second order of his argument, Blake moves inward to trace the impact of empiricist thinking on the structure of interior lives. Here he makes his most original claim: that this fearful definition of reality, and its philosophical and institutional ratification, causes the psyche to experience itself as fragmented. The sense of self-fragmentation creates passivity and paralysis. For this reason, Blake defines the Fall as a fall into self-division, and he shows that an acute sense of self-division can result from what we might term "mere" intellectual error—from misconceptions of the self and its relation to the world. In Blake's psychology, the vital metaphors used to characterize the interior life affect its experience of itself. Empiricism injures us insofar as it attempts to persuade us not only that the mind is passive with relation to material reality but also that it is divided and passive in relation to itself.

In his chapter on personal identity, Locke explicitly defines the self as no more than the "I" of present consciousness and its memories. To see the depth to which, in Blake's view, Lockean empiricism contributes to the fragmentation of subjectivity, we must go back a few steps. Locke's epistemology proposes that the mind is passive before an overwhelming external force, nature, which is irrational, insensible, and sinister. This representation implicitly formulates a concept of subjectivity in which the subject is consigned to psychic division and existential terror. Locke's views teach us terror by teaching us to regard the mind as the slave of the external world. His views consequently promote self-division by encouraging us to experience the relation of consciousness not just to the world but also to its own contents (the "impressions" and "reflections") as enfeebled.

A glance at the language of Locke's *Essay* suggests that Blake is not extrapolating recklessly. Blake detects real implications of Locke's argument: the reduction of the mind to merely natural status, and the concomitant redescription of it as narrow, mechanical, self-divided, and self-occluded. In his very first paragraph, Locke makes a rallying cry of the mind's imperfect self-knowledge.

> The Understanding, like the Eye, whilst it makes us see and perceive all other Things, takes no notice of it self: And it requires Art and Pains to set it at a distance and make it its own Object. But whatever be the Difficulties, that lie in the way of this Enquiry; whatever it be that keeps us so much in the Dark to our selves, sure I am, that all the Light we can let in upon our own Minds; all the Acquaintance we can make with our own Understandings, will not only be very pleasant, but bring us great Advantage, in directing our Thoughts in the search of other Things. (43)

According to Locke, it is a consequence of the very constitution of the mind that it should be unable fully to know itself. In this way he demonstrates the structural necessity of subjectivity's self-bewilderment. Blake would term this a deliberate act of self-sabotage.

Locke goes on to emphasize our mental limitations; he refers to "the narrowness of our Minds" (45) and says he wishes "to prevail with the busy Mind of Man, to be more cautious in meddling with things exceeding its Comprehension" (44–45). His anatomy of mental operations justifies this reduction of its status, for he describes the mind in materialist terms as a kind of natural organ with a fixed province and fixed processes. This account leads in turn to an almost willful emphasis on the mind's passivity.

> In this Part [sensation] the *Understanding* is meerly *passive;* and whether or no, it will have these Beginnings, and as it were, materials of Knowledge, is not in its own power. For the Objects of

[44]

our Senses do, many of them, obtrude their particular *Ideas* upon
our minds, whether we will or no: And the Operations of our
minds will not let us be without, at least, some obscure Notions
of them. No Man can be wholly ignorant of what he does when
he thinks. These *simple Ideas,* when offered to the mind, *the Under-
standing can* no more refuse to have, nor alter, when they are
imprinted, nor blot them out, and make new ones it self, than a
mirror can refuse, alter, or obliterate the Images or *Ideas* which
the Objects set before it, do therein produce.   (118)

Locke likens the mind to a mirror, compelled or forced to reflect images.
It is true that he describes only simple ideas here, but he treats even the for-
mation of complex ideas as uncreative. He is, as Frye says, subducting mental
processes that could be conceived of as active and imaginative into auto-
matic, reflexive, unconscious ones (22).

Locke reduces even "reflection" to a mechanical status. Reflection is "that
notice which the Mind takes of its own Operations, and the manner of them,
by reason whereof, there come to be *Ideas* of these Operations in the Under-
standing" (105). Locke defines reflection in a way that both divides and passi-
vates the mind: one half of it becomes the passive observer of automatic op-
erations in the other half. In fact—and this is startling—he says that when the
mind takes itself as an object, it incorporates the dichotomy of internal and
external into its own structure: the mind relates to its own operations in the
same way that it relates to the outside world.

> Such are, *Perception, Thinking, Doubting, Believing, Reasoning, Know-
> ing, Willing,* and all the different actings of our own Minds; which
> we, being conscious of and observing in ourselves, do from these
> receive into our Understandings as distinct *Ideas,* as we do from
> Bodies affecting our Senses. This Source of *Ideas* every Man has
> wholly in himself: And though it be not sense, as having nothing
> to do with external Objects; yet it is very like it, and might prop-
> erly enough be call'd internal Sense.   (105)

This description divides the mind into subject and object, or "I" (point of con-
sciousness) and Other (outside and alien), and thus imports into the very

structure of the interior the passivation and bewilderment of the Lockean subject in the material world. The experiencing consciousness undergoes two forms of alienation, an alienation from the outside world and from itself. For Locke's notion of consciousness creates its own abyss: the point of consciousness is diminished radically, but it remains self-conscious and, like Thel, conscious of itself, in particular, as an anomaly.

Visions of the Daughters of Albion reverses *Thel* insofar as it presents a heroine who is able to transcend the crippling mentality of empiricism, and instead it is the men of the poem who exemplify its corrosive effect on the experience of selfhood. After the rape, Oothoon asserts the integrity of her soul, and that assertion brings about major psychological and philosophical progress. She repudiates the empiricist subjectivity in which she perceives that she has been entrapped.

> Arise my Theotormon I am pure
> Because the night is gone that clos'd me in its deadly black.
> They told me that the night & day were all that I could see;
> They told me that I had five senses to inclose me up.
> And they inclos'd my infinite brain into a narrow circle.
> And sunk my heart into the Abyss, a red round globe hot burning
> Till all from life I was obliterated and erased.
>
> (VDA 2:28–34, E47)

These lines present in embryo a group of images for empiricist subjectivity that Blake will repeat and expand on all through the prophetic books. They echo the famous passage from the *Marriage* on "enclosure" in the senses, launch the description of shrinking down into the organs of the body, and end with the grim climax Blake returns to again and again—that the empiricist subject is obliterated from life. With this lament, Oothoon makes it clear that she has transcended the delusions of Bromion and Theotormon. In this respect, she is like the Gnostic Sophia (wisdom), who learns the truth by observing or experiencing the misdeeds of foolish male powers. Oothoon ridicules empiricism's reductive focus on the senses, and the uniformity of experience it consequently stipulates. Instinct, desire, knowledge, and purpose are, manifestly, not uniform: "Ask the wild ass why he refuses burdens: and the meek camel / Why he loves man: is it because of eye ear mouth or skin / Or breathing nostrils? No. for these the wolf and tyger have" (VDA 3:7–9,

E47). And what about human beings? Can everything in the mind really be traced back to sensory input? Oothoon dares the empiricist to give an exhaustive inventory of mental life, to "tell me the thoughts of man, that have been hid of old" (VDA 3:13, E47).

Theotormon and Bromion are prompted by this sally to give their two remarkable speeches. Exemplifying two different internalizations of empiricism, they address the question of thoughts and their provenance. It should be pointed out that this array of speeches does not constitute a discussion: Theotormon does not respond to the substance of what Oothoon has said, but speaks, out of his own isolation and darkness, a meditation on the topic of thoughts and feelings. Bromion seizes on what Theotormon says and gleefully menaces him with greater mental terrors. Neither Theotormon nor Bromion really hears anyone else. But why in any case are thoughts and feelings the central topic? Oothoon has correctly deduced that the real issue is not the relation of mind to body, but of the subject to her own subjectivity. A victim of rape can declare the sanctity of her soul, as Oothoon has done, but what if she does not feel herself to be in secure possession of soul, that is, what if the empiricist ideology leads her to experience alienation from her own mental life so that she becomes, to herself, a disarticulated motley of sensoria, "impressions," and thoughts? A merely empirical self cannot assert the superiority of spirit over matter—much less one that cannot call itself an essence. So Oothoon rejects the dissolution of the mystery, but naturally her argument fails to penetrate the all-absorbing circle of self in Theotormon and Bromion.

Theotormon utters the anxiety of the empiricist subject bewildered by his own thoughts, which seem autonomous and alien: "Tell me what is a thought? & of what substance is it made? / Tell me what is a joy? & in what gardens do joys grow? / And in what rivers swim the sorrows?" (VDA 3:22–25, E47). His materialist vocabulary is clearly inadequate for describing what he intuits about his mental life. If Oothoon were speaking, the questions would be rhetorical, and they would point to a source of thought unacknowledged in empiricist epistemology. But they are real questions for Theotormon, as is shown by the fact that he remains turned inward and tormented. He has been told that all thoughts are derived from experience, and, therefore, is left wondering at their strange power and provenance. This power cannot be ascribed to the "might" of the soul. Therefore thoughts are not under the control of the experiencing subject, the "I," but seem to exert some uncanny self-determination.

> Where goest thou O thought to what remote land is thy flight?
> If thou returnest to the present moment of affliction
> Wilt thou bring comforts on thy wings. and dews and
>   honey and balm;
> Or poison from the desart wilds, from the eyes of the envier.

(VDA 4:8–11, E48)

Theotormon manifests an estrangement from his own subjectivity, which takes two slightly different forms. His thoughts and emotions are not under his own power: he cannot predict whether those now developing will be consoling or poisonous. This makes some sense insofar as anticipation belongs to the future. But Theotormon is also puzzled as to the whereabouts of thoughts, especially memories and past feelings, which seem to come and go at their own volition. "Tell me where dwell the joys of old! & where the ancient loves? / And when will they renew again & the night of oblivion past?" (VDA 4:2–3, E48). He asks what has been since antiquity an important philosophical question: How does the mind preserve memories such that they can return to consciousness after having been forgotten? This question is particularly pressing for a Lockean empiricist if he or she should take literally what Locke says in his essay on personal identity: only those memories available to consciousness go to make up identity. What then becomes of forgotten experience? Is it really as if past time had never been but has instead vanished into the "night of oblivion"? Is subjective life so insignificant, so phantasmal? (This passage forecasts the antagonism to empiricist "Memory," which Blake will work out more clearly in later works; see further on in this book.) In fact, Theotormon's representation of his interiority is not such an aberration: memories are elusive, and thoughts are unpredictable. The problem lies in his reaction to these features of mental life; because he cannot refer these mysteries to the soul, he feels simply helpless. From helplessness springs anxiety, and anxiety begets more helplessness. Blake holds empiricism responsible for this downward spiral of self-estrangement.

If Theotormon represents the depressive side of empiricism, Bromion is its manic half. Theotormon feels powerless, whereas Bromion delights in an aggrandized sense of personal power that expresses itself in tyranny and sadism. He taunts Theotormon with the overwhelming plenitude of the material world. Theotormon may feel like a pip of a creature, but if he only knew how little he knows, he would feel even smaller and more insignificant.

> trees beasts and birds unknown:
> Unknown, not unpercievd, spread in the infinite micoscope,
> In places yet unvisited by the voyager, and in worlds
> Over another kind of seas, and in atmospheres unknown
>
> (VDA 4:15–18, E48)

Given the limitations of experience, an intellect that has gained all its knowledge from the senses will remain abysmally ignorant, a just object of mockery. But why then does Bromion feel so powerful? It turns out that he is thinking like the god of the law—the God both of the Hebrew Bible (as Blake saw it) and the Deists. Blake regards this god as a projection of the omnipotent agency the disempowered empiricist subject longs to have. This agency is conceived of as personal or individual. As the empiricist subject feels alone and helpless, so the dream is to be alone but all-powerful. Individual agency demonstrating its power to itself is likely to do so by exerting power over others through sadism and tyranny. Identifying with the god of law, Bromion exults in the oppressive and threatening arrangement He has stipulated:

> And is there not one law for both the lion and the ox?
> And is there not eternal fire, and eternal chains?
> To bind the phantoms of existence from eternal life.
>
> (VDA 4:22–24, E48)

The "phantoms of existence" are human subjects, that is, subjects like Theotormon who conceive of themselves as frail and insubstantial. They do not realize that they now have transcendental or eternal life, and they can continue to be distracted or "bound" from it by its deferral to a dubious afterlife—dubious partly because it is notional and partly because one might not reach it after all but be damned instead. Bromion has the makings of the punitive god, with his "Net of Religion," whom Blake will critique in detail under the name of Urizen. In fact, Blake uses the name for the first time when he has Oothoon respond to Bromion obliquely by rebuking what we are invited to imagine is his "inspiration," Urizen: "O Urizen! Creator of men! Mistaken Demon of heaven: / Thy joys are tears! thy labour vain, to form men to thine image" (VDA 5:3–4, E48). She implicitly distinguishes between the tyrannical self-imposition of a Urizen and the visionary independence she herself exemplifies. With his universal law and homogenization of desire, she says, he treats everyone as if they shared his nature, and, in fact, aims to turn them into a version of himself. (In *Milton* Blake will say that Satan—in that poem the fallen form of Urizen—"to himself [makes] Laws from his own identity" [M 11:10, E104]). By contrast, the result of Oothoon's self-assertion— if it be right to use this contemporary term—is that she discovers her freedom and generously calls on others to embrace theirs: "Arise and drink your bliss, for every thing that lives is holy!" (VDA 8:10, E51). At this point, Blake readily separates prophetic self-assertion from diseased egoism, although in later poems he will find it necessary to reexamine this distinction.

In *The Book of Urizen* Blake expands his study of the pathology of individuation in the empiricist subject, but the beginnings of his argument are evident here. Individuation of agency yields not only the will to domination but also the rigorous confrontation of self with Other. The singular agent fortifies its singularity by imposing uniformity on the multitude of others. "One law for both the lion and the ox" becomes Urizen's encompassing equation: "One command, one joy, one desire, / One curse, one weight, one measure / One King, one God, one Law" (BU 4:38–40, E72). "I" versus it. *One* God leads to *one* law: individuation to hegemony to homogeneity. In the later prophetic books, Blake will identify the double-barreled strategy of asserting selfhood and dominating otherness with moralism or "the Self righteousness / In all its Hypocritic turpitude" (M 38:43-4, E185). For the moment we see that Blake is drawing psychological connections among the desire for personal power, the perceived helplessness of the empiricist subject, and the heartless tyranny of that subject's God. Oothoon repudiates the whole package, including sexual repression and the moralizing cult of virginity. She reproaches Bromion, "Father of Jealousy," for teaching "my Theotormon this accursed thing," and she foresees that as a rejected beloved, and a dissident, she will end as "A solitary shadow wailing on the margin of non-entity" (VDA 7:11,12,14, E50). These are just the terms in which Blake will describe the prophetic Emanations; Oothoon is thus a forerunner of the exiled wisdom represented by Enion and Ahania. It is the fate of these Emanations, as of most prophets, not to be heard. So Oothoon is last glimpsed reiterating her lament "every morning," while Theotormon remains deaf, englobed in his punishing fantasies, sitting "Upon the margind

ocean conversing with shadows dire" (VDA 7:15, E50). And although Oothoon
can look back and analyze her deluded state, from now on Blake's characters
are going to spend most of their time struggling in that state. Oothoon's con-
version is swift and effective; it will not be so easy for anyone else. In fact, it
will become standard for Blake's male characters to take the route either of
Theotormon or Bromion—that is, either subsiding into passivity, like Tharmas,
or retreating into the defensive formation of atomic selfhood, like Urizen.

Atomic Selfhood

As Blake proceeds he goes deeper and deeper into a psychological analysis of
the experience of selfhood that empiricism codifies. For empiricism did not
invent the misconception of humanity; rather, it brings an age-old pattern to
its culmination. Eventually Blake extends his critique back to the Greeks, the
first "natural philosophers." To accept the reality of the natural world is au-
tomatically to be plunged into despair and paranoia about the status of the
self: What am I? How shall I endure in this wretched world of death? Why
am I cursed with subjectivity? Stoicism first addressed itself to the despair and
paranoia of subjectivity, although ultimately Stoicism works itself around
to a reconciliation with nature. But once the Stoical description of the inner
life is adopted the Stoical solution follows: all that I can govern is my own
thought and emotion, I must shape my experience of experience, and that re-
quires self-discipline, specifically, the exertion of Reason, or the select "good"
self. To Blake, the engorgement of Reason launched in ancient Greece was a
disaster, not only a social and cultural disaster but also a psychic disaster, be-
cause it isolates and reifies one aspect of the self while subjugating others,
and this can only produce internal distortion and tormenting self-alienation.
All models of faculty psychology from Plato onward that oppose Reason to
something else in the self—passion, imagination, appetite, and so forth—
propagate a noxious concept.

The empiricists and the philosophes, the thinkers of the "Age of Reason,"
recreate this destructive error by embracing the humanism of the Classical
period: so Blake will insist years later when he says, in his accusatory address
"To the Deists," "But your Greek Philosophy . . . teaches that Man is Right-
eous in his Vegetated Spectre: an Opinion of fatal & accursed consequence to
Man" (J 52, E200). The "Vegetated Spectre" is natural reason. To teach that

"Man is Righteous in his Vegetated Spectre" is to teach that Reason is the loftiest faculty and its cultivation the highest form of humanity. These teachings depend on the premise that if the natural world is reality than Natural Man is the only man, and his greatest achievement is to become the chief thing in nature; this he does by becoming its "master," dominating it through knowledge and analysis. Not only is this clearly a doomed enterprise, but even to aspire to master nature means to grasp its laws through an aspect of thought—Reason—that can know them, ironically, not because it can transcend them but because it most nearly mimes their mechanical processes. Locke's emphasis on the mechanical functions of mind tallies with the enlightenment conception of Reason to which Blake so vividly objected. To Blake, the enshrinement of Reason appallingly isolates and exalts the "legal" or logical mental processes, the aspect of mind that, although conscious, most resembles the sinister Necessity of nature with its Newtonian regulation and monotony. Exalting Reason equals exalting the aspect of *conscious* mind most like a mechanism; this is sheer paradox to Blake. The mind that cows itself with obedience to laws—the laws of nature and, just as bad, its own laws or the laws of logic—pledges itself to stultification. Enlightenment Reason is perversely self-limiting, or self-enclosing and self-englobing.

Now we begin to see why Blake calls the exaltation of Reason "an Opinion of *fatal & accursed* consequence to Man." Natural reason struggles vainly to distinguish itself from nature—vainly because it has already given up the game. It therefore inclines to defensive paranoia. The violent caprice and the punishing "clock-time" of the natural world make it, for us, a hateful chaos. We exert the "I," a fierce little node of self-consciousness against it, but that requires isolating this node out of the rest of the interior, and all else that is in us then seems alien and chaotic too—it is the inscrutable part of us conspiring with foreign Nature. Out of this increased apprehension—now of inner as well as outer chaos—we bulk up the little "I," or ego, but the more power and autonomy it tries to seize, the smaller and more helpless it becomes, because it is futile for any creature of the order of nature to crave power over it or even autonomy in it. The paranoid, grasping ego, the "condensed" or "opake" precipitate of one's anxieties is the atomic self.

Blake anatomizes the "tormenting passions" of this lonely "I" in the opening chapters of *The Book of Urizen*. Urizen falls because he individuates, separating himself out from Eternity.

Lo, a shadow of horror is risen
In Eternity! Unknown, unprolific!
Self-closd, all-repelling: what Demon
Hath form'd this abdominable void
This soul-shudd'ring vacuum?—Some said
"It is Urizen," But unknown, abstracted
Brooding secret, the dark power hid.

(BU 3:1–7, E70)

As usual in Blake, the moment of creation is simultaneously the moment of the fall; here it is the joint creation and fall of the individual soul. Anxiety results immediately, as the world divides into the "I" and the not-"I." Urizen has hypostasized the external world as everything outside him—alien to, and empty of, his own consciousness. The void he creates is the whole material universe, bereft of consciousness, and also the dark hollow in it where consciousness used to be. Naturally he finds this "external" universe to be threatening, and he develops a fearful, hostile, and violent relation to it, embarking on futile efforts to bring it under his control. "Times on times he divided, & measur'd / Space by space in his ninefold darkness" (BU 3:8–9, E70). His relation to his own "I" becomes schizoid. Sometimes Urizen exults: as the only consciousness, he is the only power ("I alone, even I"). And sometimes he feels dwarfed and disempowered: as the only consciousness, he is a mere phantasm in a dead material world. He develops power hunger as a reaction to his sense of impotence. He is a "self-contemplating shadow," spooked by his own insubstantiality (BU 3:21, E71).

But individuation deals still deeper traumas to the experience of subjectivity. By narrowing identity to the center of consciousness that is the rational self, or "I," Urizen has made an abyss of his own interiority. His consolidation of identity, his assertion and defense of the "I," results in inner fragmentation. Blake did not need Freud to tell him that defining the self as the "I" excludes powerful and importunate presences of the inner life. These intimidate the "I" insofar as they are not under its control, and so Urizen develops a fearful, hostile, and violent relation to his own interiority. He universalizes the obscure aspects of the self under the name of the "Seven deadly Sins of the soul,"—"terrible monsters Sin-bred: / Which the bosoms of all inhabit" (BU 4:28–29, E72). He seeks to legislate and punish them. In himself he finds the alien and inscrutable menace he made of the outside world. Or, perhaps, it is the other way around: he has interpreted the external world in light of his internal chaos. Urizen "strove in battles dire / In unseen conflictions with shapes / Bred from his forsaken wilderness" (BU 3:14–15, E70): is the wilderness internal or external? Blake suggests that the inner and outer void are parallel developments.

> First I fought with the fire; consum'd
> Inwards, into a deep world within:
> A void immense, wild dark & deep,
> Where nothing was; Nature's wide womb.

> (BU 4:14–19, E72)

The ambiguities here imply that the "deep world within" was created simultaneously with the void of Nature, "wild dark & deep." Both are described as abysses "Where nothing was," yet that nothing is clearly full of danger, for it is the not-"I." The dark infinity of the alien, both within and without, spring into being together upon the advent of the "I." Both are soul-shuddering vacuums: the "I" shudders at the voids it has made of the world and of itself. More deeply, these voids issue out of the shuddering or fearful self-affection of the soul, the moment in which it consolidates its identity and feels alone.

Many scholars have noted Urizen's similarity to the Gnostic Demiurge—he is a negative "creator" in the same sense, with all the same arrogance and presumption.[7] Yet he is most like the Demiurge in his haughty singularity: "I alone, even I!" The individuation "natural" to the empiricist subject is sin and error to the Gnostics. In *Urizen* Blake begins to measure the alternatives to empiricism insofar as he uses other bodies of thought to critique it. He finds a challenge to empiricism in the early heterodoxies of Gnosticism and Neoplatonism, which treat the alienation of consciousness while still investing the soul with divinity. In fact they explain the alienation of consciousness—or loneliness of the soul—as a consequence of its divinity. Blake knew the basic ideas of Gnosticism—the Demiurge and his disastrous creation, the evil of the cosmos, the hidden God, the alienation of the soul—and it is clear that he was stimulated by the Gnostic perspective when he wrote the first stanza of *Urizen*. But we have to proceed carefully because of Blake's complex relation to his sources. He rarely cites anything without critiquing and transforming it. So Blake departs from Gnosticism almost immediately, or it might be better to say that he "subsumes" it, for he performs a psychological analysis of the mythology, in the process overturning some of what are revealed to be the more literal Gnostic beliefs.

In *Urizen* Blake is inspired by Gnostic and Neoplatonic ideas, but he is hardly beholden to them.[8] He would have arrived at the same conclusions without ever hearing of these ancient religions, although where he found them, he examined them and put what he liked to use. Here we enter into the controversies surrounding the sources of his heretical ideas. In his book *Witness against the Beast,* E. P. Thompson objected to Kathleen Raine's work on Blake because she places him within a tradition (Behmen, Neoplatonism, hermeticism, Kabbalah) that is "academic to the core" (xvi). Thompson does not name George Mills Harper, who wrote *The Neoplatonism of William Blake,* but presumably he would find Harper guilty of the same elitism. Against their view, Thompson argued that Blake learned most from the radical popular religion of the English Reformation. The material he quotes from various outlying dissident sects—particularly concerning the claim that Christ is everyman and that God is "internal" to humanity—resonates beautifully with Blake. Thompson proposed that Blake's family was Muggletonian, but since Thompson's book was published, evidence has come to light suggesting that Blake's mother was a member of the less radical Moravian sect, which, like other revivalist Protestant groups, preached regeneration by faith.[9]

Raine and Thompson contend over the question of the immediate sources of Blake's thought. But one does not have to go far back to see that their contrasting traditions are in fact intertwined. In itself the opposition of heretical "popular" sources with "esoteric" ones should be treated with caution. For the radical movements Thompson admires had sources themselves, drawing on a long tradition of heterodoxy that actually goes back to the ancient heresies, including Gnosticism and hermeticism. Frances Yates made this complex and exuberant mix of ideas in the Renaissance her object of study, arguing that heretical ideas infiltrated both high and low culture. Perhaps Gnosticism and Neoplatonism should not be regarded as pieces of esoteric tradition; it is the texts that belong to the academy not the ideas. In practice it is not so easy to distinguish between what Thompson would call the "esoteric" and the "popular" tradition. Medieval Catharism, which for a period dominated rural Provence, was a Gnostic religion, a broad popular movement with a rarefied origin. Thompson agrees that some of the popular religious movements by which Blake was influenced—Behmenism, for example—ultimately had a Gnostic lineage, and that Blake may have come by his acquaintance with Gnosticism from such "second-hand sources" (35). That is good enough for me.

But I find that neither Thompson nor Raine accords Blake enough originality in his relation to his influences. He did not transcribe anyone else's ideas. He adapted whatever he knew and liked. Of course it is not just a question of sources. It is a question of what we should regard as Blake's basic inspiration, and how we should think of him as an intellectual. Here I agree in essence with Thompson that Blake was an energetic dissident emerging out of a radical popular tradition. I would simply like to name as "Gnostic" the kernel of religious humanism in all the religions in which he participated sympathetically: his family religion, the alternative religions he entertained as an adult (Behmen's and Swedenborg's), and the ancient religions he knew about. By "religious humanism," I do not mean to exclude religions with supernatural or mystical ideas, but to identify religions that treat the human as the divine. I cite Gnosticism first because it came first. Blake was a religious humanist of this kind, rejecting orthodoxy on account of its anthropomorphized Creator-God and its subjection of the human soul. As Morton Paley summarizes it, "His attitude is unabashedly Gnostic and Manichaean, which is not to say that he had been reading books on those subjects but rather that the values associated with those attitudes came to life again in him" (*The Traveler in the Evening* 295). Henry Crabb Robinson laughingly told Blake, late in his life, that he was a Gnostic, and Blake agreed enthusiastically that he was (Bentley 545). It is not a stretch to say that those Gnostic and Manichaean attitudes also came to life in English radical religion.

Blake may have an unabashedly Gnostic attitude, but he debunks the Gnostic mythology without hesitation. Blake borrows the image of the almost comical Demiurge, but he does not accept the Gnostic cosmology in which the Demiurge plays such a critical role. He does not believe that there was a demon, a nonhuman being, who wrought the material world to our sorrow. As Thomas J. Altizer points out, Urizen is not an external agency, but a psychological phenomenon (88). Urizen is a part of us—and in fact a part of Blake, an incomplete authorial surrogate. Blake often writes from his point of view, and accords him considerable sympathy. That is what the myth really tells us,

Blake would say: we have within us an imp of the perverse, a Demiurge, who incites us to anxious individuation and then "creates" the material world as an enemy of consciousness. Whereas the Demiurge is a dummy villain, Urizen is an anguishing error we commit again and again every day.

Plainly, Blake is intrigued by the psychological suggestiveness and power of Gnostic mythology. He does not care for its cosmology or theology, and he treats those doctrines as mythological, too. As Stuart Curran puts it: in relation to Gnosticism, Blake achieves, "an almost classic case of infiltration and subversion" ("Blake and the Gnostic Hyle" 130). Blake is already at work subverting Gnostic theory in the opening stanza of *Urizen,* where he dispenses with the Gnostic conception of God. "But unknown, abstracted, / Brooding secret, the dark power hid." The word *unknown* plays on the Gnostic term *agnostos theos* (the Unknown God) just as "secret," "dark," and "hid" play on the Gnostic idea of the hidden God more generally. "Brooding" comes of course from Genesis, and "abstracted" is chosen, apparently, out of Blake's arsenal of terms for mocking Natural Religion and the New Science. The "abstracted" God is the deus absconditus of Deism. By condensing these references into a single line, Blake is suggesting that all of these gods are really one: one mysterious, inaccessible object of desire. The Gnostics parodied the God of the Hebrew Bible in their portrait of the Demiurge, and Blake zestfully adopts their strategy. But he also turns the screw to suggest that their hidden God is no better. Even though it is no longer anthropomorphized, divinity is still displaced out of the human grasp, and for the present, the soul must long for union with it in vain. But, Blake counters, "All deities reside in the human breast" (MHH 11:83, E38). He embraces the Gnostic assertion that there is a "pneuma," a transcendent or acosmic self, but he jettisons Gnosticism's proliferation of divine beings including the enigmatic Unknown God. He preferred the ontology of Neoplatonism, which replaces entities with impersonal layers of being.

Blake might have read parts of the *Enneads* in the translation of his contemporary Thomas Taylor ("the London Platonist"), and in particular might have known the treatise "On the Descent of the Soul." This translation was published in 1794, the year Blake wrote *Urizen,* but he could have heard it earlier in a salon presentation.[10] Yet the value of comparing Blake and Plotinus does not turn on whether he actually knew the work of Thomas Taylor. Blake understood the basic outlines of Neoplatonism regardless of how he came by his knowledge. Comparison with Taylor's Plotinus is worthwhile because it enables us to distinguish what was original in Blake's view. Plotinus asserts that, "by a voluntary descent which is also involuntary" (M 339), the soul turns away from the All, wishing to stand alone. This is the apostasy that creates Urizen. "What was it that made the souls forget their Father God and, although parts from There and wholly of that world, made them ignorant of themselves and Him? The origin of evil was the boldness [tolma] and the entering into becoming [genesis] and the first otherness and the will to belong to themselves" (Jonas, "The Soul in Gnosticism and Plotinus" 330–31). The Eternals say that Urizen emerged as "the first otherness," and they attribute his separation to his own agency, or self-will. He is "self-closed, all-repelling," he "forms" the void, he hides. But how, in changeless Eternity, does this will to individuate arise? Following Plotinus, Blake represents it as spontaneous. It emerges of itself at some unpredictable moment. It is a strangely automatic exertion of the will. Such discriminations remove this explanation of the "fall" from cosmology to psychology. Plotinus is describing a swerve that arises from something inherent in the nature of the soul, in other words, as a psychological temptation. In fact, Hans Jonas argues in "The Soul in Gnosticism and Plotinus" that this is the point at which Gnosticism and Neoplatonism converge. Individuation is the Gnostic and Neoplatonic version of original sin, but it has almost none of the connotations of the Christian concept, which no doubt made it all the more appealing to Blake. It is not, at root, a moral but a cognitive failure. If anyone is betrayed it is oneself, not the fearsome, nonexistent Nobodaddy. Guilt is irrelevant. There is no crime—certainly nothing inherited from the days of Adam!—but error. And the error can be undone. The fall is psychological, and, therefore, reiterated every day by the individual psyche, first in its impulse to distinguish itself, and then in the loneliness and anxiety that follow.

> When they pass from their situation with universal soul, so as to become a part, and to subsist by themselves, as if weary of abiding with another, then each recalls itself to the partial concerns of its own peculiar nature. When, therefore, any particular soul acts in this manner for an extended period of time, flying from the whole, and apostasizing from thence by a certain distinction and disagreement, no longer beholding an intelligible nature, from its

partial subsistence, in this case it becomes deserted and soliary, impotent and distracted with cares: for it now directs its mental eye to a part, and by a separation from that which is universal, attaches itself as a slave to one particular nature, flying from every thing else as if desirous to be lost. Hence by an intimate conversion to this partial essence, and being shaken off, as it were, from total and universal natures, it thus degenerates from the whole, and governs particulars with anxiety and fatigue; assiduously cultivating externals, and becoming not only present with body, but profoundly entering its dark abodes.

(Plotinus, *Five Books of Plotinus* 266–68)

This description serves as an efficient summary of Urizen's fate, as dramatized in chapters 1 through 4 of *The Book of Urizen*. His is a self-amplifying error; disastrous consequences spread out like concentric waves of water. Defending his individuality, he becomes "deserted and solitary, impotent and distracted with cares." He identifies himself with his body, and finally shrinks down into it, becoming inert. The Eternals write his epitaph: he is "a clod of clay."

Blake's signal innovation here is to reinterpret both religion and philosophy in light of their psychological implications. Blake argues that Gnosticism, Neoplatonism, and empiricism have psychological content, hidden within the metaphors or "myths" of epistemology and ontology. A given philosophy has psychological implications insofar as it offers a particular view of the subject and its relation to "objects." In his address "To the Deists," Blake insists "Man must & will have Some Religion; if he has not the Religion of Jesus, he will have the Religion of Satan" (J 52, E201). As an atheist, Blake does not mean that you must believe in God, but rather than you will have a conception of what a human being is, what nature is, whether there is divinity anywhere (and if so, where), and whether you chose it consciously—Gnosticism, Neoplatonism, empiricism, and so forth—take your pick, but you will pick one.

Empiricism is to Blake the least desirable because it authorizes the error of Urizen, the evacuation of any context for subjectivity. The words Blake uses in *Urizen*—"void" and "vacuum"—subtly jibe at the New Science; they describe Newtonian space, or the vastnesses of an indifferent universe. Pascal gazed up at them and felt a Urizenic dread: "Cast into the infinite immensity of spaces of which I am ignorant, and which know me not, I am frightened" (quoted in Jonas, *Gnostic Religion*, 322). In contrast to Gnosticism, the material world has no malevolent intentions toward the soul, but that is because it is dead, and there is no soul. Locke shrinks the self down into empirical consciousness, or "personal identity," the continuity of one consciousness over time. In a modern spirit, he declines to attribute to it any transcendent capacity. The Platonic subject is lonely, too, but its loneliness is radically different. As Jonas points out, the forlornness and dread of the Gnostic arise from the awakening of the soul; it perceives its transcendence and feels anomalous, trapped, in the material world. The recognition of its exile is the first element of the liberating gnosis. It must find its real home. In empiricism, solitary consciousness fronts an alien world, and that is the final discovery.

To locate one's being in an "I" is a losing proposition, as Urizen's fate makes clear. His frantic struggles to shore up and defend his "I"—to safeguard it from internal and external menace—finally overtake and absorb him completely. He becomes lost to experience, turned in upon himself, inert. He has shrunk down into Lockean humanity, the loose affiliation of mortal body and obsolete consciousness. The Eternals say he is "Death / A clod of clay" (BU 6:10, E74): they see him as he must come to see himself, as a merely phenomenal being doomed to die. When Urizen raves about the power of consciousness ("I alone, even I"), he is reacting against his own desperate suspicion: all that is real of him is his bones. Consciousness will dissipate and leave the remains of matter. So it is his skeleton that is ultimately his "identity." In the illustration to plate 7, Urizen curls up in the fetal position, fleeing the horror of his own conception, but it is a vain effort (because you can't flee your own mind) leading to deeper paralysis (Blake, *The Urizen Books* 75). Tharmas feels the same horror. Just before he calls himself "a Nothing left in darkness," he expresses hopeless dread of the material body. As long as the body is mistaken for the subtending reality, everything else about human beings will be reduced to illusion, and nothing will be seen in them but mortal fate.

> The Infant Joy is beautiful, but its anatomy [skeleton]
> Horrible ghast & deadly nought shalt thou find in it
> But dark despair & everlasting brooding melancholy.
>
> (FZ 22:22–24, E167)

Materialism spells mortalism, and mortalism harrasses the Selfhood: the unique little "I" dreads its extinction (or Eternal Death of the soul) above all else precisely because it has learned to value its uniqueness above all else. And the threat of Eternal Death evacuates life of meaning. So suggests Luvah, the love god of *The Four Zoas,* who takes no comfort in Epicurean assurances that the soul is mortal. This means that after a lifetime of vexing passions, we will merely be scattered back into warring atoms. (Blake quotes here from Cicero's paraphrase of Democritus.)

> We all go to Eternal Death
> To our Primeval Chaos in fortuitous concourse of incoherent
> Discordant principles of Love & Hate. (FZ 27:11–13, E318)

The dissolution of identity retroactively invalidates experience in a being that has defined itself specifically *as* identity. Thus the "I" is undone and knows its futility. As Blake puts it, not unsympathetically, "The little weeping Spectre stands on the threshold of Death / Eternal" (M 28[30]:10–11, E126).

But what about the Christian promise of the afterlife? We might expect Blake to approve the Christian concept of the immortal soul (which has a Neoplatonic lineage, after all) but here his thought takes an impressive turn. He argues that Christianity identifies the soul with the "I" (the unique empirical self) and then, through its emphasis on personal salvation, fosters self-concern and more—promotes Urizenic terrors. Blake's Milton magnificently denounces the conception of the self instilled by the Christian church, which he humorously addresses under the name of "Satan."

> Thy purpose & the purpose of thy Priests & of thy Churches
> Is to impress on men the fear of death; to teach
> Trembling & fear, terror, constriction; abject selfishness
> Mine is to teach Men to despise death & to go on
> In fearless majesty annihilating Self, laughing to scorn
> Thy Laws & terrors. (M 38[43]:37–49, E139)

How does Christianity exacerbate the "fear of death," when it would seem to offer reassuring promises of immortality? It does this in two ways. First, it introduces the dread of punishment in the afterlife. (Just think of Samuel Johnson.) And second (here Blake's thought is much more original), by removing the experience of immortality to another world—hazy, fantasied, improbable—it succeeds in exposing us to corrosive doubt. Blake's theory is that anyone who accepts the Christian doctrine of the soul will be haunted by the fear that it is not true, and that the soul instead of advancing into an afterlife is going down to Eternal Death. Christianity has a crypto-materialist effect despite being putatively transcendental.

In *Milton* Blake will evolve a term for the "I" as it degenerates into a grasping ego: he calls it the "Selfhood," and rejects it as "a false Body, an Incrustation over my Immortal Spirit" (M 40:35–6, E142). The Selfhood is a misconstruction of the self, an ill-fated and delusory fragment falsely representing itself as the whole. For it is no more than the "I" or node of consciousness, a particularly pathetic entity fighting a losing battle to protect its boundaries, that is, its own sense of itself as real, substantial, and effectual. It will lose this battle because it is self-doubting—it perceives that it does not have the substance of a material thing—and it is acquisitive, imperialist, vaunting, violent, tyrannical, and defensive in proportion as it is secretly terrified. The character of Urizen, "Self-closed, all-repelling," is essentially the character of the Selfhood or Spectre, opposing, in vain, its imperiled vital singularity to an encroaching world of death. The insistence on singularity—or the uniqueness of the soul—necessarily leads to the dread of Eternal Death, and then on to gross selfishness. As the Spectre of Urthona says of himself in assaulting Enitharmon, "Thou knowest that the Spectre is in Every Man insane brutish / Deformd that I am thus a ravening devouring lust continually / Craving & devouring" (FZ 84:36–37, E360). The ego, desperate to preserve its reality, will descend into mad possessiveness. Ironically, the Spectre, as the precipitate of consciousness or the ego, is also Enlightenment Reason brought to its disassociated and distorted extreme. Instead of being the seat of objectivity, it is the source of self-concern. Blake's Milton, who has overcome his narrow rationalism, consequently pledges himself to "Self-Annihilation" and he denounces "Satan's" Churches for promoting a craven longing after personal salvation (M 38:37ff, E139, quoted in full below). The "Self" Milton pledges to annihilate is the ego, the singular soul, or what philosophical discourse calls "personal identity." To privilege one's uniqueness is a mistake, because it gives rise to a profound sense of vulnerability—and hence, as we have seen, to anxieties about loneliness, incapacity, and death. Blake thinks adherence to identity a misguided aim and a form of constraint. When it means personal uniqueness, "identity" is a hostile term in his vocabulary. Satan, the hypocrite, makes "to himself Laws from his own identity" (M 11[12]:10, E104), while the pitiful, well-meaning Tharmas can be seen "Pursuing the Vain Shadow of Hope fleeing from identity" (FZ 108:2, E383).

The final definitive error is the limitation of the true or full self to this "Identity." I use the words "true or full self" advisedly. Blake would not use them, because he treats "self," "Selfhood," and "Identity" synonymously as three names for the illusion of the unique, atomic "I"; his alternative, his term for the unbounded wealth of the interior, is "Imagination," a universal rather than individual reserve. Blake provocatively suggests that Albion, or England, "los[es] the Divine Vision" by "Turning his Eyes outward to Self" (FZ 23:2, E313), as if the Selfhood were superficial and inauthentic, outlying. This is what Blake's Milton claims, too, when he rejects his Selfhood as "a false Body" and an "Incrustation" (M 40[46]:35–36, E142). The location of all the value and power of the inner world in this "crust," this Selfhood, is manifestly reductive, and in its reductiveness it automatically creates a sense of self-division. Urizen identifies himself with his Reason, and the result is a paranoid relation to his interior life: "The Spectre is the Man the rest is only delusion & fancy" (FZ 12:29, E307). To Urizen, Reason is respectable, and "the rest"—passion and imagination, or whatever terms we wish to use—is foreign, suspicious, and disturbing. One of the worst crimes of the Enlightenment is to encourage this identification of the "real self" with Reason or the seat of consciousness.

The Books of *Ahania* and *Los* provide additional perspectives on the creation and fall of Urizen. In particular, they elaborate on his reductiveness, his precipitation out of some larger figure of mind. On this subject, *The Book of Urizen* is powerfully abrupt and cryptic, opening in medias res with the summons to behold the "shadow of horror" that has suddenly appeared. Blake did not want to tamper with this dramatic beginning, but he had more to say about the formation of Urizen, and satisfied himself (for the moment) by relegating the other ideas to satellite works. These two books portray Urizen not as a spontaneous self-creation but as a mutation from a vital form. *The Book of Los* reminds us that Los and Urizen, or imagination and Reason, are not naturally distinguishable; it is an artifact of error that they set themselves at odds. Thus, the fall of Los is described in exactly the same terms as the fall of Urizen. In *The Book of Los* it is Los who creates the "horrible vacuum / Beneath him & on all sides round" (BL 4:4092), and who sinks through it "precipitant heavy down down" for ages before he is able to stabilize his fall. It stops when "contemplative thoughts first arose" (BL 4:40, E92), which sounds like a satire on philosophy, but Blake is actually attacking his usual target: the passive Reason of the Enlightenment in which the mind merely looks on as the world acts.

> Incessant the falling Mind labour'd
> Organizing itself: till the Vacuum
> Became element, pliant to rise
> Or to fall, or to swim, or to fly:
> With ease searching the dire vacuity.
>
> (BL 4:49–53, E92–93)

Like Satan wheeling through Chaos with a false sense of freedom, Los achieves a supposititious autonomy at great cost. The mind may feel free to roam about its objects by means of contemplation but only at the expense of having first thrust them into the void of otherness. It seems strange at first to find the defensive errors of Urizen attributed to Los; the point is that Urizen himself, with his restrictive conceptions of self and world, represents a failure of imagination.

More moving is the intimation in *The Book of Ahania* that Urizen was once glorious. He is not a simply villainous principle. He has an unfallen state and is hence redeemable. In *Ahania*'s myth, Urizen falls when he rejects Ahania—"so name his parted soul" (BA 2:32, E84). In his soullessness, he "[shrinks] away from the Eternals," planting himself on a barren rock, "which himself from redounding fancies had petrified" (BA 3:57–58, E86). Wandering in disembodied exile, Ahania laments having been "cast [out] from thy bright presence / Into the World of Loneness" (BA 4:64–65, E89). She represents the self-awareness from which Urizen has shut himself off and, specifically, the awareness of what more he might be—creative, generous, life-giving—instead of what he has "petrified" himself into: punitive, defensive, death-dealing. She remembers another time:

> Then thou with thy lap full of seed
> With thy hand full of generous fire
> Walked forth from the clouds of morning
> On the virgins of springing joy,

[64]

> On the human soul to cast
> The seed of eternal science.

(BA 5:29–34, E89)

Urizen is not Reason as it must ever be, but Reason without "soul": contracted, reactive, self-policing, suspicious of itself (and the imagination in it). Urizen preexisted this contraction so the mentality he embodies must have a benign form. Here is a joyous and invigorating "eternal science," as opposed to the empiricists' "Science [of] Despair." Creative Reason is possible, Blake suggests, no matter how unimaginable in our paradigms. Ahania's memory, although logically "retrospective," is affectively Utopian: it makes us dream of experience in which the discipline of reason is not a torment to the spirit.

In the Continental Prophecies and the Books of Urizen Blake considers how to describe the problem, but in his epic prophecies he will turn to the task of imagining how either an individual or a culture can transcend empiricist subjectivity and achieve freedom. The terms of empiricism and the unholy names of Bacon, Newton, and Locke hang on as shorthand, designating a distortion of subjectivity that Blake comes to see more and more as endemic. "Empiricist" subjectivity has tempted the subject from the beginning, quite independently of philosophical history; it is a constant danger threatening to malform the psyche and pervert human relations. The Continental Prophecies and the Books of Urizen launch the mythic cast in whose struggles Blake illustrates the psychological impact—the conflicts of emotion, internal division, mistrust of others, and bad faith—that follow from empiricist subjectivity. In his epic prophecies, he proliferates the number of characters and radically intensifies the complexity of their interactions. He expands, deepens, and corrects his psychological analysis, even as he works to answer the question of how the disaster can be circumvented.

2

Wordsworth, Plato, and Blake

What writer, to Blake's mind, had manifested the despair of the empiricist subject? It certainly was not the unexcitable Locke but rather Locke's follower (at least through the 1790s), William Wordsworth. Blake recognized that Wordsworth had elaborated a phenomenology of the subject out of Locke's epistemology, and so exposed, especially in Tintern Abbey, the disappointments of Nature worship and the tormented self-division of the subject resigned to uniquely natural existence. Blake vigorously disputed with Wordsworth in his marginalia, and corrected him implicitly in his poems, yet I believe we ought to regard his opposition as sympathetic. In fact, Blake was arguing with a temptation present to his own mind, and if he sometimes seems positively aggressive in his response to Wordsworth, we should understand him to be engaged in a war of resistance against his own fears. Like any attentive reader—and Blake was much more than that—he felt the power of Wordsworth's grand melancholy, and he quarreled with Wordsworth's poetry precisely to the extent that he was moved by it.

According to Geoffrey Hartman, there is only one moment in which Wordsworth "sounds the depth of the disparity between Nature and Imagination" (59): the climactic passage from *The Prelude* 6, in which the Imagination rises up with blinding force, "halt[s]" the poet in the process of composition, and constrains him to say, to his "conscious soul," "I recognize thy glory." Imagination is glorious insofar as its autonomy testifies to its transcendent provenance:

> When the light of sense
> Goes out, but with a flash that has revealed
> The invisible world, doth greatness make abode,
> There harbours, whether we be young or old.
> Our destiny, our being's heart and home,
> Is with infinitude, and only there.
>
> (6.600–5, 1850 *Prelude* 217)[1]

Characteristically, Wordsworth chooses instead to ease the discontinuity between Imagination and Nature, to bring the mind around again to an interchange with the natural world. Why do this? The motive is psychological, Hartman seems to suggest: Wordsworth wards off enclosure in the "solitary self." For the self-consciousness that experiences of nature induce in him could be carried to the extreme of isolation. There is the prospect, in Hartman's words, "of an apocalyptic moment in which past and future overtake the present, and the poet, cut off from nature by imagination, is, in an absolute sense, lonely" (46).

We can distinguish between the everyday loneliness of someone who misses people and the intuition of the soul, or subject, that *as* a subject it is alone in the world. Hartman shows that this is a central theme in Wordsworth. It was central to Blake as well, and to the one-sided debate between them. Blake recognized that Wordsworth was haunted by apprehension of the soul's solitude. In Blake's characteristic way, he gives a polemical analysis of where this apprehension came from, and how it might be surmounted. He seems to have had the opposite intuition from Wordsworth: namely that loneliness comes from naturalism rather than transcendentalism. To overcome loneliness, Blake said, one must accept the transcendent provenance or what the Gnostics called the "acosmicism of the soul." Blake never saw the sixth book of *The Prelude*, but he thought that Wordsworth had finally come around in the Intimations Ode, where he takes the Gnostic and Neoplatonic view that the soul is not at home in the world. Here Blake and Wordsworth agree, in spirit, on the philosophical concept of the "soul in exile," which appeals to them deeply in its psychological resonance and its concentration on the *experience* of the lonely soul. (Without quickly resolving it, as orthodox Christianity does, into loneliness *for* God.) The Gnostics say the life of the soul in the world is characterized by "forlorness," "dread," and "homesickness" (to borrow Jonas's words in *The Gnostic Religion*, 65.) For Blake and Wordsworth, this picture captures the feature of phenomenal selfhood that their own poetry dwells on—its sense of itself as solitary and anomalous. Despite their great differences, they agree on the pressing importance of one topic: the uneasiness of the subject within its own subjectivity.

Blake made his indignation with Wordsworth clear in his annotations to Wordsworth's *Poems* (1815) and to the "Preface" to *The Excursion* (1814). His objections are well-known: Blake thought that in his preface Wordsworth willfully denied the priority of Inspiration or Imagination, while, by the converse logic, in his poems he timidly paid homage to the primacy of nature. Worst of all was the philosophical program that emerged out of these stances, the watery Kantianism through which, in plain bad faith, Wordsworth maintained that the mind belongs to the world and harmonizes with it. Blake expertly demolished this pious pretense: "You shall not bring me down to believe such fitting & fitted I know better & Please your Lordship" (E667). We might summarize Blake's critique in this way: against *his own* better knowledge, Wordsworth accorded too little independence to the mind and too much independence—too much inevitably fearful reality and power—to the material or natural world.

This is the critique as it has been received and paraphrased. It is certainly where Blake begins. But I think that his quarrel, or better, his engagement with Wordsworth runs deeper: Wordsworth was to Blake the contemporary poet who gave the most moving, authoritative, and persuasive rendition of subjective experience as the empiricists had—in Blake's view—misconstrued it. In fact, Blake sympathized with the misery of those who believed this version of subject life, for he thought it codified an inevitable psychological temptation: the uneasiness and despair that Natural Man must suffer. He would have heard the cry of the self "mourning lamenting & howling incessantly" (M 24[26]:53, E120) in the elegiac strain of Tintern Abbey and the Intimations Ode, poems in which the speaker has been betrayed and bewildered by Nature, regardless of how much he may struggle to deny it. And surely Blake felt it himself, for he ventriloquized this despair with great pathos in *The Four*

Zoas, *Milton*, and *Jerusalem*. He saw Wordsworth as the most eminent and most compelling spokesman of the existential sorrow he, himself, knew and was bent on counteracting. Wordsworthian sadness exemplified the damage caused by the "fatal opinion[s]" of empiricism. Blake set himself the task of proposing a counter theory that would give heart to both Wordsworth's readers and to the Wordsworth in himself.

To speak of Wordsworth as a Nature poet here, or to speak of the problem in terms of a misconception of nature, is mere shorthand. For Blake, the deepest and most dangerous effect of empiricism was its distortion of psychic experience, or the "I's" experience of its relation not only to the world but also to itself. At stake is not simply the status of nature or of man in nature, but the condition and character of subjectivity. The version of experience adumbrated in empiricism (according to Blake) and extrapolated, or given force and life (in Wordsworth), dissolves the confidence and integrity of consciousness: The "I," the mind, consciousness, or self, experiences itself as solitary, belated, and besieged; it finds that it has awoken in an object world that existed before it, and whose reality is greater than its own. This world is empty and monotonous at the same time that it is frightening and unpredictable, and the "I" feels small, isolated, and adrift; it cannot even command the contents of its own interior, but finds the self amorphous, incoherent, and mysterious, occupied by floating chunks of alterity that have somehow invaded it from the world beyond.

Locke might protest that he is not a psychologist: he has no theory of the self and gives no representation of the inner life.[2] But Wordsworth, who put the empiricist metaphors into play, wrote the autobiography of Lockean subject in his poems of the 1790s. Just think how this passage must have horrified Blake.

> I deem that there are Powers
> Which of themselves our mind impress,
> That we can feed this mind of ours
> In a wise passiveness.
>
> ("Expostulation and Reply,"
> ll.21–25, *Poetical Works* 1969, 377)

These mysterious external "Powers" exemplify what Blake meant by the "Female Will," and the subjection of the mind to them leads on to the fearful worship of "Natures cruel holiness"(M 36[40]:25, E137) by which Wordsworth often comes to grief. Meanwhile, this passive mind, stamped with the brand of external powers, must be perplexed in its experience of itself. It will be haunted by its fragmentation and made anxious by its want of self-mastery.

This is the character of interior life as Wordsworth dramatizes it—although not necessarily as he theorizes it. After all, at the end of *The Prelude*, Wordsworth seems happily to assert that the mind is "lord and master" (11.271, p. 430). But it is an open secret that its Kantian conclusion is not the most evocative part of *The Prelude*, and that Wordsworth is at his most moving, and is closest to the source of his own power, in the childhood books of *The Prelude* (1–5) when he presents the relationship of mind to world in terms that are exactly the opposite: the "I" is constantly thrown off balance by "vexing" external stimuli and baffling inward movements, neither of which it can master. It comes as no surprise that Wordsworth wrote the early books of *The Prelude* in the 1790s, when he was most under the influence of Lockean empiricism (see Grob, *The Philosophic Mind*). Wordsworth's depiction of the passive and disconcerted "I," floundering in an alien world, draws out the figure of the self that is implicit in the tenets of empiricism.

Wordsworth's Ghosts and the Model of the Mind

Wordsworth loves the words "haunt," "haunted," and "haunting." They appear in heightened moments, as when, in the Intimations Ode, Wordsworth describes the Child, the "Best Philosopher," as "Haunted forever by the eternal mind" (114, *Poetical Works* 1940–49; 461), or when in Tintern Abbey (1969) he recalls that "the sounding cataract [once] haunted [him] like a passion" (l. 77, *Poetical Works* 1940–49; 164); and when in *The Prelude* he evokes those "presences of nature that . . . Haunt[ed him] among . . . [his] boyish sports" (1:495, p. 54). It is in moments of being haunted that the mind, breaking out of its routines, perceives itself to be occupied by something powerful that has come, as it were, from another place. The word "haunt" figures the mind's uncertain relation to its own interior life. Indeed, the mind in Wordsworth is almost always not merely haunted but "self-haunting." In typical phrases from *The Prelude* (1805), Wordsworth writes of the mind "beset / With images, and haunted by itself" (6.179–80, p. 194) and of "thoughts and things / In the self-haunting spirit" (14.284). The mind is haunted—or eerily occupied—by parts of itself that have a quasi-autonomous stature: by thoughts, images, memories, and past selves. And it is also haunted, that is to say bestirred, at perceiving within it the presence of these alien forms.

I propose that this characterization of the mind's relation to itself comes out of empiricism, namely, out of Locke's picture of mental experience. I stress the word "picture" here because I mean Locke's implicit visual metaphors for the mind and the mind's operation: in Locke's picture, the mind is a screen onto which images are projected, or a box in which they are assembled. It is a repository or container and what it contains—one "idea" at a time—is, as it were, separate and independent. Wordsworth developed this picture of mental life into a conception of the self as containing entities with a life of their own from which it is partly alienated. This self is perturbed to behold its ignorance of itself and the slightness of its consciousness.

Like almost everyone else in eighteenth-century England, Wordsworth took his basic notions of psychology from Locke. But, also like others at the time, he was stimulated less by Locke's explicit arguments than by what Locke (perhaps inadvertently) implied or suggested. Locke would never have said that the mind is haunted by itself or by anything in itself. He would not have described thoughts or images as ghostly, much less as quasi-autonomous. These poetic ways of speaking were not his. In trying to explain how we come to knowledge and understanding—without having recourse to occult notions of soul or innate ideas—Locke had to invent a picture of how the mind works. But so powerful were the ramifications of his picture that they took off without him. Thus, although there is properly speaking no conception of the self in Locke, Wordsworth seized on Locke's picture of the mind and developed out of it the representation of the self that follows from this picture. Locke was not a psychologist where Wordsworth was. Out of the empiricist characterization of the mind as a substanceless thinking thing, as a blank slate, as tutored only by experience, Wordsworth created a thought of the self by which he might convey its experience of being disconcerted in its own presence. We may say that he poeticized Locke, where *poeticize* means to deepen the resonance.

This is true, at any rate, of the eighteenth-century Wordsworth. In his book *The Philosophic Mind*, Alan Grob argues that through the 1790s Wordsworth held a strictly empiricist view of mental development; he thought the mind a tabula rasa that was informed through the senses, that is to say, through its encounter with the natural world. According to Grob, the 1799 *Prelude* is a largely empiricist text (along with the first books of the 1805 *Prelude*, which contain reminiscences of this material); but in the early years of the nineteenth century, Wordsworth changed his views and adopted an opposing conception of the self in which it has a transcendental origin and an intrinsic destiny. In the late books of *The Prelude*, the self has become "lord and master" in the place of nature.

It was Grob who first noted the empiricist strain in most of the passages I will discuss in this chapter; I am considerably indebted to his book.[3] But while I accept Grob's chronological argument, I disagree with him about the consequences of Locke's influence. Grob thinks that Wordsworth was happy in his empiricism because he was able to make an optimistic theory out of it; he went beyond Locke to construe Nature as having benevolent intentions toward the human minds in its keeping. Instead of being neutral or unpredictable, as Locke would have it, Nature designs to help us by teaching us to be calm and humane. I suggest, on the contrary, that Wordsworth's empiricism enables him to articulate not a reassuring idea of Nature but rather a basic intuition about the discomfiture of interiority. Tintern Abbey and the early books of *The Prelude* describe both a childhood self bewildered at its own experiences and an adult self wondering both at these experiences and, somewhat sadly, at its present distance from them; these feelings arise out of a conception of the self in which (as even Grob observes) it has no intrinsic substance, its history is aleatory and it is not in command of its own fate. A self wholly dependent on nature or external influence is in a weak and chancy position.

Locke prepared the ground for this view by picturing the mind as a blank being stumbling about in the dark of occasional stimulation and only gradually coming to know itself by means of "reflecting" on "its own operations," that is, the effects that external stimulation produces in it. The mind cannot come to know itself by its own means but must wait on sensory stimulation both for impetus and for material on which to work. More importantly, it is the passive observer of its own operations, the moved witness of its own experience. This posture of the self, in which it stands to one side as it beholds the vagaries of its constitution, is endemic to early Wordsworth.

In an early fragment, Wordsworth adopts the empiricist account of how the mind comes to know itself. His paraphrase brings out the oddness of Locke's notion, for he intimates that by this means of self-knowledge what the mind discovers is the extent to which it is actually *un*acquainted with it-self. A bit of understanding is had at the price of sensing the self's darkness.

> In many a walk
> At evening or by moonlight, or reclined
> At midday upon beds of forest moss,
> Have we to Nature and her impulses
> Of our whole being made free gift, and when
> Our trance had left us, oft have we, by aid
> Of the impressions which it left behind,
> Looked inward on ourselves, and learned, perhaps,
> Something of what we are.
>
> (*Poetical Works* 1940–49; 5:343–44)

This account implies that the self is to itself an undiscovered country, a dark cave whose existence can only be recognized and whose contours can only begin to be fathomed through, paradoxically, the intervention of exter-nal stimuli. As usual, Wordsworth makes the point here in positive terms—Nature enables us to learn "Something of what we are"—but the troubling implication is clear: we do not already know what we are, and are only liable to find out "something" by chance. The self in early Wordsworth is not a splendid mystery but rather a baffling patchwork.

If the mind is a blank slate, then where do mental contents come from and what sort of status do they have within the mind? For Wordsworth this epistemological question becomes a psychological one: What kind of mate-rial goes to make up the self, where does it come from, and how does it get there? The 1799 *Prelude* takes up this question in its empirical account of how it was that, when he was a child, Wordsworth's mind was filled or "framed" by natural experience. As Grob remarks, the poem underscores the passivity of the self in its use of the vocabulary of "impression," "implanation," and imbibing from nature. In the most primitively empirical use of this figure, Wordsworth says that certain scenes "Remained, in their substantial linea-ments / Depicted on the brain" (1:430–31, 1799 *Prelude* 12).

But it is in the language of impression that we find Wordsworth rework-ing empirical notions into something more evocative, into a representation of a self built up out of the layering of erratic deposits. For it turns out that not merely sensations but more intangible affects and intuitions are fixed in the mind by "impression." Wordsworth recollects a "scene which left a . . . power / Implanted in my mind" (1: 329–30, 1799 *Prelude* 9); in this figure the visual scene deposits not its visual copy but its affect. These webs of image and affect can also come apart from one another and be integrated into the mind differently: he describes visual memories that remain in the mind although detached from their original affects and later grafted onto others. Thus he encountered

> tragic facts . . . that impressed my mind
> With images to which in following years
> Far other feelings were attached—with forms
> That yet exist with independent life
>
> (1:282–6, 1799 *Prelude* 8)

The images related to these "tragic facts" are described as pure images saturated, in sequence, by antithetical feelings; they have become "forms" with their own "independent life." Wordsworth uses the language of impression and implantation to convey the substantial—which is to say, autonomous—character of images or memories. And their autonomy is what gives them the power to "haunt."

Wordsworth's representation of the self as "haunted" by exoteric "impressions" turns on a paradox in the empiricist metaphor, indeed, we may say that in the full sense of the word he exploits that paradox. For how can something that is substantial be phantasmal—and hence, capable of haunting—at the same time? Something that is "impressed," "implanted," or "stamped" on the medium of the mind ought to be graven there permanently, fixed solidly in a solid medium, or so the metaphor implies. But the mind is not a solid medium, and the "impressions" or "ideas" the world leaves upon it have no solid form. The two sides, as it were, of the empiricist metaphor are not consistent: the world stamps its image upon the mind but the image is frail and ghostly. It is, however, this inconsistency that makes the metaphor powerful because it gives "ideas" or mental contents their unique status. The mind becomes a housing for phantoms that come from outside and retain something of their alterity in their discreteness and their ability to come and go at their own will. David Hume brought out these implications of the empiricist metaphor in his description of the mind as "a kind of theater, where several perceptions successively make their appearance; pass, re-pass [and] glide away" (253).

Impressions are "haunting" because they are both vital and elusive at the same time—substantial and immaterial, interior and foreign. Early Wordsworth is clearly trying to work out a means of figuring this equivocal mode of being. In "The Ruined Cottage," Wordsworth says that the Pedlar had "had impressed / Great objects on his mind" (note the passive voice)

> with portraiture
> And colour so distinct that on his mind
> They lay like substances, and almost seemed
> To haunt the bodily sense.
>
> (*Poetical Works* 1940–49; 5.381, 1.81–85)

These images, Wordsworth insists, are "like substances," yet they are haunting only because they are memories. To say that they "haunt the *bodily*"—as opposed to the mental—sense bestows a kind of substantiality on these memories, but it is dissolved again when Wordsworth concedes that they did not truly haunt but merely "almost seemed" haunting in this way. It is not easy to describe precisely how the residues of external experience come to lodge in the self. Wordsworth faces the difficulty of figuring the status of material that has been subsumed from the exterior to the interior, and has been transformed in the process yet still retains something of its tangible exoteric origin. Object-relations psychoanalysis has given us the term *incorporation,* which might be employed suggestively in this context because Wordsworth and Melanie Klein seem to work with a similar theory of selfhood. The self is formed as myriad of internalized influences: the problem is to explain how the outside gets into the inside, how the self is filled out or filled up with material from another source. In his own account, Wordsworth shows how Nature "peopled" his mind "with forms or beautiful or grand," just as Klein will say that the psyche is "peopled" by good and bad objects based on impressions of one's real parents. In Wordsworth and Klein the self is compiled out of exoteric material, and even more important, out of material that *is felt* to be exoteric.

For both, what comes from outside is never quite assimilated to the nature of the inner. In another early fragment, Wordsworth represents the dissolution of this alterity as an unrealizable ideal.

> Oh, 'tis a joy divine on summer days
> When not a breeze is stirring, not a cloud,

> To sit within some solitary wood,
> Far in some lonely wood, and hear no sound
> Which the heart does not make, or else so fits
> To its own temper that in external things
> No longer seem internal difference
> All melts away, and things that are without
> Live in our minds as in their native home.

(Poetical Works 1940–49, 5.343)

Here Wordsworth would appear to be describing a perfect assimilation of inner and outer, yet his claim that under these conditions "things that are without / Live in our minds as in their native home" should be compared with his representation of words as harboring "shadowy" things that dwell there "as in a mansion like their proper home" (5:624, *The Prelude* 184). Whatever needs a home, much less a simulated home, is out of its element. The fit of outer matter to inner form is never perfect because their modes of being are not the same. It is in these terms that Wordsworth describes the tumult of his untoward thoughts in the aftermath of the boat-stealing scene,

> after I had seen
> That spectacle, for many days my brain
> Worked with a dim and undetermined sense
> Of unknown modes of being.

(1: 417–20, The Prelude 50)

The thought of these "unknown modes of being" sprung in part from the image of the mountain that had "like a living thing / Strode after" him. But it is also the autonomy of his own fears and memories that has struck him as strange.

This is a significant crossing because when the contents of the mind per se are described as autonomous—the thoughts themselves, rather than impressions—then they too take on the qualities of "haunting": they come and go, tenuous and unpredictable. Wordsworth figures the sense of estrangement from the contents of one's own mind in *The Prelude* when he describes his experience of writing block.

> I had hopes
> Still higher, that with a frame of outward life
> I might endue, might fix in a visible home,

[76]

> Some portion of those phantoms of conceit
> That had been floating loose about so long,
> And to such beings temperately deal forth
> The many feelings that oppressed my heart.
>
> (1: 127–33, *The Prelude* 34)

Here the mind is imaged as a drafty housing of thoughts that "float loose" about in it, like ghosts whose spirits have not been laid to rest. The language of housing ghostly beings in mind or words comes ultimately out of the empiricist metaphor, even where, as here, the alien material consists of one's own "home-grown" thoughts. But now the self has been constitutively disintegrated.

Wordsworth spelled out and bequeathed to psychoanalysis the notion of self-estrangement that is inherent in Locke's picture but which Locke would have abjured because he precisely did not wish to make an occult thing of selfhood. Yet Locke ended up doing so unintentionally, for the inert material, the "ideas," that take up residence in the interior are lodged there like alienated extensions of the mind, and a mind with properties of this kind has become the site of an enigma. From this thought Wordsworth powerfully reconceived the self as containing vital, unassimilated parts to which its central consciousness has an anxious, sometimes wistful, sometimes grateful relation.

But in order to bring out this implication of the empiricist metaphor, Wordsworth had to defy something Locke said explicitly. In his account of personal identity, Locke argued that self should be defined neither as soul nor substance (we have no evidence either for or against their existence) but simply as "that conscious thinking thing (whatever substance, made up of whether Spiritual, or Material, Simple, or Compounded, it matters not) which is sensible, or conscious of Pleasure and Pain, capable of Happiness or Misery, and so is concern'd for it *self,* as far as that consciousness extends" (341). Personal identity consists merely in the "Identity of consciousness": "That with which the *consciousness* of this present thinking thing can join itself, makes the same *Person,* and is one *self* with it, and with nothing else; and so attributes to it *self,* and owns all the Actions of that thing, as its own, as far as that consciousness reaches, and no farther" (341). In other words, the present self is merely consciousness, and its continuity with the past self is established by the iteration of consciousness. Experiences in the past count as experiences of the same self because the consciousness that registers them in memory *now* feels itself to have been the same consciousness that registered the reality *then*. Material lost to memory is not part of the self. Wordsworth nuances this account simply but dramatically in his crucial observation:

> A tranquillizing spirit presses now
> On my corporeal frame, so wide appears
> The vacancy between me and those days,
> Which yet have such self-presence in my mind
> That sometimes when I think of them I seem
> Two consciousnesses—conscious of myself,
> And of some other being.

> (2.28–33, *The Prelude* 66)

When Wordsworth says that he seems to himself to be, at one and the same moment, "Two consciousnesses," he defies Locke's analysis of personal identity. He represents it as reductive. For the past self, instead of being smoothly continuous with the present self, instead of showing itself to have been the same self that now surveys it, asserts its difference, floats about in the present self as an opaque and alien being. Yet it would not be there at all if it were not an ancestor of the present self. That is the paradox, the subtlety Wordsworth implies that Locke missed: past consciousness exercises authority over the present self precisely because it both belongs to the present self and is differentiated from it. Consciousness does *not* recognize itself unproblematically in its past experience; on the contrary, it feels itself to have diverged so much from its former constitution that it hardly knows itself in its old self. Of all the alien bits and pieces that press on the self and make it aware of its elusiveness, the most commanding for Wordsworth are these estranged residues of former selves, the old consciousnesses that haunt the present self in which they have become obsolete.

Wordsworth brought out the notion of self-division that is inherent in the empiricist picture of the mind separated out between ideas and the observer of those ideas, between mental operations and the observer of those operations. These divisions will be carried into psychoanalysis in the form of the topographical model, where the self is dispersed into diverse entities that are competitive, obtuse, and detached from one another.[4] While scholars such as Ernest Tuveson and Terry Castle have noted the continuity from Locke through Romanticism to psychoanalysis, they have traced the contribution of Romanticism to the idea of the autonomous Imagination whereas I find it in Wordsworth's representation of the self as porous, fragmented, haunted, and half blind.

Wordsworth's poetry of self-alienation partakes of the diffused elegiac tone that is typical of him. It makes sense that he should turn elegiac when he is clearly sorrowing—as when the "hiding places of his power" close. More interesting is that he sounds elegiac even when nothing has gone missing— when, for example, he evokes being stimulated by "a dim and undetermined sense / Of unknown modes of being." We might be content to say he is typically elegiac because he is typically describing the past. But to be more accurate, elegy is related to anxiety in Wordsworth, and anxiety is related to loneliness. In Tintern Abbey, Wordsworth is plainly threatened with loneliness because he is threatened with separation from nature. In the passages I have quoted from *The Prelude,* loneliness arises from the experience of self-fragmentation. Consciousness experiences itself as alone within the self: on the inside looking in.

Twentieth-century (nonexperimental) psychology has tended to share Wordsworth's intuition. Certainly the idea of the lonely and besieged central consciousness will recall to us Freud's dictum, "The ego is not master in its own house," as well as Lacan's focus on the failure of self-coincidence. It is not clear whether these filiations bear witness to a convergence on the "facts," or a more complicated phenomenon of intellectual history in which Freudian notions resemble Romantic ones because they descend from them. In any case, thinkers in the Freudian tradition are Wordsworthians and not Blakeans: the splitting of the self is constitutive of selfhood and cannot be "cured." Perhaps that is the truth, but it is obviously beyond the scope of this book to explore the question. What is important for our purposes is to identify the "Wordsworthian" psychology Blake meant to correct.

Melanie Klein, in particular, sounds strikingly like Wordsworth in her account of the isolation of consciousness. Her essay "On the Sense of Loneliness" analyzes what she calls *internal loneliness*—"the sense of being alone regardless of external circumstances, of feeling lonely even when among friends or receiving love" (300). One source of loneliness is the experience of self-fragmentation: the feeling that one is broken up into "split-off parts" (some of which are then "projected" into the outside world, a dynamic that

reverses empiricist "introjection"). One feels "that one is not in full posses-
sion of one's self, that one does not fully belong to oneself, or, therefore, to
anybody else. The lost parts too, are felt to be lonely" (300). Wordsworth's
"phantoms" and "strange forms" do seem to share in his loneliness. However
stimulating his inner world, it is not festively populated. The alien presences
remain elusive, and their separateness inspires Wordsworth with his classic
yearning. As in Klein, the discovery of the exotic within the self (paradoxi-
cally) causes loneliness. Blake had had the same thought expressed nega-
tively: without a window into the transcendent, Natural Man experiences the
inner life as a huddle of forlorn parts.

Blake's Answer

To Blake's mind, the anxieties of selfhood in Wordsworth play out the im-
plications of empiricist psychology. When Blake writes in his annotations
to Wordsworth's *Poems* (1815), "I see in Wordsworth the Natural Man ris-
ing up against the Spiritual Man Continually" (E665), he employs a favorite
shorthand, but there is much more in this than a philosophical objection.
His very formulation—the Natural Man *rising up* against the Spiritual Man
Continually—shows that he is making a psychological observation, seeing in
Wordsworth's poems a pattern of self-division, self-occlusion, and denial.[5]
The Wordsworthian experience of self is dominated by fearfulness and psy-
chic conflict; he clings to the being of Natural Man despite the anxiety this
generates. This compulsion can be seen most clearly in Tintern Abbey. The
poem fulfills Blake's prophecy: a man who conceives himself as merely
"Natural" will one day come to recognize that consciousness and nature
are not of the same order, that consciousness really has no place in nature,
and that insofar as consciousness is only empirical (and not transcendent),
it has no place anywhere. It is a sad evanescent singularity. Wordsworth
may say Nature "never doth betray the heart that loves her," but in fact he
feels, or dreads to feel, that he has been betrayed. The "I" or solitary con-
sciousness has been cast adrift, severed from other forms of being, and iso-
lated in time because it was wrong in the past, and it shall be empty in the
future. Wordsworth hastens to assure himself that knowledge is recom-
pense, and that Nature remains "the nurse, the guide, the guardian of my
heart."

Wordsworth was closest to empiricism in the 1790s when he wrote Tin-
tern Abbey and also the childhood books of *The Prelude* (1–5). Blake would
not have known the early books of *The Prelude*, but he could have anticipated
something of their content from hints in the autobiographical poems that
Wordsworth did publish in this period, especially Tintern Abbey. Empiricist
psychology isolates the node of consciousness as the real self, and thus opens
up the possibility of regarding other material in the self as alienated. Of
course Western psychology since Plato has allowed for the existence of inner
promptings unowned by consciousness. What distinguishes empiricist psy-
chology is its representation of (some of) the alien material as alien because
it was originally *extraneous*—it was "impressed" upon the mind—and it re-
tains a measure of its foreign character. Further, the identification of con-
sciousness as the real self removes other parts of the self to a greater distance
than any previous psychology. The "I" is dwarfed by the amorphous dark-
nesses moving around it. In the early books of *The Prelude*, such a gap opens
up between the "I" and the interior. Important passages dwell on the state of
internal alienation. The "I" experiences selfhood as a haunting: phantasmal
interior phenomena dislocate and baffle consciousness.

Blake recognizes that Locke's philosophy gives scientific authority to the
subject's apprehension that its advent is belated: Locke's rejection of the doc-
trine of innate ideas stipulates that the subject brings nothing of its own into
the world—it merely stumbles into awareness of a prior and supervening re-
ality. This is the experience of floundering subjectivity as it is adumbrated in
Tintern Abbey, where the self awakens to find itself deracinated and spectral.
In this poem, Wordsworth entertains the anxiety (characteristically expressed
as denial) that Nature will—or already has—"betray[ed] the heart that loves
her": having honored the grandeur of an external force in Nature he now
finds it asserting its autonomy, departing from him, and leaving him a tran-
sient anomaly upon the earth, "an atom in darkness," as Blake might say. For
to Wordsworth, the withdrawal of natural ministration, or the suspicion that
it was never there, spells the dissolution of ontological security. Without his
special bond to Nature, the "I" of his present consciousness is now adrift,
haunted by memories of a delusional past and aghast at the prospect of an
empty future. Wordsworth entertains his anxiety tentatively, acknowledging
that the new unmeaning Nature leaves him in "somewhat of a sad perplex-
ity," and that his old confidence may have been "but a vain belief." He is

compelled to be circumspect because the stakes are so great. If his anxieties are justified and nature is no thoughtful guide but rather a dead world withdrawn and inert, then he is plunged into an abyss, condemned, like Urizen, to a ghostly singularity. Blake might sigh for him and say, "The little weeping Spectre stands on the threshold of Death / Eternal" (M 28[30]:10, E126). No wonder Wordsworth is reluctant to remain in this predicament: as the poem goes on, he tries to reinvent his faith in Nature, and to contrive a benevolent scheme of "compensation" to redeem his loss. He can claim thereby that he remains "a worshipper of Nature" and that she is still "the nurse, the guide, the guardian of my heart." Blake would have heard such claims as symptoms of desperation: Wordsworth has foreseen the inevitable defeat of his attempt to lodge value and benignity in nature, and now he is trying vainly to regress.

In his empiricist phase, Wordsworth's "I" is consciousness severed from belonging either in the world or in the self. In later poems, particularly the later books of *The Prelude* and the Intimations Ode, Wordsworth changes his idiom, adopting Platonic or Kantian terms that allow for the mind's (or soul's) transcendence. Blake, naturally, approved of the Intimations Ode: we have Crabb Robinson's account of reading the poem to Blake, who responded with "The same half crazy crochets about the two worlds," and with praise for the parts of the Ode that, says Robinson, "were the most obscure & those I the least like & comprehend" (Bentley, *Blake Records* 544). As Leopold Damrosch points out, these were surely the Neoplatonic passages (88). Wordsworth finally surrenders his reverence for Nature in favor of the Gnostic and Neoplatonist view that Nature is inferior to the soul, and in this world the soul, remaining alien, must be forlorn. Wordsworth likens this life to death, as Blake had done: the child knows "those truths . . . Which we are toiling all our lives to find / In darkness lost, the darkness of the grave" (ll. 115–17, *Poetical Works* 1969, 461). The Intimations Ode was published in 1807 after Blake had written his major poetry. But Blake clearly interpreted it as a confirmation of his general views and of his interpretation of Wordsworth. He "enjoyed" the Intimations Ode presumably because in it Wordsworth comes as close as he ever does to dismissing the siren song of Nature. He nearly acknowledges that nature has no meaning without the contribution of human imagination. When the veil of glory, which is a projection of imagination, drops away from the phenomenal world, it becomes a place of dreary repetition: "But yet I know, where'er I go, / That there hath past away a glory from the earth" (ll. 17–18) and "The Pansy at my feet / Doth the same tale repeat" (ll.54–55, *Poetical Works* 1969, 460). The truth has been revealed: nature is dull and vacant. But if the power of projecting "glory" unto it is lost with childhood, how is the adult to endure the monotony of merely natural existence? In the first four stanzas, the speaker finds himself, like the speaker of Tintern Abbey, struggling precariously to keep his balance in the void created by his estrangement from Nature. The exacerbating effect of this estrangement is that it throws consciousness itself into turmoil—as the speaker oscillates from wishfulness to panic to denial—so that at last he has only invidious alternatives from which to choose: the tedium of the world or the frenzy of the interior.[6]

Blake would say that Wordsworth is finally facing up to the consequence of Nature worship—abandonment and terror. These are the result of his abject dependence on Nature, for anyone who thinks Nature is a Mother (our source and origin, the authority and reality that supervenes over the subject) must sooner or later doubt her, and then come to think of her as treacherous. The speaker is both sad and resentful when he calls Nature a "homely Nurse," who "doth all she can / To make her Foster-child, her Inmate Man, / Forget the glories he hath known" (ll. 81–83, *Poetical Works* 1969, 461). Here Wordsworth is letting his maternal metaphor play out to its logical end. As Tintern Abbey demonstrates, the notion of nature as good mother cannot be sustained. It is impossible consistently to regard the material world as animated by a principle of benevolence. When Blake said, "I *fear* Wordsworth loves Nature," he must have meant that he feared for him because Nature worship becomes its own torture. Thel's morale collapses in just this way, as her attempts to contrive a redemptive vision of natural reality fail, and she is left alone with her alienation from the insatiate mortal body. The logical conclusion of any attempt to redeem nature is paranoia and horror of it, or of it insofar as it is in us. We will turn bitter against nature in the end and say, with Stevens: "what good is it that the earth is justified?" ("World Without Peculiarity," 453).

Of course it is at this point that the Intimations Ode takes a surprising turn into mythography. Blake liked these Neoplatonic passages of the Intimations Ode because they propose, against Locke, that we do have innate ideas—and they recur to us in the form of episodes of Berkeleyan idealism— or occlusions of natural reality. Locke scoffs: "'Tis strange, if the Soul has *Ideas* of its own, that it derived not from *Sensation* or *Reflection*, (as it must have, if it thought before it received any impressions from the Body) that it should never, in its private thinking . . . retain any of them, the very moment it wakes out of them, and then make the Man glad with new discoveries" (113–14). Blake took the Intimations Ode as a riposte to this kind of argument.

But even here, where Wordsworth is most acceptable to Blake, they diverge crucially. Wordsworth solves the puzzle, "Where is it now, the glory and the dream?" with a metaphysical assurance that comes at the expense of this present and this life. The soul discovers itself to be stranded here in two related ways: (1) it is stranded here, in this place, because it has found that the material world is barren and (2) it is stranded here, in this moment, because it is merely passing the time until it returns to its true home. In Wordsworth's revised view of nature, it is not invested with spiritual reality, which belongs to soul alone, and in fact, contact with Nature is detrimental to the soul: the effect is "To make her-Foster-child, her Inmate Man, / Forget the glories he hath known, / And that imperial palace whence he came" (ll. 82–84, *Poetical Works* 1969, 461). The image of earth as a prison house for the soul is common to Gnosticism and Neoplatonism; it goes back to their shared source, Plato, and beyond, to an Orphic and Pythagorean origin. Orthodox Christianity, which inherits Platonic dualism, maintains that the Creation is good (Genesis clearly says so), and Plotinus argued vigorously, against the Gnostics, that matter, although debased, has some share of the divine. Wordsworth's solution seems to incline him toward Gnostic devaluation of natural experience.

Wordsworth's ontology differs somewhat from the Gnostic and Neoplatonic because in both of these early heterodoxies, the child is no spiritual authority; it is born into the material world in complete ignorance and must awaken to knowledge rather than struggle to recover intuitions it had at birth. In a deeper sense Wordsworth's idea is clearly consistent with the basic Platonic view and he might be seen as temporalizing the phenomenon implied in Plato, the Neoplatonists, and the Gnostics: the self-awareness of the soul is eroded (or threatened with being eroded) by experience. The Socrates of *The Phaedo* says that the task of the philosopher is to "practise death"—to concentrate on the intelligible and so evade as much as possible the distractions of the empty phenomenal world. Wordsworth's incremental "forgetting" is the result of such distractions, or the converse of what Gnostics called awakening. But, once it has "remembered" its transcendental original, what is the Wordsworthian soul, still marooned in the material world, to do? Try to stay awake—try to keep remembering—and wait.

Because it was his project to educe the bewilderments of selfhood (and not to cure them), Wordsworth attended to psychological intuitions rather than final results in philosophy. Thus he was able to "reject" empiricism and "adopt" Platonism with relative ease because to him they had an underlying continuity. I take my cue here from A. D. Nuttall, who points out that as psychologies of individual consciousness, empiricism and Platonism can be made to coincide (see *A Common Sky* 25–29, et passim). Tintern Abbey and the Intimations Ode demonstrate the result of this coincidence: the Neoplatonist soul is just as lonely as the dwarfed "I" in the dark box of Lockean consciousness, because Wordsworth's Neoplatonist soul must still await its reunion with infinitude. Blake does not wish to accept this tragic conclusion. He claims that Neoplatonist idealism is the cure for the despair of the subject. This means ceasing to identify one's "real self" with the ego or Selfhood and identifying it instead with the impersonal Plotinian soul, or as Blake calls it, the "Imagination." The Imagination can escape, at this very moment, from the stranglehold of the material world into the freedom of the "Eternal Now."

And yet to make this argument, Blake must share with Wordsworth some of the ideas we might be taking him to refute: that consciousness is an anomaly, that the soul is lonely, alienated, and mourning. Crucially, Blake starts from the same assumption as Wordsworth: that the "I" will feel adrift. His argument takes effect at the meta-level of response to this experience. Blake sees empiricism and Platonism as rival explanations for the essential uneasiness of consciousness. But empiricism leads to despair where the Platonist "religions" of Gnosticism and Neoplatonism offer a graceful, and hopeful, explanation of the soul's bewilderment. The acosmic soul's true home is a transcendental realm beyond; this transcendental realm is anonymous or unknowable, yet it is present in the innermost soul, here and now. This approach appeals to Blake, who collapses all spiritual hierarchy, finding godliness in "the Universal Divine Humanity," in which the soul participates and by which it has access to the Eternal Now.

Herein lies the major philosophical difference between Blake and Wordsworth, persisting despite their Gnostic rapprochement. In the Intimations Ode, Wordsworth summons the Platonic myth of origins in order to explain (and solace) a strange, radical affect of selfhood, what we termed in another idiom the sadness and loneliness of the soul. The myth does have explanatory and consolatory power—we derive from it an assurance of the

immortality of the soul—but it confirms rather than denies the soul's imme-
diate affect. If anything, the soul is more "forlorn" in the here and now than
it was before, because the myth has decisively devalued phenomenal reality.
The only balm—the nursing of memories—is inherently imperfect. One lives
off the past and anticipates the future, but the present is a dead end. Thus the
soul is thrust back into passivity and helplessness. These are the affects Blake
adapts Gnosticism and Neoplatonism to counteract. For Blake, the recogni-
tion of its transcendence gives the soul access not to the promise of immor-
tality but to the Eternal Now. One opens the window in the present and there
it is: an exit into a higher reality. He does not ask us to wait until we return
from earth to the transcendental realm beyond. The soul participates in eter-
nity and a leap of faith can take us there at any time.

Wordsworth and Blake draw opposite conclusions from the metaphor of
"awakening." In Wordsworth the soul awakens to an intensified alienation and
loneliness for which there is no immediate remedy, whereas in Blake the soul
awakens to an invigorating awareness of its own power and freedom. Ulti-
mately, Blake is a spiritual philosopher where Wordsworth is and remains a nat-
ural psychologist. Yet Blake's mission remained unknown, while Wordsworth's
spurious cures—his "recompenses" and "benedictions"—were taken literally
and entered the culture through his Arnoldian reception. That is the official
Wordsworth. Blake responded to the other Wordsworth—the Wordsworth
who so movingly articulates the sheer remediless anxiety of selfhood. As we
have seen, whatever the source of the connection, this Wordsworth persists
in psychoanalysis. He persists as well, more plainly and for more obvious rea-
sons, in a major strain of post-Romantic poetry, exemplified by Stevens, John
Ashbery, and A. R. Ammons. I have staged the contrast between Blake and
Wordsworth from Blake's point of view—deliberately attempting to channel
his polemical verve—but that is not to say that he was either right or perfectly
convincing.

Indeed, it takes effort not to regard Blake's solution as rhetorical. And yet
it is not so easy or automatic as paraphrase makes it sound. He perceives that
the hold of Selfhood is very hard to break despite the promptings of the soul
in its forlornness. Experience of the inner world is characterized by incoher-
ence and self-mistrust, or what Blake called the "torments of love and jeal-
ousy" between different parts of the self. The "prophetic spirit," the inner
prompting that would recall to us our transcendent provenance, has difficulty

exerting its proper authority; it is dismissed as illusory by the Selfhood (and its "Reason") whose superior reality is assured by so much in our worldly experience. Blake himself had to work hard in his three epic prophecies to imagine how the internal deadlock might be broken. In *The Four Zoas, Milton,* and *Jerusalem* Blake addresses himself to the psychology of emergence: how the empiricist subject might escape from the cave and how the culture at large might be transformed. He will discern stages and obstacles, and his scenarios will accordingly grow more detailed and complex. Yet the intensity of his Utopian moments, when the Selfhood is undone, conveys such force of longing as to suggest that even to Blake they were elusive. In a central formulation, Blake images the revelation as scarce, imperiled, and magical. This stirring passage pays homage to a precious illumination surrounded by darkness.

> There is a Moment in each Day that Satan cannot find
> Nor can his Watch Fiends find it, but the Industrious find
> This Moment & it multiply. & when it once is found
> It renovates every Moment of the Day if rightly placed.
> In this Moment Ololon descended to Los & Enitharmon
>
> (M 35[39]:42–45, E136)

This passage is celebratory, but observe the surprising and sobering qualifications: revelation is limited to moments, and although they are powerful, there is no guarantee that one will discover them or know how to place them rightly. There is a peculiarly Blakean pathos in this economy. It is a careless critical habit to think of Blake as confident, if not dogmatic, in his assurance of salvation. In his later works (at least), he is not so naïve as to suppose the way ready and easy. More often, he evokes the desperate conditions that create the need for reprieve, and then images the reprieve as a delicate possibility supercharged with desire. He largely reserves apocalyptic imagery for the redemption of the culture as a whole (the end of *Milton* looks forward to "the Great Harvest and Vintage of Nations"). By contrast, the aspiring prophet, who is perforce isolated, has a "Moment" to escape through a transcendental window. Will she or he find it?

This characteristic way of creating pathos is exemplified by the extraordinary lyric called "The Smile," which builds up an atmosphere of dismay and dread before it yields a reprieve at the last moment.

There is a Smile of Love
And there is a Smile of Deceit
And there is a Smile of Smiles
In which these two Smiles meet

And there is a Frown of Hate
And there is a Frown of disdain
And there is a Frown of Frowns
Which you strive to forget in vain

For it sticks in the Hearts deep Core
And it sticks in the deep Back bone
And no Smile that ever was smild
But only one Smile alone

That betwixt the Cradle & Grave
It only once Smild can be
But when it once is Smild
Theres an end to all Misery.

(E483)

There is only one gracious smile, whereas there are several forms of vicious smiles and frowns; the latter evidently will not disappear altogether. They form the oppressive background against which the star of the Smile rises. The poem expresses no doubt that this emparadising smile will come. Yet its invocation in the last stanza is somehow painful—poignant, literally "stabbing"—rather than happy. The Smile comes as a powerful departure from the deep pessimism of the earlier stanzas without entirely dispelling it. The reprieve is a little window of grace, a rare antidote encompassed by poisons. That is what seems typically Blakean about the movement of affect in the poem: he begins with a gripping and persuasive account of suffering in which he perseveres so effectively that the ray of light, when it comes, is invested with all the pathos of remission. Each of the Epic Prophecies as a whole moves this way, with redemption arriving at the end by complex means against the odds even though mandated. Blake reconstitutes in us our desperation as empiricist subjects, pierced by the thought of relief. The individual stands in need of heartening and invigoration, the escape through the window of that moment that "renovates every day if rightly placed." The word

[88]

"renovate" is startlingly Wordsworthian and Coleridgean. It shows Blake's essential connection to mainstream Romanticism: he too meditates on the nature of despair and the means of recovery. Frosch notes this parallel when he remarks of *The Four Zoas,* "Blake's first epic tells on a mythic and historical plane the same story that the 'crisis' poems of Wordsworth and Coleridge do on an individual level, that of a crippling dejection and an inability to create, now in civilization itself" (36). I would add that Blake often tells the story at an individual level as well. The Blakean idealism of Wordsworth finds its inverse in the Wordsworthian pathos of Blake.

<u>3</u>

The Four Zoas:
Transcendental Remorse

There is in every respect a great leap from the *Urizen* books to *The Four Zoas*. In style, form, and content, the development is so profound that it is a wonder Blake made it all at once. It was like skipping from *Dubliners* straight to *Finnegans Wake*: the degree of subtlety increases exponentially. Blake was moved to make dramatic changes because the *Urizen* books, although terse, had opened up a field of speculation. He had explored the psychological life of the individual, or, as he called it, "the state of the soul," in *Songs of Innocence and of Experience, The Book of Thel,* and *Visions of the Daughters of Albion.* (The *Songs* is subtitled "Shewing the Two Contrary States of the Human Soul" [E7].) In *Europe* and *America* he had employed his psychological acuity in portraying the relationships between the members of his mythological family (the father–son agon of Orc and Urizen, the vicious interdependency of Orc and the shadowy female). They figure in an explanation of history that focuses on the dominance of Mystery Religion and the ensuing cycle of repression and reaction. In writing the *Urizen* books, particularly the central *The Book of Urizen,* Blake realized that he wished to go further.

Although there are hints of a synthesis in the earlier works, it is *The Book of Urizen* that fully compounds Blake's twin interests. Here Blake realizes that

he can analyze the errors of ideology and history and the distortion of the in-
dividual psyche *at the same time,* because they are inherently related. *Urizen*
combines *The Book of Thel* and *Europe.* Urizen has a mythological identity that
plays its role in Blake's epitome of history, but he is also a character with psy-
chological experience whose own interiority displays the ravages of reason.
In turning to this examination of his psychological development, Blake moves
beyond *Thel,* for, unlike Thel, Urizen does not merely entertain a distressing
misconception: his errors cause systematic psychological damage. His interior
life is *structurally* compromised, the "I" enlarged at the expense of the imper-
sonal soul. Thus, with *The Book of Urizen,* Blake discovers an interest in dis-
secting the deformed psyche. The topic seems suddenly to open up as one he
has the means to explicate in detail through his critical ideas and his mytho-
logical method. He can create a new psychological discourse. This is the elec-
tric recognition that gives rise to *The Four Zoas.* Because Blake was adventuring
in this long poem, thinking things through, the work is passionate, exploratory,
sometimes tentative. It is important and thrilling writing.[1] Northrop Frye was
right to call its abandonment "a major cultural disaster" (269).

    The Book of Urizen provides Blake's point of departure, but he does more
than expand on it in *The Four Zoas.* His thinking develops, and the poem de-
velops accordingly. To accommodate the accelerating sophistication of his
analysis, Blake increases the size of his mythological family, which permits
more elaborate interplay between characters. He modifies his style of pres-
entation, switching more frequently than in earlier works from third-person
narration to a seeming cacophony of competing monologues, heated ex-
changes, and passionate laments. The characters give variant, often conflict-
ing, interpretations of events, and no omniscient narrator discriminates
among them. These changes shift the balance from polemics to analysis; they
slow up the pace, introduce ambiguities, and allow for more comprehensive
thinking. But subtlety is not the only goal. The most striking difference be-
tween *Urizen* and *The Four Zoas* lies in form and feeling: *The Book of Urizen* is
a satire whereas *The Four Zoas* is a drama, and, consequently, the *Zoas* gives
occasion to much greater pathos. *Urizen* and its satellite books contain tragic
moments and tragic potential, but *The Four Zoas* concentrates on the anguish
of its characters. Its original subtitle, *The Torments of Love & Jealousy in the
Death and Judgement of Albion the Ancient Man,* identifies emotional suffering
as its topic. Blake's earlier works certainly explore suffering—especially the

Songs of Experience—yet with The Four Zoas he changes his emphasis. Blake wants now not only to work out his analysis of intellectual and historical error but also to dramatize the sorrow (the daily sorrow of the soul) that, Blake would say, it has precipitated in every human heart. This is ontological unhappiness—the anxiety of subjectivity or the soul's unease in itself. The Four Zoas focuses on this form of unhappiness and its provenance with an intensity that distinguishes it from the rest of Blake's prophetic books.

How does Blake deepen his representation, and his account, of this unhappiness? The Zoas and Emanations express it in many speeches, as Blake stages new ideas about its nature and its origin. He makes several major innovations in the poem in order to incorporate his new ideas. Most importantly, he pushes his analysis of the psychological issues farther back, now finding it insufficient to place all the blame on the greed of the Selfhood. The problem, he determines, began at a more primitive level with an earlier resignation of personal agency. Blake adds two characters, Tharmas and Enion, whose roles are specifically to embody passivation and despair. In the revised version of the poem, they are the first characters to appear so as to suggest that the process of disintegration begins with the collapse of agency. This conceptual adjustment produces others. Now that Urizen is no longer responsible for every error, Blake modulates his meaning and character. He is more sympathetic toward Urizen, who comes into his own, as it were, as not simply a caricature of Reason, but rather the approximation of a larger consciousness, something like the ordinary sense of self. For the first time Urizen laments—he is unhappy and aware of it—as if to suggest that the mind intuits its own failure and, reproaches itself instead of remaining complacent and obtuse. His acts have more destructive consequences than he intended—he perceives the stuntedness of human beings for which he is responsible—and he feels remorse, although he remains unable to reform.

The appearance of these empirical people constitutes an innovation in itself. Not since the Songs of Experience has Blake directly portrayed the loneliness and misery of ordinary people. In the middle Nights, these ordinary people crowd the poem as anonymous hoards of "the spectrous dead," sad casualties of the Zoas's disasters. The Zoas witness the anguish of the spectrous dead and grieve for them—for a time rather ineffectually. The Zoas have much greater contact with their human "subjects" in this poem than in the other prophetic books. There is something moving in this: it shows that

their suffering is mutual and that it stems from causes closer to tragic acci-
dent than complacent wrongdoing.

In Nights Eight and Nine, Blake will present a scenario of emergence in
which the decadence of the culture gives way to apocalyptic rebirth. For our
purposes, the most significant feature of this eventful narrative lies in the
identification of a new psychological principle—or better, a new emotion—
which plays a role in bringing about change. This is the emotion of dismay
felt by the emanations Enion and Ahania, who share the intuition that some-
thing has gone wrong, and something is missing. Enitharmon, who behaves
like a vixen in *Europe*, comes to share their dismay. At first triumphant and
nasty (as is Los), Enitharmon later becomes a troubled figure, harassed by the
Spectre of Urthona and deceived by Urizen. The gate of her heart "breaks,"
and the spectrous dead descend through it "upon the wind of Golgonooza"
(FZ 99:24, E372). Los says her heart breaks when it is "astonished melted into
Compassion & Love" (FZ 99:16, E372). Like Enion and Ahania, Enitharmon's
dismay results from her empathy with human beings. Thus, although their
anguish entails suffering, it is valuable; it represents the pricking of con-
science. The spectrous dead, poor zombies, have lost all intuition of their
higher being. But Enion, Ahania, and Enitharmon, with her "broken heart
Gate," reach a more advanced stage; they have awoken, they perceive the truth,
and they feel an appropriate sorrow. When translated into the experience of the
individual, this sorrow becomes regret on behalf of the soul. Awakening from
the stupor of materialism, one recognizes the "Eternal Life" one "forgot"; one
feels guilty for having ignored the transcendental intuition and betrayed the
proper vocation of humanity. I call this affect "transcendental remorse."

The Loss of Parent Power

The first version of *The Four Zoas*, titled *Vala*, began with the opening lines of
what subsequently became "Night the Second":

> Rising upon his Couch of Death Albion beheld his Sons
> Turning his Eyes outward to Self. losing the Divine Vision
>
> (FZ 23:1–2, E313)

Blake launched his epic by summarizing the essence of the catastrophe:
forgetting the impersonal soul in favor of identification with the "I" or

empirical self. Blake's ironic formulation, "Turning his Eyes outward to Self," calls attention to the delusion involved. This "I" is an imposter, masquerading as the real self, insofar as it constitutes (so it says) the unique individual—but its claims are spurious. Not particularly authentic, and certainly not original, this "I" is merely an artifact of accretion and thus "outward" by contrast with the impersonal soul, which is an ontological inheritance, a deeper reality within—as Blake terms it, an Opened Center. When Albion turns outward to Self, he loses power of action; suddenly he feels "weary" and, after resigning his "Scepter" to Urizen, he falls into a Gnostic "dark sleep of Death." A contest between Urizen, Luvah, and Vala ensues. While Albion sleeps, while the human being is divided from knowledge and capacity, pernicious ideas spring up—dissolution of agency, degradation of humanity, craven fear of nature and God, and so forth—with all the distortions of conscious and passional life, which lead to them and follow from them. At the end of "Night the Second," we see Los and Enitharmon quarreling, their quarrel manifesting the prophetic impulse disarmed by doubt and divided against itself. In this first version, in other words, Blake begins by picking up the story of Urizen, Los, Enitharmon, and Orc (now Luvah) from his earlier prophetic books. He transforms the story, but it is easy enough to see where he begins.

When Blake reworks *Vala* into *The Four Zoas,* he makes a more basic change, naming a new source as the origin of disaster. "Night the First" of *Vala* becomes "Night the Second" of *The Four Zoas,* and the new "Night the First" introduces despairing Tharmas and Enion to the saga. They have been invented, like neologisms or new terms of art, to allow Blake to say something he had not said before. It is as if Blake had reviewed these original opening lines and seen the possibility of going deeper. He decided not to open on a scene of Urizen, that is, *not* to begin with the bad faith of consciousness, but to start the story of unraveling with a more inchoate psychological moment: what I will term "the anxiety of interiority." He condensed a great deal of thinking and rethinking into the first few plates of *The Four Zoas.* I will be following them closely.

The text proper begins by introducing the reader to Albion, the "Giant Man," or figure of humanity whose deterioration and redemption the poem will describe.

His fall into Division & his Resurrection of Unity
His fall into the Generation of decay & death & his Regeneration
by the Resurrection from the dead.   (FZ 4:4–5, E301)

Here Blake practices his characteristic strategy of employing the language of Christian orthodoxy to invert its meaning: the "Resurrection from the dead" is not the resurrection of the body at the Last Judgment but rather the reawakening from the death-in-life of empirical subjectivity. To show how humankind fell into this state of inertia, Blake starts with Tharmas, who enters the poem announcing the confusion inspired in him by his psychological experience. He is mystified by his interior life and laments that he does not understand what is happening to him.

> Lost! Lost! Lost! Are my Emanations Enion O Enion
> We are become a Victim to the Living We hide in secret
> I have hidden Jerusalem in Silent Contrition O Pity Me
> I will build thee a Labyrinth also O pity me O Enion
> Why hast thou taken sweet Jerusalem from my inmost Soul
> Let her Lay secret in the Soft recess of darkness & silence
> It is not Love I bear to [Jerusalem] It is Pity
> She hath taken refuge in my bosom & I cannot cast her out.
>
>   (FZ 4:7–14, E301)

Tharmas's story is completely incoherent and so are his affects. He strays from self-pity to guilt, accusation, and denial. He recognizes that he does not know his motives. But he attempts to explain to himself the source of his anxiety: it is the fault of "Jerusalem," an importunate presence in his inner life that inspires ambivalence. In Blake's mythology, Jerusalem is a figure for heart, hope, and vision. Tharmas knows Jerusalem is there but cannot embrace her; he wants and does not want her. He is agitated by this internal incoherence, but is also agitated *because* he is agitated, troubled by the bewildering nature of his own interiority. No wonder he seeks to hide himself, or hide Jerusalem, "in the Soft recess of darkness & silence." But he senses that there can be no escape: his anxiety will be endless now because it is now the anxiety *of* interiority, the uneasiness of being subjected to one's own feelings. He feels not simply helpless in an empirical sense, but helpless in relation to his own psyche.

[95   ]

Tharmas's Emanation, Enion, speaks next, reflecting the internal split. Enion regards him with horror and disappointment, confirming his own view that his inner world is sinister: "I have lookd into the secret soul of him I lovd / And in the Dark recesses found Sin & cannot return" (FZ 4:26–27, E301). To compound their terrors, both feel an obscure sense of guilt, translating the anxiety of interiority into a moral register. Tharmas begs Enion not to inquire too closely into his inner life because she will find it a morass of unsavory affects.

> Thou wilt go mad with horror if thou dost Examine thus
> Every moment of my secret hours Yea I know
> That I have sinnd & that my Emanations are become harlots
> I am already distracted at their deeds & if I look
> Upon them more Despair will bring self murder on my soul

> (FZ 4:29–38, E302)

Here Tharmas sounds like Urizen who, as we have noted, hypostasizes his quasi-alienated affects under the name of the Seven Deadly Sins. Tharmas calls them whorish Emanations, things of darkness that he acknowledges as his own. Both Urizen and Tharmas follow Augustine in characterizing interiority as the source of sin and guilt, precisely insofar as the consciousness does not govern all of it. ("The ego is not master in its own house.") According to Augustine, one does not know oneself and cannot trust oneself. "For that darkness is lamentable in which the possibilities in me are hidden from myself: so that the mind, questioning itself upon its own powers, feels that it cannot lightly trust its own report: because what is already in it does for the most part lie hidden, unless experience brings it to light" (*Confessions* X. xxxii). The unpredictability and inscrutability of the inner world create paranoia toward it on the part of consciousness, and this paranoia naturally leads on to denigration and rejection. In an easy move, Tharmas universalizes his shame, extending his self-contempt to others: he turns Enion's horror of him back on her: "O Enion thou art thyself a root growing in hell" (FZ 4:39, E302).

Both Urizen and Tharmas project sinfulness onto unacknowledged parts of the self, and from thence onto others, with their own obscure inner lives. But with his new opening, Blake shifts the focus from the engorgement of the "I" to a primary internal chaos. We can see him rethinking the opening chapters of *The Book of Urizen*. Where *Urizen* begins with individuation and alienation from the external world, *The Four Zoas* starts with self-division and the anxiety of interiority. In *Urizen* the "I" emerges, and the hypostasis of the "I" makes an eerie realm of the interior: Urizen simultaneously projects and introjects the fearsome "void" he cannot control. But in *The Four Zoas* Blake presents the alienation of the inner world first. The experience of the interior as a frightening chaos is the principal experience. We may be reminded of Melanie Klein's phrase, "inner chaos," and her claim that newborns feel that they are chaotic inside. But unlike Klein—and this is all-important—Blake does not offer a developmental paradigm. Tharmas is neither a child nor a representative of a childhood feeling. Tharmas represents a fundamental experience of subjectivity that is ever pertinent to anyone and everyone. Nor is Blake presenting a chronological scheme: it is not that the anxiety of interiority *predates* the creation of the "I"; obviously, some kind of "I" or central consciousness must exist to experience the alienation. (And Tharmas speaks as an "I.") But the hypostasis of the ego is no longer the essential problem, and it is no longer, as in *Urizen,* an error or caprice that is theoretically avoidable. The "I" inevitably calcifies in reaction to the primal terror of subject life which there is no avoiding. Why does Blake create this new scheme? He makes the change, I believe, because he has changed his definition of the fundamental evil in empiricist subjectivity: it is not the egoism of the isolated Ratio but the assumption of helplessness. The anxiety of interiority, in Blake's view, brings with it this radical passivation. One neither grows out of it nor into it by getting older; it is an always-available concomitant of subjectivity, and the only way to transcend it is to replace one experience of self with another. Although Blake continues to use the metaphor of the fall, he does not mean it literally: there was no time we were not as now—not in childhood, not in the "childhood" of humanity. Instead, Blake retains the metaphor because it captures something about the phenomenal experience of the self: namely, that endemic anxiety and passivity feel like damage; they make one feel *as if broken.*

We will understand Blake's argument more clearly if we define Tharmas in his so-called unfallen form—his benign apparition. Critics have found Tharmas a puzzling figure, and there is no exact consensus about what he signifies. Because Blake introduces him with the epithet "Parent power, darkning in the West" (FZ 4:6, E301), Tharmas is interpreted as some sort of capacity or potential, although critics disagree about its nature. As a "Parent power,"

Tharmas is clearly a radical power. But perhaps he also represents a projected power, specifically, the benevolent power the child attributes to the parent. (Suggestively, the mother figure in the *Zoas* is Enion, the emanation of Tharmas: in her fallen state she becomes the helpless prophetess, the Rachel who cannot save her children.) The power of the parent becomes a power in the child, an ontological security that is a mighty possession in itself. Wordsworth illustrates this process in the poems describing the exaltation of his childhood, when he was inspired by faith in Nature's "ministry"; conversely, when he grew disillusioned with Nature, his glamorous sense of self subsided. "A power is gone which nothing can restore," he says in "Elegiac Stanzas," written after his brother was drowned at sea (*Poetical Works* 453). The lost power is not that of Nature, which has demonstrated its might, but rather the power of his own soul, which "a deep distress hath humanized," or humbled. For Wordsworth, this ontological confidence is not a delusion that one outgrows; it is a faith we are unfortunately compelled by experience to discredit.

But Blake departs sharply from Wordsworth, for again, Blake does not work with a developmental paradigm, even an inverted one in which the child is the Father of the Man and is the "best Philosopher, the eye among the blind." Blake's Innocents possess not agency but an illusion of it. Therefore, Blake promotes not the *recovery* of an empirical agency (which was never possessed) but the *discovery* of agency of another kind, and this is the work of a mature intelligence. The form of agency he promotes is not that which the speakers of Experience long for and sometimes claim they have—that of empirical confidence, or trust that one can enact one's will in the world; it is a larger assurance, the conviction of one's *transcendental* power. Blake knows that no form of empirical power can dispel helplessness, but transcendental agency—Vision if it helps to call it that—moves in another realm over which materiality has no purchase. Rightly considered, this power is absolute. Nothing can contravene or disprove it. One is free to believe in it; in believing, to experience it; and in experiencing it, to feel free. Enemy of the Enlightenment though he was, Blake, I think, would have approved of Kant's argument that humanity has a vocation for transcendence that is necessary to discover, and would have agreed that this discovery is critical because of its moral and psychological consequences. In Kant's analysis of the "dynamic sublime," the acknowledgement of empirical helplessness (before nature) reverses into an exhilarating recognition of transcendental invulnerability:

Now in just the same way the irresistibility of the might of nature forces upon us the recognition of our physical helplessness as beings of nature, but at the same time reveals a faculty of estimating ourselves as independent of nature, and discovers a pre-eminence above nature that is the foundation of a self-preservation of quite another kind from that which may be assailed and brought into danger by external nature. This saves humanity in our own person from humiliation, even though as mortal men we have to submit to external violence. In this way, external nature is not estimated in our aesthetic judgement as sublime so far as exciting fear, but rather because it challenges our power (one not of nature) to regard as small those things of which we are wont to be solicitous (worldly goods, health, and life), and hence to regard its might (to which in these matters we are no doubt subject) as exercising over us and our personality no such rude dominion that we should bow down before it, once the question becomes one of our highest principles and of our asserting or forsaking them. Therefore nature is here called sublime merely because it raises the imagination to a presentation of those cases in which the mind can make itself sensible of the appropriate sublimity of the sphere of its own being, even above nature. (III)

We may quibble about whether Blake would have endorsed this degree of alienation from nature, or whether by "mind" Kant means Reason of the kind Blake questions. Nor would Blake have admired Kant's hierarchy of the faculties. But, nonetheless, he shares with Kant the notion that people can possess themselves of an unassailable transcendental agency, and that this discovery is of great therapeutic value insofar as it reverses the condition of helplessness to which we are otherwise largely condemned. Everyone knows that Blake is a species of Platonic idealist, championing Imagination over Nature, and the transcendent realm over the world of matter. These are evidently his dogmas. I argue that they are *not* dogmas, but rather urgent therapeutic interventions designed to ameliorate the radical unhappiness of passivation.

Returning now to *The Four Zoas,* Tharmas, in his fallen state, represents surrender to empirical helplessness, and the consequent slide into paralysis and despair. He has relinquished his "Parent power," and made a universal *assumption,* a reflexive axiom, of his incapacity. His impotence takes on the incontrovertible status of fact. With his second sentence he utters a cry of defeat: "Enion O Enion / We are become a Victim to the Living" (FZ 4:7–8, E301). The world has him in its grip, and there is nothing that he can do. From this point on, Blake works to show that the assumption of incapacity has effects that are pandemic. In his second speech, Tharmas picks up the topic of *Urizen:* the trials of consciousness that suspects itself of infirmity. But unlike Urizen, Tharmas actually voices the contradictions and anguish of empirical subjectivity; he describes what passes within when one feels oneself to be merely an "I." Here we return to the passage discussed in my introduction as exemplifying the predicament of the empiricist subject: "I am like an atom / A Nothing left in darkness yet I am an identity." Straightened between the double voids of inside and outside, the "I" contracts, stripped of substance and agency, although remaining, strangely, self-conscious.

Out of this essential pessimism of selfhood comes the invention of Fate. We see Tharmas setting the "Circle of Destiny" in motion. That is to say, it is only after perceiving the futility of consciousness that Tharmas discovers a principle of necessity in the world. In a paradox that captures the essence of projection, Tharmas creates this Circle of Destiny by which he imagines himself to be bound. He shapes confines in the same manner as the Urizenic "Ancient of Days," Blake's version of the Gnostic Demiurge, who draws a circle in the void with his compass.

> Tharmas groand among his Clouds
> Weeping, then bending from his Clouds he stoopd
> his innocent head
> And stretching out his holy hand in the vast Deep sublime
> Turnd round the circle of Destiny with tears & bitter sighs.
>
> (FZ 5:8–11, E302)

Tharmas rationalizes the anxiety of interiority by locating a force of determination outside the self. Something out there oppresses him; something else has the power of agency, and that allows him to explain why he feels incapable. Once invented, his concept assumes authority. It hardens into truth. Enion completes the Circle of Destiny by weaving it into "a watry Globe self-balanced" (FZ 5: 25, E302), that is, a self-sustaining entity.

(The phrase is Miltonic.) The Daughters of Beulah try to limit the damage by confining this fatality to the space of "Ulro," or the physical world. With this act, Nature comes into its own as a site of necessity, a sphere in which the human being is subject. Nature is no longer, as in *Urizen*, simply the void or not-"I" that springs into being with the "I"; it is the force of compulsion, or Newtonian law. What Tharmas first creates in the Deep is not nature itself, not the Earth, not the physical universe. It is the assumption on which our concept of materiality is predicated: the supposition of binding fate or final agency external to the self. This idea then informs our view of materiality.

Blake names this supposition of Fate the "Spectre of Tharmas"—a shadow or projection out of Tharmas's passivity. The hardening of Fate begins when Tharmas collapses and his Spectre "[issues] from his feet in flames of fire" (FZ 5:15, E302). Enion draws the Spectre out, "every vein & lacteal threading them among / Her woof of terror" (FZ 5:17–18, E302). She weaves these combined elements into "the Circle of Destiny Complete," but she works involuntarily and with foreboding. She creates a monster.

> Terrified & drinking tears of woe
> Shuddring she wove—nine days & nights Sleepless her
>   food was tears
> Wondring she saw her woof begin to animate. & not
> As Garments woven subservient to her hands but having a will
> Of its own perverse & wayward   (FZ 5:18–22, E302)

Blake emphasizes the fact that we are witnessing a transfer of agency. The Circle of Destiny Complete—the attribution of all power to nature—springs from humanity's conspiracy in its own subjection, which it imagines itself to have accepted only reluctantly. Nature assumes the might surrendered by the transcendental and immortal Human. Therefore, the benign Daughters of Beulah remark, "this Spectre of Tharmas / Is Eternal Death" (FZ 5:41–42, E303), the death of the soul. Enion is horrified when she beholds her creation, the Circle of Destiny, and in her guilt she turns inward to find that a ghastly change has taken place.

> A life is blotted out & I alone remain possessd with Fears
> I see the Shadow of the dead within my Soul wandering

In darkness & solitude forming Seas of Doubt & rocks
  of Repentance
Already are my Eyes reverted. all that I behold
Within my Soul has lost its splendor & a brooding Fear
Shadows me oer & drives me outward to a world of woe
So waild she trembling before her own Created Phantasm

(FZ 5:44–53, E303)

Something within the self has perished and left consciousness alone, "possessed with Fears." And yet what has died has not disappeared; it lingers on as a forlorn ghost, a strange absence-as-presence that consciousness feels to be alien but by which it is somehow inspired with remorse. This "Shadow of the dead" is the abandoned intuition of transcendental agency. Interiority has undergone a drastic decline: "all that I behold / Within my Soul has lost its splendor." Enion sounds Wordsworthian here. Her soul has been ontologically evacuated, stripped of its transcendental splendor or "glory," as Wordsworth would say. To adapt a phrase of John Ashbery's, the soul is not a Soul. A power is gone, which nothing can restore. Deprived of transcendental purchase, soul collapses into psyche. The different strands of the inner life—affects, memories, thoughts, impulses—are unmoored, attenuated, and detached from one another; each floats about on its own. From this haunted world the mind flees outward, but it can find no stability or comfort in a world defined as the sphere of Fate, the "world of woe."

This phantasm of Enion's subjection, before which she wails, does indeed take on a life of its own: The Spectre of Tharmas emerges out of her woof and begins his assault on her. In the frightening encounter between them that follows, he enacts a gross misappropriation of agency, seemingly engorged with the power Tharmas / Enion has resigned. The Spectre evinces vindictive pride and he harangues Enion with self-righteous hauteur—he tells her he is pure where she is polluted—but the message he proffers does not concern morality or sin. He menaces her with sadistic ontology.

This world is Thine in which thou dwellest that within thy soul
That dark & dismal infinite where Thought roams up & down
Is Mine & there thou goest when with one Sting of my tongue
Envenomd thou rollst inwards to the place whence I emergd.

(FZ 6:13–16, E303–4)

The Spectre scoffingly accords to Enion "this world"—the material world—while claiming her inner world for himself. The inner world ought to be a refuge for thought—it is, after all, the mind's "proper sphere"—but in Enion's experience, this inner world is even more scary and disorienting than the fearsome world of matter. Gothic language recurs as thought (or the central consciousness) feels itself to be straying up and down in the self's "dark & dismal" void, languishing in the oubliette of the interior. Thus far the characterization is familiar from the earlier speeches of Tharmas and Enion, but in this passage the central consciousness seems even worse off than before because now it faces not only interior bewilderment but also some principle of internal hostility: the Spectre proclaims that when it stings thought with venom, and thought rolls inward for safety, it meets the vicious serpent there too because the inner world is actually its nest. The whole process is figured in terms that are almost vertiginously circular: "and there thou goest when with one Sting of my tongue / Envenomed thou rollst inwards to the place whence I emerged." (In fact, in keeping with the vertigo of the passage, the participle *envenomed* is a squinting modifier; it goes with both "tongue" and "thou.") What is Blake's point?

Let me note that Blake did something very curious in this passage: it is something he does elsewhere in *The Four Zoas* but not, as far as I know, in any of his other works. Blake revises antithetically, replacing a word with its antonym. In the earlier version of this passage, the possessive pronouns were reversed: "This world is *Mine* [not Thine] in which thou dwellest" and "That dark & dismal infinite where Thought roams up & down / Is *thine* [not Mine]" (*The Complete Poems* 280, emphasis mine). Why did Blake reverse the pronouns, especially when he is describing a power dynamic? How can he invert his account of whose world is whose? I think he began with the idea that follows most logically from what the poem has just shown. The Ulro has been formed, and the Spectre emerges to insist on the separation of inside and outside: the threatening outside world is his and only the enveloping inside world is hers. But then Blake bethought himself: in fact, the dualism of inner and outer not only makes the outer world forbidding but also ends up, more traumatically, darkening the experience of interiority. The Spectre becomes more frightening when he grants Enion "this world" while claiming "the dark and dismal infinite" of the interior for himself, because he thereby shows that there is nowhere the "I" can be master. It encounters its ineffectiveness in every sphere. Enion has submitted ontologically—thought accepts its helplessness—and experiences in the outside world seem to demonstrate its infirmity. But when consciousness takes refuge in its proper domain, it feels disempowered there as well, because that is where it grew this demon of impotence. This estrangement of the interior life is harsher than alienation from nature because it can be cruelly all-absorbing. From one's own affects there is really no escape. As we shall see, when Urizen tries to rouse people in "Night the Sixth," he gets no response: "no one answer every one wrapd up / In his own sorrow howld regardless of his words" (FZ 70[First Portion]:41–42, E347). Thought has a hard time righting itself by thought, especially thoughts about itself. Are "mind-forg'd manacles" all that easy to break?

To compound the torment, Enion blames herself for her confusion and dismay. In her delusion, she says, she has murdered the Emanations of Tharmas, finding out too late "that all those Emanations were my Childrens Souls" (FZ 7: 3, E304). In his first speech, Tharmas had lamented the loss of his Emanations, and now Enion says she killed them or drove them "into the desarts" with her "Cruelty." The Emanations of Tharmas seem to represent positive emotional resources (hope, kindness, confidence)—the resources that Tharmas in his ontological terror has to do without—in the same way that Jerusalem represents the alienated benevolence of Albion. Of course it is the Spectre of Tharmas who has induced Enion to murder these Emanations: they are casualties of the fear and paranoia that result from the loss of agency. Let us recall that Enion herself is an Emanation of Tharmas, so that what we are witnessing is a form of self-mutilation, the emotional damage a person does to herself when she perceives herself as radically helpless. Enion's guilt represents a further emotional complication. She feels that she is somehow implicated in her own contraction or self-loss. She must add self-reproach to grief, like the speaker of "The Angel."

> Soon my Angel came again
> I was arm'd, he came in vain;
> For the time of youth was fled
> And grey hairs were on my head.
>
> (E24)

Both this speaker and Enion have arrived at a perspicuous representation of their plight—they are correct to blame themselves. The perversity of this whole spiral of feeling is reflected by the fact that it ends in apt self-castigation. This is the economy of Sin—and Enion accuses herself of

sinning—but Blake in his ironic way has demonstrated that the error of Thar-
mas and Enion has nothing to do with sin as Christianity defines it, quite the
reverse. Guilt over sin creates its own effect, increasing self-alienation and
self-dread and so escalating, or re-escalating or re-re-escalating, the mystifica-
tion of interiority: "dark I feel my world within" (FZ 7:7, E304).

The last moment in the fall of Tharmas and Enion follows. Congress be-
tween Enion and the Spectre of Tharmas produces Los and Enitharmon,
vampiric offspring who siphon off their mother's vitality. Full of maternal
passion, she nourishes them at her breast, and they grow strong as she grows
"Weaker & weaker . . . wearier and wearier . . . her bright Eyes decayd
melted with pity & love" (FZ 8:8–10, E304). In "pride and haughty joy," they
disdain her and desert her, but, ironically, the effect is beneficial: in her agony,
Enion "rehumaniz[es] from the Spectre in pangs of maternal love" (FZ 9:3,
E304). Enion returns to herself—she recovers some of her status as an intu-
iter of truth—but only after a compromised form of it, prophecy, has en-
tered the empirical world. Thus she is reduced to straying in the void as a
murmur of conscience while Los and Enitharmon—the remains of imagina-
tive agency—glory in an illusory sense of power. It is illusory because deraci-
nated, "grounded" in the false authority of empirical presence, while cut off
from the real source of power, which is transcendental intuition. Under these
circumstances, imaginative agency cannot cooperate with itself, it cannot
gather its own force. Los and Enitharmon enter into a nasty affair and a sullen
marriage, as the decadence of the other Zoas quickly proceeds. Vala appears,
the evil omnipotence of nature; she and Luvah (yearning) fly up "from the
Human Heart / Into the Brain" (FZ 10;11–12, E305). Helpless fear becomes
doctrine. Then Urizen wakes up and seizes power, the mind struggling vainly
to regain the agency the human being has resigned.

Meanwhile, Enion becomes the poem's most articulate prophet of de-
spair. In the only well-known speech from The Four Zoas, Enion deplores
the bitter character of natural experience and the selfishness of Natural
Man: "I am made to sow the thistle for wheat; the nettle for a nourishing
dainty / I have planted a false oath in the earth, it has brought forth a poison
tree" (FZ 35:1–2, E324–25). Her speech rises in a crescendo of self-accusation:
"I have chosen the serpent for a councellor & the dog / For a schoolmaster to
my children / I have blotted out from light & living the dove & nightingale"
(FZ 35:3–5, E324–25). The rhetoric is superb, the argument simple: our life is

nasty by nature—perverse and cruel—and so are we. There is nothing to be done about this; it is inevitable. Again we see the characteristic feature of despair—the sense of being enslaved to necessity—here, in particular, to the "laws" of nature and society. But Enion's despair does not settle here. It overflows into her evaluation of her own knowledge. We may be incapable in relation to natural experience, but we can cognize it, we can even cognize our incapacity—we can know the truth. Are we not then capable in the realm of mind? Enion in her despair answers, Yes but so what? Who would desire such an unwelcome burden? Knowledge of necessity is by definition ineffectual (necessity cannot be altered), and so it becomes oppressive, even painful. Nor shall we be permitted to arrive at it by means of contemplation. It will be forced on us by grim ordeal. Therefore, knowledge is bound to its own tragic law.

> What is the price of Experience do men buy it for a song
> Or wisdom for a dance in the street? No it is bought with the price
> Of all that a man hath his house his wife his children
> Wisdom is sold in the desolate market where none come to buy
> And in the witherd field where the farmer plows for bread in vain.
>
> (FZ 35:11–15, E325)

Enion has become the representative of despairing knowledge, knowledge that knows its own truth but finds itself empty to the extent that it cannot be acted on. Soon she will communicate her despair to Urizen's Emanation, Ahania. Ahania, the wisdom which rationality affords, hears Enion's lament, and she is haunted by it: "never from that moment could she rest upon her pillow" (FZ 36:19, E326). Ahania floats about, intuiting truth but remaining unheard and unseen, like Enion: "Where Enion, blind & age bent wanderd Ahania wanders now" (FZ 46:8, E331). Enitharmon will become a figure of desolation in "Night the Fourth" and following. These Emanations represent the perception that their Zoa refuses, or denies, and is therefore rendered powerless. Thus they are reduced to the pure lamentation of Cassandra.

From their own perspective, their knowledge is useless and their sorrow is vain, because they believe in the compulsion of nature. They have reached an impasse, believing that fate is the "lesson" of experience. Blake does not agree: he sees belief in necessity as productive of despair (rather than the other way around), because it is a belief intertwined with passivation. He breaks this cycle of necessity, redefining natural "law" as an illusion created by our spontaneous or unnecessary resignation of agency. We think ourselves powerless in relation to nature—there are good reasons for thinking so—and we forget that agency in the physical world is not the only form agency can take. Yet Blake believes that the restless apprehension of the Emanations is valuable. It keeps opposition to "fate" alive by lamenting it. Something is wrong, they say, which we cannot accept. Enion is compassionate and her great speech ends in a moment of moral resistance: "It is an easy thing to rejoice in the tents of prosperity / Thus could I sing & thus rejoice, but it is not so with me!" (FZ 36:12–13, E325). In their very anguish, Enion and then Ahania represent a vestige of idealism or transcendental intuition for they recognize that they experience a lack of agency where they should not. Insofar as they feel helpless, they have lost a power that rightfully belongs to them. This murmur of their resistance will endure throughout the first eight Nights of *The Four Zoas*. It is a major source of hope, because without it, humanity could never awaken and redeem itself. The chagrin of Enion and Ahania recalls the proper status of humanity, lost to view among "the spectrous dead," or empirical human beings, in their inert humiliation.

The Spectrous Dead

In Nights Six and Seven of *The Four Zoas*, Blake concentrates on the fate of ordinary people who are represented as a dismal anonymous mass. This feature of *The Four Zoas* distinguishes it from both *Milton* and *Jerusalem* in which Blake does not explicitly describe the impact of the mythological action on the lives of empirical human beings. Nancy Moore Goslee perspicuously describes the contrasting strategy in the *Zoas:* Blake "weaves a tenuous connection between the giant forms who split and fragment, and the individual humans who are both subject to the actions of the splitting forms of the Zoas and whose subjectivities in some sense are represented by them" (396). In the *Zoas* Blake wished to make plain the translation to individual experience; he seems to have been particularly moved by the subject at this moment. As Nights Six and Seven unfold, portraying the progress of history, the plight of the "ruind spirits" darkens considerably to the extent that although they begin as Miltonic figures of some grandeur, as "ruined spirits," they end up as "piteous spectres." Their story climaxes in a poignant scene at the end of Night Seven, when Los and Enitharmon, moved by what they see, try to comfort and revive the supine "spectres of the dead."

How did they acquire this name and what does it signify? The penultimate chapter of *The Book of Urizen* first hints at this characterization. Dramatic action pauses as Urizen goes out alone to "explore his dens." It is a reflective moment, as befits Urizen: he looks and judges, and in this case he hates what meets his eyes. His offspring inspire him with revulsion because they are weak and corrupt: "for he saw that / That no flesh nor sprit could keep / His iron laws one moment" (BU 23:25–6, E81). He loathes life and the debasement of the living:

> For he saw that life liv'd upon death
> The Ox in the slaughter house moans
> The Dog at the wintry door.
>
> (BU 23:27; 25: 1–2, E81-2)

Urizen's words echo Enion's in her great speech on natural experience. But even if he shares her vision, he responds differently. Whereas she is grieved and resistant, he merely feels disgust, which he quickly masks under hypocritical "Pity." From this "cold" rejection of his mythological "sons and daughters," "a cold shadow" arises: the "Net" or "Web" of Religion. Urizen's religion repudiates humanity by disparaging it and then requiring human beings to participate in their own degradation. He passivates them in the name of compassion. With the formation of this "Net of Religion," ordinary people (as opposed to mythological characters) first appear in the poem. They are the "Inhabitants of those Cities" "Whereever the footsteps of Urizen / Walk'd . . . in sorrow," and they adopt his distorted views without question (BU 25:13–14, E82). A hoard of the unnamed, "They" take the empiricist view that they are bodies without souls, doomed to extinction: "They lived a period of years / Then left a noisom body / To the jaws of devouring darkness" (BU 28:1–3, E83). In their desperation, they embrace Urizen's religion, with its reductive ontologies and its false benevolence. By this they are further diminished.

> Six days they shrunk up from existence
> And on the seventh day they rested
> And they bless'd the seventh day, in sick hope
> And forgot their eternal life.
>
> (BU 27:39–42, E83)

They have contracted transcendental amnesia. Their ears now are "wither'd, & deafen'd, & cold" to the murmurs of resistance. The prophets despair of them: at the end of the poem, the few souls uncaught by the "Net of Urizen" depart from Egypt for the Promised Land.

When Blake reworks this material in Nights Five and Six of the *Zoas*, he greatly expands his account of the individual's existential suffering, and he also rethinks the relation of consciousness to suffering of this kind. Urizen makes his tour of the fallen world in Night Six, lighting his way with a "Globe of Fire." The first creatures Urizen meets are his three daughters (a new invention not present in *Urizen*). At first, he does not know them, and they do not know him. They appear as three women of "terrible" power, three sisters like the Fates, the Erinys, and the Eumenides. But as soon as Urizen recognizes them, "they [shrink] into their channels, dry the rocky strand beneath his feet / Hiding themselves in rocky forms from the Eyes of Urizen" (FZ 68:3–4, E345). They had been productive possibilities of thought; but now they have been desiccated, somehow, by thought itself. Like Lear, their father perverted them in confronting them. Now Urizen curses them to be reversed into their opposites—destructive misuses of the mind. Instead of wisdom, thoughtfulness, tolerance, and self-respect, he proclaims, they shall have "Chains of dark ignorance & cords of twisted self conceit / And whips of stern repentance & food of stubborn obstinacy" (FZ 68:23–24, E345). When this corruption of intellect and emotion has been accomplished, the daughters will "curse & worship" the violent God, "the obscure Demon of destruction" (FZ 68:25–26, E346). With these lines, Blake summaries the contortions by which the mind brings itself to participate in harmful religion. But Blake's myth also tells of a family romance: because the obscure demon is none other Urizen himself, Urizen means to draw his daughters into a pathological relationship with him, suffering themselves to be cursed by him while they furiously curse him in return but also fearfully "worship" him.

Soon Urizen witnesses the effect of his curse on humanity. For people there is no divided, no shared if dysfunctional dynamic. Each person is reduced to a feeble isolate by self-thwarting passion and self-vitiating intelligence. As Urizen forces a path among "the terrors of the Abyss," he stumbles upon something more pitiful than his daughters—ordinary human beings, Dantesque in their desolation.

For Urizen beheld the terrors of the Abyss wandring among
The ruind spirits once his children & the children of Luvah
Scard at the sound of their own sigh that seems to shake the immense
They wander Moping in their heart a Sun a Dreary moon
A Universe of fiery constellations in their brain
An Earth of wintry woe beneath their feet & round their loins
Waters or winds or clouds or brooding lightnings & pestilential plagues

(FZ 70:5-15, E347)

This passage is unprecedented in Blake; he nowhere else gives a picture
of the inner life, in this plain descriptive mode, with this much plangency.
This is his portrait of emotional evacuation. Weary, lost, oppressed, the ru-
ined spirits mope because they are materialists estranged from the material
world. They have internalized the view of it as impassive and threatening.
This view has sunk so deep as to seem like an inborn fact, a truth known in-
tuitively: "*in their heart* a Sun a Dreary Moon / A Universe of fiery constella-
tions *in their brain* / An Earth of wintry woe beneath their feet & round their
loins" (emphasis mine). The "reality" of nature's power has been sealed by
the subject's resignation and dread. The "Earth of wintry woe" figures the in-
different necessity of the material world, echoing Enion's and Urizen's image
of "the dog at the wintry door." The sigh of the suffering soul—of experience
and consciousness—echoes hollowly in this dead world; therefore, ruined spir-
its are "scared at the sound of their own sigh that seems to shake the im-
mense." Each expression of their existence reminds them of their isolation.

Blake does not give moping its contemporary pejorative sense in which it
is related to self-indulgence and self-pity. He seems to mean it in several dif-
ferent, earlier, senses. An archaic meaning, "to wander aimlessly, bewildered,"
is clearly relevant along with two intransitive uses given by the *Oxford English
Dictionary:* (1) "to be in a state of unconsciousness, to move and act without
the impulse and guidance of thought" (Obs.) and (2) "to yield oneself up to
ennui, to remain in a listless, apathetic condition, without making any effort
to rouse oneself, to be dull, dejected and spiritless." The ruined spirits com-
bine these qualities: they stray about aimlessly in a state that links confused
fear with a general emotional retrenchment. Their repertoire of feeling has
been severely curtailed, but the negative affects that remain have lost none of
their force. In "Night the Eighth" people will be briefly "humanized," but

then they will regress: "Relapsing in dire torment they return to forms of woe / To moping visages returning inanimate" (FZ 102:7–8, E374). This description seems paradoxical at first—tormented but inanimate?—until we realize how Blake is using the word. *Inanimate* means lacking in soul—unsouled, or better, de-souled, "dishumanizd" (FZ 70:31, E347). Far from being impassive, the soul that does not think it is a soul suffers, feeling the burden of its futility. Like Tharmas, who complained of being a lonely "identity" tormented by vain feeling, these "compeers" undergo the loneliness and disequilibrium of ensouledness without the sustenance of its pride.

In *Urizen* Blake called people the offspring of Urizen, but in the *Zoas* he gives them a new lineage emphasizing the ruination not just of their ideas but of their emotional lives. Now people are the children of Urizen and Luvah, the product of an intellectual *and* affective distortion. Blake had concentrated on the malformation of reason and ego in *Urizen;* in the *Zoas* he introduces the characters of Luvah (love) and Vala, Luvah's tormenting consort, to show how passional life is thwarted. The capacity for love we manifest in our relation to other creatures, and to nature, is diverted by insecurity and self-mistrust into malign affects (hatred, jealousy, fear). Frustration results, then contraction and surrender. When Urizen in his tour arrives at the domain of Luvah, he finds it emptied out: "No form was there no living thing" (FZ 71:17, E348). Love has been utterly routed.

When Urizen first comes across these "ruind spirits," he finds them embedded in self-enclosure, incapable of love. Not only is each isolated in the world as a possessor of consciousness, but each is also trapped *within* his or her own consciousness.

> Beyond the bounds of their own self their senses cannot penetrate
> As the tree knows not what is outside of its leaves & bark
> And yet it drinks the summer joy & fears the winter sorrow
> So in the regions of the grave none knows his dark compeer.
>
> (FZ 70;12–15, E347)

This is the "Forgetfulness, dumbness, necessity" that descended on Urizen, now witnessed in the ordinary human psyche. But none of the blame that attaches to Urizen belongs to these poor benighted souls. They are seen as victims, not perpetrators of error. Indeed, they are ignorant of their condition. But their very lack of awareness is a symptom of how they, who

should be mighty, have fallen. They sink below the vocation of humanity.
Blake reminds us that they should be grander with the Miltonic phrase, "his
dark compeer." In "the regions of the grave" (i.e., life, Gnostically transvalu-
ated), each unsouled soul lives in loneliness, not recognizing that its suffering
is shared or that it is an exalted "peer" surrounded by like-souled "compeers."

Dread is isolating: it buries each frightened soul in its own anxiety. The
image of Urizen as a skeleton, curled in upon himself in the fetal position, is
emblematic of this contraction. But in this scene, touchingly, Urizen tries to
penetrate the rigid self-absorption of his "children," steeped in their terrors.
As he goes on, Urizen encounters animal forms that represent Circean meta-
morphoses of "dishumanizd men" (FZ 70:31, E347). And he meets even stranger
attenuations of humanity. Like Dante in the underworld, Urizen feels sympa-
thy; he wants to draw them out. But they cannot hear him above their own in-
coherent mouthings.

> His voice to them was but an inarticulate thunder for their Ears
> Were heavy & dull & their eyes & nostrils closed up
> Oft he stood by a howling victim Questioning in words
> Soothing or Furious no one answerd every one wrapd up
> In his own sorrow howld regardless of his words, nor voice
> Of sweet response could he obtain tho oft assayed with tears
> He knew they were his Children ruind in his ruind world.
>
> (FZ 76:36–45, E347)

During this initial survey of the fallen world, when Urizen first beholds
the devastation he has caused, he feels genuine dismay. The deterioration of
human beings makes him cry; he speaks to them through tears. We are re-
minded of Satan's response to the sight of his troops when first assembled in
Hell: "cruel his eye, but cast / Signs of remorse and passion to behold / The
fellows of his crime, the followers rather . . . condemned for ever now to
have their lot in pain / Millions of Spirits for his fault amerced / Of heav'n"
(*Paradise Lost* I.ll.604–10, pp. 20–21). Like Satan—and unlike Dante—Urizen is
responsible for the suffering he beholds. He recognizes his guilt, and evidently
desires to reverse the damage, but it is too late. He cannot lift the curse.

> He saw them cursd beyond his Curse his soul melted with fear
> He could not take their fetters off for they grew from the soul

Nor could he quench the fires for they flamd out from the heart
Nor could he calm the Elements because himself was Subject.

(FZ 70:46–47; 71:10–13, E348)

Like Enion weaving the "Circle of Destiny," Urizen sees the consequences
of his retrenchment spiral out of his control. It is suggestive that he cannot
calm the Elements "because himself was Subject." Clearly this idea alludes to
the passivating materialism Urizen practices; he thinks himself a conscious-
ness without power over the Elements. But Blake, capitalizing the word "Sub-
ject," may very well intend a pun. In that case, the word might function not
only as an adjective (subject to) but also as a noun (a subject). It is precisely be-
cause he has described himself, to himself, as a Subject that he has no power.
The fetters now grow *from* the soul. This figure signifies that self-limitation has
been so thoroughly internalized as to seem intractable, but it also means that
self-limitation has infected the concept of the soul. These two ideas are re-
lated: the beggarliness of the human being appears to be fated because it ap-
pears to subsist in the nature of the human soul. The individual reprises the
"fall" of Tharmas, adopting his ontological fatalism. Thus human beings are
cursed "beyond" the original curse; a thought has grown into a necessity, and
Urizen cannot reverse the process even when he wants to.

Urizen's remorse constitutes a striking new development, because he had
expressed no guilt or chagrin in *Urizen*. To his analysis of affects in the fallen
soul, Blake apparently wants to add the *sorrow of reason*, which is to say,
awareness on the part of reason that it has failed. Urizen takes over the mid-
dle books of *The Four Zoas* because he instantiates consciousness's day-to-day
recognition of its own inadequacy. He is the one who beholds the suffering of
the "ruind spirits," who hears us and comes close to us, because he represents
the power of mind capable of explicitly formulating the failure of mind. How
could we know the deracination of consciousness except by means of con-
sciousness? And yet how much can thinking do? It has neither given the
mastery it promised nor brought the soul the equilibrium it craves. This is
conscious recognition of disaster as opposed to Enion's intuitive recogni-
tion. It is not Enlightenment Reason that has failed us but rather the power
of consciousness altogether. Urizen bears witness to the suffering of his chil-
dren; he even wants to help them, but he cannot. Consciousness cannot pro-
vide happiness in itself, without the assurance of transcendental agency, and

it will at some point perceive its own limitations. Then it will recognize that it has reached an impasse, and it will feel a restlessness for which there is no proper outlet. It will see itself, wrote Wallace Stevens, as a river "that flows nowhere, like a sea" ("The River of Rivers in Connecticut," 533). More spiraling self-division results.

Urizen wishes to "on high attain a void / Where self sustaining I may view all things beneath my feet" (FZ 72:23–24, E349) but when he discovers that such mastery is not possible, and he finds himself instead "down falling thro immensity ever & ever" (FZ 73:7, E350), he determines to reverse his fall through retrenchment. At this point his compassion and sorrow become meretricious. They revert to self-pleasing indulgence, and he resumes his familiar sadistic style as "the sorrower of Eternity in love with tears" (FZ 103:1, E375). Blake records that Urizen laments the fate of his children in "a selfish lamentation." Urizen's failure evidently suggests that the problem he exemplifies is refractory, but it also suggests something about why that is so: namely that it is hard for the mind to dissolve its own chains. In *The Four Zoas* Urizen is not merely arrogant and obtuse, as he is in *The Book of Urizen*. The crux lies deeper: he has knowledge, but knowledge in itself does not provide salvation (as it does in true Gnosticism) or even enlightenment. Perhaps solitary consciousness cannot correct itself, at least not at will.

Urizen's lamentation is exposed as selfish because he immediately sets to work building up the methods of empirical science, thus reaggrandizing the authority of reason, and "Gaining a New Dominion over all his sons & Daughters" (FZ 73:24, E350). The Mills and Circles of science prosper at the expense of the Eternal Great Humanity Divine: the soul loses more ground. Notions like that of the so-called harmony of the spheres work to intimidate our sense of agency: "every human soul terrified / At the turning wheels of heaven shrunk away inward withring away" (FZ 73:22–23, E350). If this is an act of compassion, who needs hate? Urizen's hypocritical sympathy once again produces the noxious religion that claims to offer consolation: "a white woof coverd his cold limbs from head to feet" (FZ 73:27, E350).

This is the turning point at which we begin our descent from "ruind spirits" to "spectres of the dead." With the advent of religion and science, the poem picks up the trajectory of Western civilization. The reader beholds Urizen growing ever more devious and malevolent, and accumulating greater and greater power, as he successively institutes priestcraft and class duplicity.

These ideological formations require the aid of the imagination, so Urizen contrives to suborn the scattered energies of prophetic mind, currently reduced to attenuated forms: the Shadow of Enitharmon (frail, self-doubting dreams) and the Spectre of Urthona (prophecy's worldly ambitions). Urizen instructs his daughters to capture these remnants of intellectual autonomy for service to his obfuscating religion, "the Tree of Mystery." They should go at their task with zeal, making their hearts "harder than the nether millstone," so that Los "may evaporate like smoke & be no more" (FZ 80:4, 6, E355). They should subdue people with the hypocrisy of religion and class society:

> Compell the poor to live upon a Crust of bread by soft mild arts
> Smile when they frown frown when they smile & when
>   a man looks pale
> With labour & abstinence say he looks healthy & happy
> And when his children sicken let them die there are enough
> Born even too many & our Earth will be overrun
> Without these arts . . . Flatter his wife pity his children till we can
> Reduce all to our will as spaniels are taught with art.
>
> (FZ 80:4–21, E355)

Urizen had felt sorry for his human "children" in "Night the Sixth," but now he conspires to make them suffer and sadistically enjoys the prospect. A new malignity has entered the scene: we can think of it as a principle of historical decline or as a development in the relation of human beings toward one another. Once the Shadow of Enitharmon and the Spectre of Urthona delude themselves into joining the ranks of Mystery, a new and more destructive Vala is born. The Spectre of Urthona first calls people "spectres of the Dead" (FZ 84:40, E360) but it is their emergence through Vala a few lines later that illustrates what he means. Vala is a revitalized succubus of materiality that "recreates" human beings in a more diminished form than ever. In the parodic "resurrection" that ensues, human beings arise as vicious zombies: "this wonder horrible a Cloud she grew & grew / Till many of the dead burst forth from the bottoms of their tombs" (FZ 85:17–18, E360). The ruined spirits have undergone a spiritual degeneration, figured as a mutilation, becoming "male forms without female counterparts or Emanations" (FZ 85:19, E360). Later they will be called "spectres," which are always male in Blake. The want of an Emanation suggests transcendental amnesia. They have completely forgotten their human vocation: no longer graced with bewilderment, they dwell in blind fixation on the material world, "in dreams of Ulro dark delusive" (FZ 85:21, E360). They have lost all memory or intuition of another reality and all capacity to sense that something is wrong. Therefore, they are "dead."

The advance of civilization contributes to this deadening. As "Night the Seventh" moves forward in human history, Urizen introduces economical and technological innovations that speed the society but consume the individual. In other words, Blake recognizes the phenomenon Marx will later call the alienation of labor, or, as Blake represents it, the conversion of a human being into a zombie. Urizen's energetic pursuit of progress leaves such casualties in its wake, particularly among child laborers, who "Of dire necessity still laboring day & night till all / Their life extinct they took the spectre form in dark despair" (FZ 95:27–28, E361). Here Blake focuses on the psychological effect of exploitation. Laboring "of dire necessity," the children are subjugated and stripped of agency. As ghosts of former human beings, they take "the spectre form." They look to others and to themselves like automata, but it is an excess of feeling—frustration and hopelessness—that makes them so. They are overwhelmed, first by the nature of their labor and then by the despair it creates.

The malignancy at work under the name of Urizen induces people to use their powers to their own detriment, to deploy the self against the soul. In a chilling passage, Blake portrays workers compelled to labor at their own mental evacuation. Urizen replaces the implements of pastoral life—the plow and harrow, the hammer and chisel—with weapons, machinery, and scientific instruments in order to stupefy his children.

> And in their stead intricate wheels invented Wheel without wheel
> To perplex youth in their outgoings & to bind to labours
> Of day & night the myriads of Eternity. that they might file
> And polish brass & iron hour after hour laborious workmanship
> Kept ignorant of the use that they might spend the days of wisdom
> In sorrowful drudgery to obtain a scanty pittance of bread
> In ignorance to view a small portion & think that All.
>
> (FZ 92:26–32, E364)

Mechanized labor subdues humanity to the robotic rhythms of clock time. It empties the mind as it is fixated on trivia. Worse still, workers are encouraged to find their work meaningless—they are, in a special sense, alienated from their labor—for the express purpose of demoralizing them so that "they might spend the days of wisdom / In sorrowful drudgery," dissipating the prime of creative life. In this way class society designs to waste the remains of transcendental power.

The Broken Heart Gate

One version of "Night the Seventh" ends with the consummation of this stupefying process. Human beings lose all contact with the Divine Vision and thus become perfectly "opaque." In the last stanza, the "myriads of the Dead burst thro the bottoms of their tombs," then pass through the Garden into the Ulro, "Beyond the Limit of Translucence on the Lake of Udan Adan" (FZ 95:13, E367). They have reached their nadir and now take the aggregate name of "Satan," or (as Blake calls him elsewhere) "the Limit of Opacity" (FZ 56:19, E338). In another version, Blake concludes more optimistically with the tumultuous reunion of Los, Enitharmon, and the Spectre of Urthona, who join together to repair some of the damage done to humanity. In this second version, their intervention provides the first step in the long process of transcending the effects of the fall. *The Four Zoas* launches the effort Blake pursues in all his epic prophecies: imagining how individuals and cultures can emerge out of their Urizenic stupor.

The Spectre of Urthona, the prophet's worldly will, is the first to perceive the deterioration of human beings, and he is conscience stricken: "I began the dreadful state of Separation & on my dark head the curse & punishment" (FZ 87:33–34, E369). He articulates the guilt of the prophet who has abandoned his proper task in favor of wordly ambition. (Milton will voice guilt of the same order.) The prophet's vital mission is to lift transcendental amnesia—to remind people of their own constitutive divinity. The empirical "eye" of the prophet has, logically, been first to recognize that the mission is unaccomplished: people have sunk to such a low as to be spiritually extinguished. "Urthonas Spectre terrified beheld the Spectres of the Dead / Each male formd without a counterpart without a concentering vision" (FZ 87:29–30, E369). As Jerusalem constitutes the Divine Vision of Albion (which he has lost), so here a "counterpart" is an emanation and an emanation is a "concentering vision," a perception that opens the Center. Lacking this vision, lacking consciousness of their transcendental provenance, people grow desperate: "they ravin / Without the food of life." Therefore, the Spectre exhorts Los, "Let us Create them Counterparts" (FZ 87:36–37, E369).

Los and the Spectre set to work, although what they are able to do has the character of palliative care rather than transformation. They create Golgo-nooza, the City of Art, which offers a site for the recovery of transcendental intuition: beneath its pillars and domes "Was opend new heavens & a new Earth beneath & within / Threefold within the brain within the heart within the loins / A Threefold Atmosphere Sublime" (FZ 87:8–10, E368). But in the next line, Blake cautions us that Golgonooza remains subject to the impedi-ments of material existence: "yet having a Limit Twofold named Satan & Adam." Adam is the "Limit of Contraction" or diminishment of humanity. The twofold limits of Satan and Adam set boundaries to the degree of re-demption achievable in Golgonooza. Art provides a circumscribed remedy. Even Los is not immune to the undermining insinuations of empirical reality. We see him in the very next lines standing "on the Limit of Translucence weeping & trembling / Filled with doubts in self accusation" (FZ 87:12–13, E369). Enitharmon lingers under the Tree of Mystery, gripped by her own form of self-doubt—the fear of Death Eternal, or the mortality of the soul. But Urthonas Spectre comforts them, and they enter, together, into the strug-gle of prophecy to sustain itself through the course of human history: "But This Union / Was not to be Effected without Cares & Sorrows & Trou-bles / Of six thousand Years of self denial and of bitter Contrition" (FZ 87:26–28, E369).

Specifically, Los and Enitharmon labor to make counterparts for the Spectrous Dead. This is evidently the chief task of art, but the language in which Blake describes the work remains enigmatic, as we shall see. Enithar-mon is intimidated by the task, but Los encourages her. Her "bosom translu-cent" provides "a soft repose" where the "piteous victims of battle . . . sleep in happy obscurity." Los wants to revive them, "to fabricate embodied sem-blances in which the dead / May live before us in our palaces & in our gar-dens of labour" (FZ 90:5–10, E370). Los draws a distinction between the nar-cotic or infantilizing effect of escapism and the fortifying effect of vision. So far prophetic power has been reduced to comforting the exhausted detritus of civilization, but Los now looks forward to a true resurrection of human-ity to be catalyzed by his fabrication of "embodied semblances." As Enitharmon elaborates on it, to fabricate "embodied semblances" means to fabricate "forms sublime" that the spectrous dead "may assimilate themselves into" (FZ 90:23, E370). The plan works, and we next see the spectres of the dead being transformed by assimilation into their young and beautiful selves.

> And first he drew a line upon the walls of shining heaven
> And Enitharmon tincturd it with beams of blushing love
> It remaind permanent a lovely form inspird divinely human
> Dividing into just proportions Los unwearied labourd
> The immortal lines upon the heavens till with sighs of love
> Sweet Enitharmon mild Entrancd breathd forth upon the wind
> The spectrous dead Weeping the Spectres viewd the
>   immortal works
> Of Los Assimilating to those forms Embodied & Lovely
> In youth & beauty in the arms of Enitharmon mild reposing.
>
> (FZ 90:35–44, E370–71)

Los draws a Platonic form of ideal humanity, and Enitharmon colors the form. After assimilating to forms such as these, "Embodied & Lovely," the spectrous dead assume their own ideal forms, and they take comfort in prophetic hope. What, then, is this process of assimilation? It is nothing so banal as modeling oneself after painterly beauties or literary characters. Instead Blake means to adduce the role art plays in reawakening transcendental intuition, insofar as it escapes a measure of confinement to empirical reality. He seems to share something of Percy Shelley's thought in his "Defence": "poetry defeats the curse which binds us to be subjected to the accident of surrounding impressions . . . It makes us the inhabitants of a world to which the familiar world is a chaos . . . [it] creates for us a being within our being" (533). Shelley's "being within our being" resembles Blake's "Center," the "World within" that "Open[s] its gates" (FZ 86:7–8, E368). This is the transcendental capacity of the soul that art inspires us to remember. But before anyone accuses either poet of naivete, let it be recalled that in both Blake and Shelley, the idealizing effect of art is short lived. For Blake, the power of art (and sex) is singular but also local, yielding only one of those moments in each day that Satan cannot find. The work of Los and Enitharmon brings "comfort" to Orc and "hope" to Tharmas at the end of "Night the Seventh," but the battle resumes in "Night the Eighth."

"Night the Eighth" witnesses a heightened contest over the fate of the spectres, waged between Urizen on the one hand and Los and Enitharmon on the other. Urizen introduces rabid warfare, violent repression and pietistic terrors, the Cruxifixion, and the renewal of Mystery in the form of Natural Religion. Los forges and Enitharmon weaves, trying jointly to nourish the spirituality of the spectres with art, passion, and pleasure. Enitharmon becomes a sympathetic emanation. The work she undertakes on behalf of humanity is limited but not ineffective. Once an obstacle, she is now a conduit to transcendental awakening, as is exemplified by her new relation to Jerusalem. Together she and Los and their children form "a Vast family wondrous," which (Blake now says) can also be called Jerusalem, a figure for human spirituality, "a Universal female form created / From those who were dead in Ulro from the Spectres of the Dead" (FZ 103:37–39, E376). It is Enitharmon who recognizes Jerusalem, names her, and perceives her significance.

> And Enitharmon namd the Female Jerusa[le]m the holy
> Wondring she saw the Lamb of God within Jerusalems Veil
> The divine Vision seen within the inmost deep recess
> Of fair Jerusalems bosom in a gently beaming fire.
>
> (FZ 104:1–4, E376)

Using the Plotinian metaphor of occulted internal presence, Blake has Enitharmon behold the divine Vision nesting "within the inmost deep recess" of Jerusalem's heart. Enitharmon fathoms the Divine Vision because she represents something close to it, linked to it, or sensitive to it. Once she was "obdurate" against the vision; now she can perceive it, but, as I will demonstrate further on in this chapter, she acquires this perception at the cost of sorrow. Blake figures her painful awakening in the image of her "broken heart gates."

When Los urges Enitharmon to descry the Divine Vision within her own "deep recess," he pictures gates at the entrance to the heart.

> Tremble not so my Enitharmon at the awful gates
> Of thy poor broken Heart I see thee like a shadow withering
> As on the outside of Existence but look! behold! take comfort!
> Turn inwardly thine Eyes & there behold the Lamb of God.
>
> (FZ, 87:40–43, E369)

To apprehend the vision, Enitharmon must first have her heart broken, or to use Blake's full metaphor, the gates of her heart must be broken open. Los has seen her at these gates, despairing as an abject creature "on the outside of Existence," deprived of life and power. If she looks *through* the opened gates, she will see the life and power within. Behind this image is the image of the Garden of Eden, its gates blocked by the Covering Cherub. One does not seek to escape without the gates, but to fling them wide apart and return to the paradise within. The image of "Opening a Center" is consistent with the image of the garden, and Los combines them when he exclaims, "Even I already feel a World within / Opening its gates" (FZ 86:7–8, E368). In Blake's landscape of the interior life, transcendental power awaits recovery in a *hortus conclusus*, an "inmost deep recess," whose gates have been shut by opacity or blindness.

But something remains to be explained about the figure of the "broken heart gate": by definition it involves *heartbreak,* sorrow, rather than the exhilaration we might expect. What is the source of this sorrow? Enitharmon's heart-gates were shattered in a scene we studied previously: the creation of Super-Vala, which propels the spectrous dead out of their graves. The hideous progeny of the Shadow of Enitharmon and the Spectre of Urthona, Vala is the putative might of nature, made all the more titanic when prophecy misguidedly joins forces with Urizenic religion. Enitharmon suffers a sympathetic labor as her shadow "in the deeps beneath" gives birth to the new monster, and the monster once born crashes open the gates of her heart.

> She burst the Gates of Enitharmons heart with direful Crash
> Nor could they ever be closd again the golden hinges were broken
> And the gates broke in sunder & their ornaments defacd.
>
> (FZ 85:5–18, E360)

This imagery is manifestly destructive, and the horror of the scene seems to be confirmed when in the next moment the zombies arise. Yet, if the figure of the open gates signifies access to vision, then the breaking of the gates signifies enlightenment. Enitharmon has had an awakening as a dialectical reaction to the apotheosis of nature; total passivation can provoke a response. How then is her awakening related to the false "resurrection" of the spectres? In a later reprise of this imagery Los insists on the positive meaning of the broken gates, even though they are again associated with the degradation of humanity: "Los said I behold the Divine Vision thro the broken Gates / Of thy poor broken heart astonishd melted into Compassion & Love" (FZ 99:15–16, E372). Los and Enitharmon are inspired with wonder; they perceive "the Divine Hand upon [them]" (FZ 100 (First Portion): 6, E372). But it is to "Ulros night" that the spectres descend.

> And Enter Urizens temple Enitharmon pitying & her heart
> Gates broken down. they descend thro the Gate of Pity
> The broken heart Gate of Enitharmon She sighs them forth
>   upon the wind
> Of Golgonooza Los stood recieving them
> For Los could enter into Enitharmons bosom & explore
> Its intricate Labyrinths now the Obdurate heart was broken.
>
> (FZ 99:21–26, E372)

Enitharmon's heart is no longer "Obdurate" to the extent that it is no longer Opaque. But she is not exalted; in fact, with her new understanding, she grieves for the oblivious spectres whom she now regards with "Compassion & Love" (FZ 99:16, E372). They descend through her Gates of Pity because she represents the awareness of their stupefaction that they, of course, cannot have. She has attained consciousness of how far prophecy and humanity have strayed from their vocation; her broken heart gates stand for the regret following upon this consciousness. But as yet she is pure regret. In Los's image of her lingering "at the awful gates of [her] poor broken heart . . . like a shadow withering," she reveals her sadness but also her continued vacillation. She stands on the threshold. She glimpses the Divine Vision within her, but she sees it *at a distance,* not feeling herself to be possessed of it or—even better—to be possessed by it. The sight is tantalizing enough to remind her of transcendental potential but not to let her grasp it. Like the speaker of the Intimations Ode, she becomes conscious of a gap in nature, with the displacement of the transcendental out of the grasp of the present self. She encounters her own power under the aspect of mourning, and feels that in her natural self she has failed *it,* reneged on the vocation of the soul. She experiences transcendental remorse. This affect is equivocal and divided because it arises from what is at once both a positive and a negative discovery. That is why Los sees Enitharmon standing at the gates of her heart—on the limen—looking both ways like Janus, outside to the natural self and inside to the Divine Vision. "Tear bright Enitharmon" weeps, but Blake portrays the development as auspicious because heartbreak comes from the acquisition of essential knowledge, like the dismay of the Gnostic novice: "The recollection of his own alienness, the recognition of his place of exile for what it is, is the first step back; the awakened homesickness is the beginning of the return" (Jonas, *Gnostic Religion*, 50). Nothing has changed in the world, but something has risen to consciousness that has the effect of divorcing consciousness from the world and imbuing it with respect for the transcendental.

In this first phase of sorrow, Los and Enitharmon can give only very limited aid to the spectres. Los creates "the times & spaces of Mortal Life"; he instills "the terrific Passions & Affections of the Spectrous dead" (FZ 113:7–8, E376). Enitharmon weaves them "Vegetated Bodies" to alleviate the pains of material existence, "Clothing their limbs / With gifts & gold of Eden" (FZ 113;12–13, E376). As a result the spectres enjoy a dim pastoral happiness, "Opened within their hearts & in their loins & in their brain" not to the Divine Vision but "To Beulah" (FZ 100:20–21, E373). Rather than awakening the spectres, Enitharmon seeks to induce oblivion, like a mother rocking a child: "Singing lulling Cadences to drive away / Despair from the poor wandering spectres" (FZ 100:4–5, E372). Their struggle is eased, but they remain in suspended animation until the Divine Vision does what is proper and "awakes the sleepers in Ulro" (FZ 113:36, E377). Enitharmon's temporary anodynes, by contrast, are bound to fail. Indeed, her own faith is still tenuous; later in "Night the Eighth," after the Crucifixion, we see her and Los—and even Jerusalem—"Despairing of Life Eternal" (FZ 105:16, E379). Finally, it is left to Enion to articulate the desperate hope remaining—what she calls "bitter hope"—that "the time approaches" when transcendental confidence will be recovered. Death will be "as a thing / Forgotten when one speaks of thee he will not be believd / When the man gently fades away in his immortality / When the mortal disappears in improved knowledge cast away" (FZ 109:30–32, E384–85). In Enion's state of mind, hope remains once removed from happiness; it is longing, not expectation, longing of the kind to which Enitharmon was awakened when her heart gates burst. Then she herself became like Enion, conscious of error and murmuring her resistance, or, to put it inversely: through Enitharmon the lament of Enion rises to a higher level of awareness. In Nights Eight and Nine of *The Four Zoas*, Blake starts to sketch out a theory of how his culture can emerge out of its benighted state. In the figure of Enitharmon's broken heart gates, he shows that for the individual psyche, the momentum of change begins in transcendental homesickness.

4

Milton:
The Guarded Gates

Thou percievest the Flowers put forth their precious Odours!
And none can tell how from so small a center comes such sweets
Forgetting that within that Center Eternity expands
Its ever during doors, that Og & Anak fiercely guard.

(M 30[33]:46–49, E131)

As Donald John has shown, Blake followed contemporary trends in identifying salvation with the remaking of the self. But the subtle psychology Blake evolved to explain why and how such a remaking should take place was his own. According to Blake, the error of isolated natural consciousness can be transcended: the task is to imagine self and world differently. Specifically this means dissolving the tyranny of the "I"—whose passions and interests exact an unending, futile vigilance—and identifying inner capacity with something larger than the empirical or phenomenal self. This solution is ultimately Neoplatonic, but with decisive amendments. First, Blake replaces the "All-Soul" with the "Imagination" as the power within us affiliated to the noumenal world. The immortality of this power can be experienced in this life, in the present moment, within what Blake calls, as opposed to the "Eternal Death," the "Eternal Now." In Plotinus's argument, one reaches spiritual reality by ceasing to seek it in the degraded external world, and returning instead to the immaterial reality harbored within: "Withdraw into yourself and look" (*Enneads* 54).

> When you are self-gathered in the purity of your being, nothing
> now remaining can shatter that inner unity, nothing from without
> clinging to the authentic man, when you find yourself wholly
> true to your essential nature, wholly that only veritable Light
> which is not measured by space, not narrowed to any circum-
> scribed form nor again diffused as a thing void of term, but ever
> unmeasurable as something greater than all measure and more
> than all quantity—when you perceive that you have grown to
> this, you are now become very vision. (55)

Intense introspection finally isolates "the authentic man" but that man
is infinite Spirit or Light. Blake also identifies Imagination as the hidden re-
source of the interior. In his spatial metaphor, or map of the interior life, the
Selfhood is a superficies concealing a reality that lies deeper in the psyche. We
have seen this metaphor already in Milton's characterization of the Selfhood
as "a false Body, an Incrustation over my Immortal/Spirit" (M 40: 35–36,
E142), and in Blake's image of Albion "Turning his Eyes outward to Self"
(FZ 23: 2, E313). *The Four Zoas* uses this metaphor in an especially arresting
formulation when Enion complains: "Already are my Eyes reverted all that I
behold / Within my Soul has lost its splendor." The "I" is the outward part of
the inner life; to go further inward is to discover not a personal identity but an
impersonal Divine Vision. You expand by going inward and contract by going
outward. Blake calls this reversal from contraction to expansion opening a
Center, and he uses the Plotinian figure of internal dilation in describing his
notion of how to rehabilitate the psyche.

> Trembling I sit day and night, my friends are astonish'd at me.
> Yet they forgive my wanderings, I rest not from my great task!
> To open the Eternal Worlds, to open the immortal Eyes
> Of Man inwards into the Worlds of Thought: into Eternity
> Ever expanding in the Bosom of God, the Human Imagination
> O Saviour pour upon me thy Spirit of meekness & love:
> Annihilate the Selfhood in me, be thou all my life.
>
> (J 5:16–22, E147)

"Withdraw into yourself and look"; turn your eyes "inwards" to behold
Eternity. Behind the minuscule atomic self the vastnesses of the noumenal

world lie concealed. This "Human Imagination," being divine, resides in "the Bosom of God." One may implore the grace of the Savior to liquidate the atomic self so that one may reach this "Eternity" within. Indeed, free of the Selfhood, one becomes the Savior. (Crabb Robinson asked Blake if he thought Jesus was God, and Blake replied yes, *"He is the only God . . . And so am I and so are you"* [Bentley 310].) Here Blake is practicing a favorite technique of amalgamating terms; he seems, surprisingly, to amalgamate Plotinus with Christianity, naming the Plotinian Light "the Bosom of God" and calling on the "Saviour" to help him open the Center. Yet, although Blake may admire some Neoplatonic ideas—and even some Christian ones—we always find him practicing his alert revisionism. In this passage he actually departs from both Christianity and Plotinus and does so in the same way, by collapsing the hierarchy of spiritual orders and conflating the human with the divine. The "Human Imagination," the "Saviour," and "the Bosom of God" are all one. No spiritual power resides outside humanity. With his characteristic insouciance, Blake has taken what he likes from Plotinus, and from Christianity, and left the rest: he adopts the idea of spiritual expansion at the center, but discards the idea of referring it to any superhuman order (God, the All-Soul, the Intellect, the One).

This is a significant revision of tradition, but Blake makes his most original contribution in his epic prophecies, where he gives a psychological analysis of what stands in the way of the soul's rehabilitation. Knowledge is not a cure in itself; the internal obstacles are too tenacious to be dispelled by epiphany. The key is to dissolve the grip of individuation and to regard one's true self, instead, as immortal and impersonal Imagination. But the task is by no means easy because so much in experience and education nourishes the anxieties and cravings of the "I," as well as its more basic illusion of being substantial. Blake admits that is hard for us to uncover the inmost soul. We are in a deep "sleep" of worldliness; we instinctively prefer this soporific superficiality to the dread of "awakening." Obstacles arise not only from social (including philosophical and religious) conditioning but also from the leanings of the natural or empirical self. How is any one person to dispel the force of these pressures—the innate inclination to identify one's being with the little "I," and then the support this inclination derives from religious and philosophical ideologies, from the harrying trials of natural experience, and from the very tendencies of the inner life—especially the tendency to precipitate out a defensive identity, a "Spectre," with all the anxious energy it needs to enforce its claims? To dispel the Selfhood one must reintegrate the psyche and reintroduce the soul to its own cognizance: this is no easy task, where the psyche resists of its own nature. How can anyone succeed in "putting off Self" and becoming a noumenal subject?

Fetters of the Soul

Blake wrote *Milton* to work out how such an inner transformation might occur. He seems to have composed *The Four Zoas* (in some form) before he began *Milton*, and *Milton* issues from a decision to scale back from the epic scope of *The Four Zoas*. *Milton* has all the sureness and economy of an epitome written after a long and ragged exploration. In *The Four Zoas* Blake deals with a number of different problems raised by his ideas, but in *Milton* he productively narrows his scope. As distinct from *The Four Zoas* and *Jerusalem,* which are dense with allegorical figures representing diverse aspects of the psyche, *Milton* describes the reformation of one particular mind—an actual person and a historical figure. Whereas in earlier and later prophetic books Blake diagnoses the ills of "six thousand years" of Western history, in *Milton* he focuses on the stop gaps, shrinkings, and failures of an individual mind. He sets himself the task of imagining, in detail, how an individual can successfully put off Self. Blake chooses Milton as his model, most capable and most in need of such a reformation.[1] But it is clear that Blake means to instruct and inspire himself.

The critical turning point in *Milton* is a recognition scene: it occurs when Milton, having already spent one hundred years in Eternity, suddenly apprehends that he is still unredeemed, still dwelling in error. He is awakened to self-knowledge by a cautionary tale that he hears in Eternity. A character called the Bard, who is in fact an aspect of his own critical intelligence, sings an allegorical epic in which prophetic power feebly betrays itself to worldly interests. The ego, or Selfhood, pursuing those interests is now called "Satan." In his epiphany, Milton sees that he yielded to pride, vanity, and power hunger, and consequently he emulated tyranny when he promulgated his unsavory portrait of God and, in patriarchal fashion, abused his wives and daughters. He became a despot in his home, a little Urizen. Now Milton recognizes that he confused his true prophetic authority with the will-to-power of the wordly self, or "I." That "I," whose cravings he sought to satisfy, is the

"Satan" of the Bard's song, selfish, imperious, and violent. Milton gave way to the Satan in himself: "I in my Selfhood am that Satan: I am that Evil One! / He is my Spectre!" (M 14[15]:30–31, E108). This is the decisive mental act: Milton estranges his "I." He sees it no longer as himself but as merely a facet of himself, prolific in illusion and error, which he is free to suppress or reject. When it is put down, what will appear in its place is "His real and immortal Self," which has been dormant, awaiting his recovery "as One sleeping on a couch / Of gold" (M 40[46]:35–36, E142).

But rehabilitation is arduous. It is already suggestive of difficulty that Milton's recovery has been so long delayed. He had to die first, and dwell in his tedious heaven for a century before illusion began to falter. And his break with illusion only makes a start: there is much for him to struggle through before he is reunited with his emanation, Ololon. Milton has to go backward and disentangle himself from error. First he has to get an education: he meets his estranged wives and daughters, but sees now "that they might be resum'd / By giving up of Selfhood" (M 17[19]:2–3, E110); he beholds the truth about Rahab and Tirzah, and Orc and the Shadowy Female, who represent noxious ideas about the Creation he helped to propagate. Milton bears witness, as from out of the tortures of desperate humanity and sadistic nature emerges Urizen, the God of *Paradise Lost*.

At this point the mode of the narrative changes. Milton ceases to be a student and a spectator. He takes on the correction of his errors, striving with Urizen, who is his worst legacy. But Urizen also represents a tenacious internal obstacle, the "inner Urizen," or Milton's attraction to absolute masculine authority. This is Milton's patriarchal overidentification, which accounts for the streak of authoritarianism in his personality and hence his misogyny, pride, and self-righteousness. He struggles with Urizen in silence because the struggle is an internal one.

> Silent they met, and silent strove among the streams of Arnon
> Even to Mahanaim, when with cold hand Urizen stoop'd down
> And took up water from the river Jordan: pouring on
> To Miltons brain the icy fluid from his broad cold palm.
> But Milton took of the red clay of Succoth, moulding it with care
> Between his palms: and filling up the furrows of many years
> Beginning at the feet of Urizen, and on the bones

Creating new flesh on the Demon cold, and building him,
As with new clay a Human form in the Valley of Beth Peor.

(M 19[21]:7–14, E112)

This is a powerful scene; in answer to Urizen's aggression, Milton rather
tenderly seeks to recast and warm "the Demon cold." He turns the tables,
acting as God to Urizen's Adam; now the human is reforming the divine. This
means in part its *idea* of the divine. But Urizen also represents something
within Milton's particular psyche, and at this moment it is something subtler
than the Selfhood that requires "annihilation." It is a part of Milton that can-
not be extirpated but has to be remade or redeemed. The illustration shows
Milton as a heroic nude commanding the inert blue Urizen, although the ges-
ture is ambiguous: is he caressing Urizen, or trying to strangle him? (Blake,
Milton: A Poem Pl. 15). The equivocations here reflect Blake's own ambiva-
lence toward Urizen, whom Ahania had imaged as a figure of sexual and cre-
ative generosity in his pre-fallen state. Apparently at this point Blake is not
thinking of Urizen as Satan or the Selfhood but as internal powers and capac-
ities for whose benign manifestation one might long. Thus Blake envisions
Urizen's rehumanization with a subtle wishfulness. This is Wordsworthian
pathos, a combination of longing with self-conscious dream. Its presence
here gives the scene a Utopian air, suggesting that Blake recognizes how ex-
traordinary such a remaking would be.

In *The Four Zoas* Urizen finds that, even though he feels remorse for the
plight of human beings, "he could not take their fetters off for they grew
from the soul" (FZ 71:11, E348). *Milton* considers the fetters that grow from
the soul and how hard they are to cast off. That they "grow" from the soul
means that they emerge from it spontaneously; the soul is the source of its
own constriction and obstruction. While Milton confronts "the darkend Ur-
izen," Blake turns to Albion, and simultaneously to the reader, exhorting us
to recognize the self-obstruction "in every human heart." This obstruction
causes the kind of blindness—or "Opacity to the Divine Vision"—that made
someone like Milton believe in Nobodaddy instead of in his own "Eternal
Great Humanity Divine." A fly can do better.

Seest thou the little winged fly, smaller than a grain of sand?
It has a heart like thee; a brain open to heaven & hell,
Withinside wondrous & expansive; its gates are not clos'd

> I hope thine are not: hence it clothes itself in rich array;
> Hence thou art cloth'd with human beauty O thou mortal man.
>
> (M 20[22]:27–31, E114)

This passage gives the reader a sharp rhetorical shock: it is the only time in *Milton* that the narrator turns to the reader and speaks to her directly. In fact, it is one of the only times in his epic prophecies that Blake (or the Blake narrator) ever uses a second-person address. Here he pivots and makes a pointed, even somewhat accusatory, remark—I hope *your* gates are not closed—designed to render us suddenly self-conscious. Blake reminds us that he intends his comments to have a universal application: we are to recognize that this is our story, too. Thus the passage continues in the second-person imperative: do not look for power in an external God—"Seek not thy heavenly father then beyond the skies," for such a projection of God can become a spiritual blocking-agent: "There Chaos dwells & ancient Night & Og & Anak old." (Og and Anak are biblical giants, enemies of the Israelites.) The passage segues from this fairly familiar argument into material that is new in Blake: a universal psychology of the blocking agents *within* the self, the Og and Anak who may be keeping our own gates closed.

> For every human heart has gates of brass & bars of adamant,
> Which few dare unbar because dread Og & Anak guard the gates
> Terrific! and each mortal brain is walld and moated round
> Within: and Og & Anak watch here; here is the Seat
> Of Satan in its Webs.   (M 20[22]:33–38, E114)

We have already seen the necessity of "broken heart gates" in *The Four Zoas*. The heart's gates remain closed here because they are guarded by Og and Anak, figures for self-created fears and self-imposed limitations. Og and Anak are not beyond the skies but within: with typical inversion, Blake reminds us that the imposing forces we perceive outside are actually internal— not only internal insofar as they are fantasies ("all in the mind") but also insofar as such forces do occupy the inner life. All deities reside in the human breast, and so do the devils.

According to Hans Jonas, the Gnostics were the first to claim that the deepest threat to the soul comes not from the distractions of matter but from the development of a false self. "That this *body* is a fatality to the soul had

long ago been preached by the Orphics, whose teachings were revived in the
era of Gnosticism. But now the *psychical* envelopments too are considered
impairments and fetters of the transmundane spirit" (*The Gnostic Religion*
158). These "envelopments," or "appendages," conglomerate into a separate
entity, as is suggested by the title of Isidorus's lost treatise *On the Accreted Soul.*

> Now, what are these foreign accretions? In their sum they are the
> empirical character of man, comprising all the faculties and
> propensities by which man relates himself to the world of nature
> and society; that is, they constitute what would normally be
> called his "psyche." And what is the original entity overlaid by
> these accretions? It is the transcendent acosmic principle in man,
> normally hidden and undiscovered in his earthly preoccupations,
> or only negatively betraying itself in a feeling of alienness, of not
> completely belonging.   (Jonas, *The Gnostic Religion* 158)

The Orphics, the Pythagoreans, and the Platonists all spoke of the soul as
the "psyche," but the Gnostics revisionistically contrast "psyche," or empiri-
cal self, with "pneuma," or "divine spark." The person who has come to con-
fuse his psyche with his pneuma, his false with his real self, has degenerated
into a "son of the house," a creature of phenomenality. Iamblichus stipulated
that there are in fact two souls: a soul "from the First Mind," and a debased
"planetary soul," imposed on us by the astronomical "spheres" of the mate-
rial world. (Planets and stars are our enemies.) In Gnostic times, these beliefs
give rise to what Jonas calls "an entirely new idea of human freedom," an
idea that Jonas terms "unGreek" and that Blake clearly shares: "However
profoundly man is determined by nature, of which he is part and parcel—
and plumbing his own inwardness he discovers in layer after layer this
dependence—there still remains an innermost center which is not of na-
ture's realm and by which he is above all its promptings and necessities"
(*Gnostic Religion* 160).

In Blake the opposed terms are "Selfhood" and "Imagination," or any of
its cognates. Blake's figure of "incrustation" ("an Incrustation over my Im-
mortal / Spirit") reminds us of the Gnostic theory, and he seems to take over
the notion that introspection reveals the presence in us of an inauthentic em-
pirical Selfhood, which has become more and more entrenched over time. It

is not that we are born without it, and should, therefore, seek to restore that condition of "Innocence." Selfhood can never be simply elided; it has to be confronted and transcended. Thus Blake has no desire that we should return to an infantile psychological state. But in his view experience does tend to enhance the claims of the Selfhood insofar as it increases anxiety and the need for self-defense. From *The Book of Urizen* onward, we have seen Blake working out an analysis of how the Selfhood grows on one, how it conspires with the pressures of experience to bulk itself up at the expense of spiritual wellbeing. The "Real Man, the Imagination" cannot by definition participate in wordly concerns; it is exclusive of the empirical man and vice versa. Freedom consists of dissolving the empirical man.

But Blake goes beyond Gnosticism in describing how the "accreted" soul or empirical man arises not from the impositions of the outside but from the dynamics of the inside: the experience of interiority positively *encourages* the development of the false self. As we have seen, the "I," or grasping Selfhood, is a significant blocking agent, usurping identity and obscuring the sight of the Eternal World within. It is a defensive and reductive definition of self, fostering an anxiety on its own account that can never be allayed. And the more anxiety the "I" generates, the more one seeks to stabilize and consolidate identity with the result that the definition of self becomes ever more reductive. Finally, the inklings of Imagination, Spirit, Light, and Infinity become fearful in themselves, so that the self has perversely succeeded in defeating the interests of the soul. Each heart constructs for itself the means of its own frustration.

Where Plotinus blames the soul's distraction on its embodiment, and proposes introspection as the cure, and where the Gnostics say simply that the "accretions" of experience overlay the soul, Blake gives a deeper analysis in which the psyche works against itself. It is the very nature of interiority to precipitate out a false self, an "I" that goes on to deform the inner life. The subject–object distinction is an intuition that has to be countered, but in Western culture it is instead reinforced. The subject apprehending itself as a unique node of consciousness builds and builds on this apprehension, hardening its position and accreting around itself layers of protection and defense. Og and Anak represent such inner bulwarks, the force of the "I's" selfpreservative instinct. Thus "every human heart" maintains in itself the principle of resistance to the Divine Vision. It has posted guards at its own gates to freedom. That is why it requires heroic labor—such as that which Milton undertakes when he wrestles with Urizen—to undo the error and the damage. The self has to subvert something in itself. Twentieth- and twenty-first-century psychology have made this form of struggle familiar to us and also revealed how difficult it is. Blake emphasizes the difficulty when he shows that the "I" is a special kind of obstacle, deriving its tenacity from the very nature of the inner life.

I believe Blake had not thought through the phenomenon of self-obstruction until he came to write *The Four Zoas* and *Milton*. The *Urizen* books present an analysis of the division and malformation of the self. Urizen figures the characteristics of the "I" insofar as he is willfully blind and self-torturing. Certainly he embodies a force of resistance to enlightenment. But Urizen is not yet represented as an obstacle with a power of psychological necessity. When Blake in *Milton* sets out to imagine the transcendence of the "I," he is brought by reflection to recognize the strength of the internal impediments. Or perhaps it was the other way around, and Blake wrote *Milton* because he had come to perceive the strength of internal impediments, and he wanted now not only to enlarge his theory to accommodate the new ideas but also to provide the hypothesis of a cure for a disease that seemed harder to deracinate than before.

Perhaps recent experience—and the self-examination it precipitated—caused Blake to ponder the intransigence of Selfhood. He begins *Milton* with a long meditation on how the prophet comes to betray his vocation. The topic is relevant to Blake's critique of Milton, whom he regarded as a failed prophet, but the meditation also seems to offer some cryptic self-reproach. Blake was just recovering from an attempt to compromise with circumstances by indenturing himself to the dreadful poetaster Hayley of Felpham. He started *Milton* in Felpham and completed it after he returned to London. It may be that what Blake regarded as his own faltering made him reflect on the power of the obstacles, especially those that reside in one's own "heart." Milton reenters the world through Blake's left foot, from which "a black cloud redounding spread over Europe" (M 15:50, E110). This is the scourge of war and religious militancy, or self-righteousness, and in this strange figure Blake, rather than representing himself as "inspired" by Milton, suggests that he has been complicit in Milton's failings. From now on he will reconsider the delinquency of Imagination. He will devote major parts of *The Four Zoas* and

Jerusalem to analyzing how and why the prophet figure Los undermines himself—compromising, doubting, losing his nerve, and dallying with worldly temptations—succumbing, in other words, to an internal encumbrance.

The Inner Landscape

As Blake zeroes in on the divisions of the interior, he begins to make psychotopographies. Near the end of *Milton,* Blake the narrator descends into the chaos of Satan's interiority, as Thel had passed through "the eternal gates" and entered the land of death. In "Satan's bosom" the traveler finds an infernal region that Blake evokes in a rich bricolage of Miltonic and biblical language.

> I also stood in Satans bosom & beheld its desolations!
> A ruind Man: a ruind building of God not made with hands;
> Its plains of burning sand, its mountains of marble terrible:
> Its pits & declivities flowing with molten ore & fountains
> Of pitch & nitre: its ruind palaces & cities & mighty works;
> Its furnaces of affliction in which his Angels & Emanations
> Labour with blackend visages among its stupendous ruins
> Arches & pyramids & porches colonades & domes.
>
> (M 38[43]:15–22, E139)

The scene of desolation widens out as the passage progresses in a manner that reflects Blake's anxiety and dismay: the ruin is first a building, then a landscape with forbidding mountains and plains, then a vast foundry of molten rock, then whole cities of ruined palaces with "Arches & pyramids & porches colonades & domes." The sublime dereliction testifies to extinguished greatness. Satan's inner world is like Nineveh, a crumbling capital, a blasted civilization. That is what the degradation of human potential amounts to: a tragedy of this or even greater magnitude. Poignantly, what was good in this world lingers on, in reduced form, in subordination and neglect: "Angels & Emanations" toil on in the wreckage as slaves. The spark of divinity has been mishandled and forced to labor against itself.

In this scene Blake gives us a fairly straightforward unitary "picture" of the inner life, a rendering of it as a landscape or cityscape. In other more intricate passages, he creates a differentiated topography in which specific parts of the self are situated in relation to one another. When Ololon recognizes "Milton's Shadow" (i.e., his Spectre or Selfhood), she perceives it as possessing its own complex inner organization.

> I saw he was the Covering Cherub & within him Satan
> And Raha[b], in an outside which is fallacious! within
> Beyond the outline of Identity, in the Selfhood deadly.

> (M 37[41]:8–10, E137)

Blake characteristically scrambles inside and outside in a manner that seems confusing at first. The "outside" that is fallacious is actually inside; it is not outside but "an outside," that is, a false appearance worn by certain illusions: Rahab (seductive and cruel nature) along with Satan (the greed of the "I"). The two of them are encompassed in the Covering Cherub guarding the gates to the Divine Vision with bristling, fiery arms. The Covering Cherub is another name for Og and Anak old—that within us that blocks access to the Paradise or Divine Vision, which is also within.

Blake creates this complex inner landscape to embody a new idea. Although elaborated out of Urizen, Satan represents an even greater force for deception (and self-deception) because he is an unconscious hypocrite, concealing his hostility and greed from himself so as to be able to act on them. He is self-concern that does not recognize itself and, therefore, cannot disavow itself. "What could Los do? how could he judge, when Satans self, believ'd / That he had not oppress'd the horses of the Harrow" (M 7:39–40, E101). Satan's own "fallacious outside" imposes on him, as the "I" imposes on the subject. "The Selfhood," it turns out, has its own layers: one ventures in and encounters first the "outline of Identity," the atomic person, then "beyond" it, the Covering Cherub, and within the Covering Cherub, Satan and Rahab. Blake often runs most of these terms together as synonymous, but here he has visualized them in an arrangement like that of Chinese boxes, nestling one inside another. Presumably he wants to show the genetic connection between these malformations. The fallacy of the Selfhood includes the other fallacies (sadistic nature, needy "I"), meaning that they are all mutually predicated, as Blake had already demonstrated in *The Book of Urizen*. Now he invents a psychotopography that illustrates this notion schematically. It also has the merit of suggesting how fallacies of this kind survive—because the Selfhood is disassociated and one part of it does not know another.

In *Milton* Blake is also thinking evolutionarily; he pauses to chart the growth of the Selfhood. In the Bard's song, he pictures the process by which the Covering Cherub calcifies in the heart of Satan. It occurs at the moment when Satan assumes the identity of the Genesis God and creates the Seven Deadly Sins, along with "Moral laws and cruel punishments," which prompts the evolution of prudential morality. "Saying I am God alone / There is no other! let all obey my principles of moral individuality" (M 9:25–26, E103). In other words, Satan is reprising the actions of Urizen, but whereas in *The Book of Urizen* Blake represents the ensuing course of collapse in physical and external terms—Urizen becomes a "clod of clay"—in *Milton* Blake images Satan's degeneration as interior.

> His bosom grew
> Opake against the Divine Vision: the paved terraces of
> His bosom inwards shone with fires, but the stones becoming opake!
> Hid him from sight, in an extreme blackness and darkness,
> And there a World of deeper Ulro was open'd, in the midst
> Of the Assembly. In Satans bosom a vast unfathomable Abyss.
> Astonishment held the Assembly in an awful silence: and tears
> Fell down as dews of night, & a loud solemn universal groan
> Was utter'd from the east & from the west & from the south
> And from the north; and Satan stood opake immeasurable
> Covering the east with solid blackness, round his hidden heart.
>
> (M 9:30–40, E103)

The imagery is apocalyptic and evocative. It seems quite confusing at first—I have quoted it at length to show this—but what looks like incoherence is actually meaningful. The fire goes out in Satan's heart, chilling the stones and leaving them their natural color, black. This change "hid[es] him from sight"—that is, it hides his soul from his Selfhood, and his Selfhood isolates him, hiding him from others. The reduction of self to Selfhood extinguishes Divine Vision, leaving only an empirical self in a material world whose authority is now greater than ever; it has become "a World of deeper Ulro." Without Divine Vision, Satan is plunged, like Urizen, into an internal as well as external void. He has become the type of the Selfhood that covers the east in everyone. He obstructs his view of the light in himself, cloaking it "with solid blackness," which encircles and conceals "his hidden heart." Occlusion of the Divine Vision hides the heart in the sense that it isolates emotional life from the rest of the self. We witnessed this in *The Four Zoas* in the confusion and belligerence of Luvah (love). Emotion is disassociated from its relation to transcendence, and reduced to mere phenomenon, competing for power with other empirical parts of the self, such as "reason" and "appetite."

The Work of Golgonooza

Despite these compelling images, we should not look for a consistent psychoto-pography in *Milton*. Although Blake repeats the general pattern of imagery—blockage versus light, Selfhood versus Center—his changes in perspective lead to kaleidoscopic reorientation. He treats Satan sometimes simply as one element of interiority, and sometimes as a figure with his own inner life. In some passages the force of blockage appears within Satan, but in others the view is reversed, and one sees Satan within the Covering Cherub. In the central appearance of Og and Anak, quoted previously, the giants act as modes of defense for Satan, or the calculating, grasping Selfhood; he stands within them ("And each mortal brain is walld and moated round / Within: and Og & Anak watch here; here is the Seat / Of Satan in its Webs [M 20[22]:27–28, E114]). Blake condenses Satan into a single actor here because he wants to make room for something else in the self.

At this point we move from the analytical to the therapeutic intention of Blake's psychotopographies. Blake goes on to posit the existence of a third power in the self beyond the opposition of Satan and Divine Vision.

> for in brain and heart and loins
> Gates open behind Satans Seat to the City of Golgonooza
> Which is the spiritual fourfold London, in the loins of Albion.
>
> (M 20[22]:38–40, E114)

It turns out that there is another set of gates, apparently obstructed by Satan himself insofar as they lie "behind" his throne. They are the gates of Golgonooza, Los's city, the City of Art.

Golgonooza serves a crucial function in Blake's psychology. Although it is not in itself the Plotinian light or Center, it serves to reawaken the soul, and remind it of its transcendental vocation. Golgonooza belongs to the fallen world as an aid for the empiricist subject who requires such encouragement.

In *Jerusalem* Los builds Golgonooza "Outside of the Gates of the Human Heart, beneath Beulah / In the midst of the rocks of the Altars of Albion" (J 53:16–17, E203). The City of Art does not reside in Beulah, the regressive fantasy land, but rather in the world of experience, where it is real and necessary, among the hardships and misconceptions of Natural Man. Therefore, the gates of Golgonooza lie *behind* Satan's Seat: one has to pass through the Selfhood to reach them, which is to say, it is having a Selfhood that makes one need a Golgonooza. As Blake puts it later in *Milton*, one cannot "behold Golgonooza without passing the Polypus / A wondrous journey not passable by Immortal feet" (M 35[39]:19–20, E135). (Similarly, in Shelley's *Prometheus Unbound*, Earth tells Prometheus he cannot hear her voice because he is immortal.) The Polypus is the gross nexus of the material world; only a mortal being knows the experience of being subject to it—of fearing harm from it and "Eternal Death." You have to have suffered—or at least truly apprehended—the despair of materialism before you can perceive the beauteous inspiration of Golgonooza.

> For Golgonooza cannot be seen till having passd the Polypus
> It is viewed on all sides round by a Four-fold Vision
> Or till you become Mortal & Vegetable in Sexuality
> Then you behold its mighty Spires & Domes of ivory & gold.
>
> (M 35[39]:21–24, E135)

But Golgonooza does not yield a permanent cure. It palliates current suffering and gestures toward redemption, but it does not itself recreate the soul. Blake is often particularly moving when he describes the work of Golgonooza, because its effect is lovely but limited. It arouses longings it cannot satisfy.

The long middle of *Milton*—between the title character's first and final epiphanies—is devoted to weighing the value of temporal remedies for the despair of Natural Man. Climaxing the description of Milton's encounter with Urizen, the passage on Og and Anak closes with a reminder that although the self harbors blocking agents, it can also share in the regenerative agency of Golgonooza. With this reference as a prelude, the focus of attention now shifts to the power of prophecy. Milton enters a latent phase. He is said to fall "thro Albions heart, travelling outside of Humanity" (M 20[22]:41, E114), but he is still psychologically wrestling with Urizen, as we discover when the perspective shifts back to him at the end of Book II. (Ololon makes her own descent and finds him "striv[ing] upon the Brooks of Arnon" [M 39[44]:53, E141].) For now Los takes center stage, along with his Sons and Blake himself, as the recipient of prophetic inspiration. Los, and Blake through Los, are both possessed by the fire of their vocation. But Los has a struggle with his sons Rintrah and Palamabron, who are angry and restless. This interlude figures the continued incoherence of the prophetic impulse, and the vain fits and starts of its historical expression. Blake seems to endorse Los's assurance that "Six Thousand years are passd away the end approaches fast" (M 23[25]:55, E119), but his sons dislike being exhorted to patience.

On this unresolved note, Blake shifts perspective again to show what the "World of Los" can do for us in the long interim of imperfection. Blake is at his most compassionate and lyrical for much of this section, which occupies the poem to the end of Book I. The poor souls of human beings descend to the body "wailing," but Los and his sons take pity on them, and succor them with Promethean gifts. They provide technologies of sustenance: food, clothing, houses, fields (see M 26[28]:23–30, E123). One might say that they bestow "the arts of civilization," but these images of home comforts are partly metaphorical. Blake gives a deeper analysis of the comfort they represent: their gifts enable us to live at greater ease not only in our lives but also, specifically, in our inner lives. As it is, we "sleepers" are lost in emotion, experiencing our own interiority as a storm of "Passions & Desires." But the Sons of Los channel the chaotic power of emotion into literature and philosophy where it can become a source of enchantment, a "beautiful House for the piteous sufferer."

> Some Sons of Los surround the Passions with porches of iron & silver
> Creating form & beauty around the dark regions of sorrow,
> Giving to airy nothing a name and a habitation
> Delightful! (M 28[30]:1–4, E125)

Alluding to Theseus's definition of poetry, Blake concurs that its "form & beauty" encompass the "dark regions of sorrow." Poetry converts incoherent emotion and mental abyss into "most holy forms of Thought" (M 28[30]:1–4, E125). To Theseus's notion Blake adds that it thereby reshapes the experience of the inner life. It soothes the embattled "I," "the piteous sufferer," with its doubts and fears, its dread of Eternal Death, and its attraction-repulsion to other selves. One plate earlier, Blake had portrayed the emotional torture of the fallen subject, especially in the form of "love." "But in the Wine-presses the Human grapes sing not," they "howl & writhe" "In pits & dens & shades of death" reminiscent of Milton's Hell.[2] These human beings take "shapes of torment & woe" while Luvah's Sons and Daughters stab and whip them. "These are the sports of love, & these the sweet delights of amorous play" that Luvah, the distorted Eros of the fallen world, has to offer (M 27[29]:30–41, E124–25). When Blake turns to erotic reconciliation in "the World of Los," the contrast is sharp and poignant. While the sons of Los make

> Cabinets richly fabricate of gold & ivory;
> For Doubts & fears unform'd & wretched & melancholy
> The little weeping Spectre stands on the threshold of Death
> Eternal; and sometimes two Spectres like lamps quivering
> And often malignant they combat (heart-breaking
>   sorrowful & piteous)
> Antamon takes them into his beautiful flexible hands,
> As the Sower takes the seed, or as the Artist his clay
> Or fine wax, to mould artful a model for golden ornaments.
> The soft hands of Antamon draw the indelible line:
> Form immortal with golden pen; such as the Spectre admiring
> Puts on the sweet form; then smiles Antamon bright
>   thro his windows.   (M 28[30]:8–18, E125–26)

Antamon is a son of Los and Enitharmon. Associated with sexual satisfaction, Antamon first appears in *Europe* where Enitharmon beholds him as a cloud form, "Floting upon the bosomd air: / With lineaments of gratified desire" (Eur 14:18–19, E66). Here he labors on behalf of humanity. What is he doing? S. Foster Damon thinks he is making "physical forms for the yet unbodied Spectres" (25) so that they can mingle in erotic love. This reading is plausible, although I propose that Antamon's act of creation remains more complex. His innovation corresponds to a moment in *The Four Zoas* in which Los "fabricate[s] forms sublime / Such as the piteous spectres may assimilate themselves into" (FZ 90:23–24, E370). Los fabricates the forms by drawing a design in the "shining heaven"—a "permanent . . . lovely form inspird divinely human"—and when the Spectres behold it, they "assimilate" into the shape, reposing "Embodied & Lovely / In youth & beauty in the arms of Enitharmon" (FZ 90:42–43, E371). Such glowing refers not so much to the actual as to the ideal, or visionary, body in which even the aged are restored to "youth & beauty." Beyond this it is apparently an ideal human form, an ideal manifestation of humanity itself, not just the human body. When the spectre "assimilates into this form," it identifies the form as its own. It recasts itself in light of the ideal, attaining its level and rising to proper self-esteem. Although it does not include confidence of transcendence, this new self-definition has a profound therapeutic effect. The spectre's loneliness and anxiety, its fear of death and of otherness, abate. By elevating its phenomenal self-description, the empiricist subject can achieve some measure of erotic happiness and some peace.

Yet the touching nature of this scene reminds us that it describes the making of a temporary reprieve. This is not the revelation or the coming of Blake's Eternity that will bring energy, determination, and preparedness for "Mental Fight." Throughout this section of *Milton*, Blake continually juxtaposes the ameliorations of Los with the depredations of Urizen and Luvah, and at the end, he sums up by emphasizing that he has so far delineated only the record of history in which the revelation has not come, and Los has worked simply to keep hope alive: "Such is the World of Los the labour of six thousand years" (M 29[31]:64, E128). Although lyrical in its evocation of the comforts afforded to the wretched Spectre, Blake's survey makes it clear why we need a revolution, a transformation of the psyche, a greater Milton. The consolations of art and love are inadequate. We are left longing—recalled to our transcendental vocation but not raised to it. The human soul still does not know that it is divine, and that is why it requires Blake's more radical therapy.

Blake figures the desperation of the mortal soul in the person of Orc, who rebels against oppression without knowledge of the transcendental window. Orc has lost some of the rebel charisma he had in the early prophecies, and has become more clearly a principle of frustration, unease, and chaotic resistance. Blake now pointedly describes the state he represents as the universal inheritance of Natural Man. Orc himself is the "Polypus," the unwilling submission to materiality: he howls "Within the vegetated mortal Nerves; for every Man born is joined / Within into One mighty Polypus, and this Polypus is Orc" (M 29[31]:27–31, E127). We might say that Orc is every man of woman born—everyone who resents his incarnation and rejects the "Mother of [his] Mortal part" (like the speaker of "To Tirzah"). It comes as a surprise, and a thrill, when Blake adds that "Satan is the Spectre of Orc." He has not offered this definition before and, although it accords logically with the old pairing of Orc and Urizen, it embodies a further psychological observation: Satan, or the Selfhood, is the precipitate of the empiricist subject's despair. The desires of Natural Man are inevitably balked, and the shadow being, the "I" or ego, arises to address that frustration in necessarily contradictory ways: by condensing it, by denying it, by claiming to control it, by expressing it without self-knowledge. Satan is a false face of mastery. The Selfhood, like the inchoate Orc from which it springs, continually exerts its power only to fall back in an acknowledgment of its helplessness. Empiricist subjectivity cannot compensate for lost transcendent agency. For this reason Blake also characterizes Orc as "the generate Luvah," the human Christ or Man of Sorrow. He epitomizes the fate of transcendental longings—of love and passion—in the materialist's world.

The set piece on Los and his sons at the end of Book I represents art as the achievement either of palliative care or of qualified encouragement. Art is the "masculine" remedy associated with Milton's prophetic calling, but it is only a half measure. Book II opens with a beautiful but circumspect examination of Beulah, the "moony" shadow land of respite created for the Emanations. It is also inadequate. Beulah is the earthly paradise just below Eden; a "feminine" remedy, it embraces the escapist elements of domestic and pastoral happiness. Blake specifically links it to regression: "Beulah to its Inhabitants appears within each district / As the beloved infant in his mothers bosom round incircled / With arms of love & pity & sweet compassion" (M 30[33]:10–12, E129). Beulah is best understood as a form of psychological retreat. The Emanations request it as "a habitation & a place / In which we may be hidden under the shadow of wings" when they shrink from the Wars of Eternity and "unboundedness" of the life of Man (M 30–33:24–25, E129). Sexist as Blake's terminology sounds, he is identifying what he regards as a universal failure of nerve common to both men and women—the psychological temptation of willed innocence. Ololon descends into "this pleasant Shadow Beulah," as Milton descends into the sublunary world. In both cases descent reflects a catharsis and an undoing of error. But Ololon is an aspect of Milton, an estranged "feminine" principle, and so whatever error is undone in her is undone in Milton too; or to put it the other way around, Milton's prophetic calling must have been compromised by an attraction to Beulah-land.

Of what did this attraction consist? Milton was, after all, hardly a passive figure. Perhaps Blake is criticizing the terms in which Milton depicted Paradise, for the fierceness of Blake's "Eternity" makes Milton's Eden look not merely pastoral but imbecilic. Certainly Blake is attacking the benignity of Milton's nature—think of the gorgeous hymns in *Paradise Lost*—which he would consider the product of willed innocence. At this point Blake offers his own praise of nature in two exquisite lyrics, but each astonishingly ends by characterizing what we have just read as "a Vision of the lamentation of Beulah over Ololon" (M 31[34]:45, E131). Does this sound like a lamentation?

> Thou hearest the Nightingale begin the Song of Spring;
> The Lark sitting upon his earthy bed: just as the morn
> Appears; listens silent; then springing from the waving
>   Corn-field loud
> He leads the Choir of Day! trill, trill, trill, trill,
> Mounting upon the wings of light into the Great Expanse:
>   ⋆   ⋆   ⋆
> All Nature listens silent to him & the awful Sun
> Stands still upon the Mountain looking on this little Bird
> With eyes of soft humility, & wonder love & awe.
>
> (M 31[34]:28–38, E130–31)

Clearly it matters that Blake does not call this stirring pastoral hymn a lamentation in itself, but "a Vision" of a lamentation. The Daughters of Beulah weep when Ololon descends, because they behold "the Lord coming in the Clouds" of Ololon (M 31[34]:10, E130). When Satan and Rahab see this, they weep with terror, but the Daughters weep with relief and longing. The hymn of the Nightingale is a "vision" of this longing. No matter how perfect the loveliness of nature, it cannot satisfy transcendental desire; it only sharpens it. That is evidently Blake's thinking as he concludes the second of the two lyrics. Following a glorious description of fragrant flowers and herbs, "filling the air with an innumerable Dance / Yet all in order sweet & lovely," Blake comments, "Men are sick with Love!" (M 31[34]:61–62, E131).

Socrates in the *Symposium* defines love as the desire for that which one lacks. This is the "love" with which nature inspires Natural Man, making him "sick" with unfulfilled desire. Love gestures beyond itself to transcendence it does not embody. Thus the highest satisfaction of Natural Man provokes a sense of deprivation. Beulah laments over Ololon because even in Beulah uneasy consciousness cannot find rest. Desire shines through the sleep like light through a veil. There is no refuge from one's own transcendental longings; far from being at peace, the Gnostic "sleeper" twists and turns in the grip of nightmare. Blake worked on simulating this fugue state in *The Four Zoas*, subtitled (after Young's *Night Thoughts*) "A Dream of Nine Nights." In *Milton* he demonstrates why the temporal remedies—the Golgonoozas and the Beulahs—fall short.

On the Threshold of Transformation

Blake devotes a large part of *Milton* to demonstrating how the mind may take refuge in fantasy or find amelioration in art, but in either case it has not yet engaged the real "Mental Fight." For all his bravery and polemical vigor, Milton the poet did not entirely fight this better fight himself. Through intellectual error and flaws of character, Milton did not think up to the capacity of his own understanding. The Selfhood subtly tempted him to shirk the harder work of self-reformation in favor of authority and righteousness. That is why he ascended into a false Heaven, where we find him at the beginning of the poem—a wearisome, conformist place, bearing no relation to Blake's Eden of dynamic intellectual exchange. Milton got the Heaven he deserved. It is also, of course, the Heaven he created in *Paradise Lost*—a palace of dull piety, or so Blake had asserted in *The Marriage of Heaven and Hell*.

Milton the character fully emerges out of his spiritual purgatory in Book II when he completes his expulsion of Satan and his reunion with Ololon. The expulsion and the scenes leading up to it emphasize the mirror relationship between the Selfhood and the punitive God, both of them dependent for their existence on the occlusion of the true human divinity. In a Song of Beulah—that is, a hopeful vision of what is passing within Milton—he repudiates the angry God, or "Heavens builded on cruelty" (M 32[35]:3, E131). The Angels of the Presence point out that the outward deity *is* Satan, "Who made himself a God &, destroyed the Human Form Divine" (M 32:13, E131). Their remark clearly reiterates the Gnostic view of the Creator God as an imposter, arrogating to himself the status of divinity that rightly belongs to human beings. In his epigrammatic poem "To the God who is the Accuser of this World," Blake identifies Satan and God systematically, conflating the official deity with Satan as portrayed in The Book of Job. His point is that Christian theodicy makes them partners—testing and punishing people—and beyond this, that the orthodox God (Milton's God) has an evil personality; he is Satan "Worshipd by the Names Divine" (E269). But Satan is also the Selfhood, and we can see readily enough that the Angels' gibe applies to the Selfhood too, which has made itself the "God" of the self by displacing the "Human Form Divine." (This is a dig at Milton too, who only went as far as "the human face divine," a phrase sanctioned by Genesis, which affirms that we are made in God's image, but not that we *are* divine.) "To the God who is the Accuser of this World" ends by reminding God / Satan that he does not exist, but was hallucinated out of our exhaustion and uncertainty. To borrow a phrase from the poet A. R. Ammons, he is a false god for real human needs.

> thou art still
> The Son of Morn in weary Nights decline
> The lost Travellers Dream under the Hill.
>
> (E269)

To be lost, travelling, dreaming, to lie in the shadow of the hill: these are all limbo states, reflecting the bewilderment of Natural Man. To dispel his errors, the Angels of the Presence encourage Milton to introspect, distinguishing his immortal "identity" from transient "States" such as the ego of the empirical being: "States Change: but Individual Identities never change nor cease . . . Judge then of thy Own Self: thy Eternal Lineaments explore / What is Eternal & what Changeable? & what Annihilable" (M 32[35]:30–31, E132). Note that in this passage, Blake wrests the term "identity" away from the empiricists, redefining and transvaluating it. Here identity is the eternal, the soul, and also the Eternal is the Divine Voice, Jesus, the Opened Center, the Human Form Divine. The annihilable is Satan the Selfhood, the Covering Cherub that silences that Voice, solidifying itself into an illusory power and projecting its tyrannical likeness onto the heavens. As a mere "incrustation," it can be removed.

Ololon is comforted by this Song of Beulah, and she continues her descent through Beulah to Ulro. In a beautiful inversion of Milton's Sin and Death creating the highway to Hell, her descent opens "a wide road . . . to Eternity" (M 35[39]:35, E135). Ololon emerges through the "Moment in each Day that Satan cannot find" (M 35:42, E136), and enters Blake's Garden at Felpham in the form of "a Virgin of twelve years." She sees Milton's Shadow and recognizes it as the Covering Cherub, this time especially as the delusive religion precipitated out of the Selfhood. Blake sees it too: he beholds the "desolation" of Satan's bosom. (The passage is quoted above.) Now Milton reappears, not yet reunited with Ololon but clearly strengthened by her arrival, for he stands "[i]n the Eastern porch of Satans Universe" and denounces him. Milton now perceives the paradox of countering Satan with the Satan in himself. He could "annihilate" Satan "And be a greater in thy place" but that would be to replicate Satan, becoming "thy Tabernacle / A covering for thee to do thy will, till one greater comes / And smites me as I smote thee & becomes my covering" (M 38[43]:30–32, E139). (This is the paradox of the murderous chain figured in Frazer's *Golden Bough* in the anecdote of the King of the Wood at Nemi.) What this means is that righteousness cannot counteract righteousness. No assertion of authority that comes from the Selfhood can reform the Selfhood, and the "I" that polices itself recreates the Urizenic spiral. At this turning point Milton wants to make a more radical change: to quell the needs and ambitions of the empirical self, including the pride it takes in its Christian "virtue." Such pride enables prudential morality to devolve into mere selfishness, and puritan discipline into mendacity and aggression.

> I come to discover before Heavn & Hell the Self righteousness
> In all its Hypocritic turpitude, opening to every eye
> These wonders of Satans holiness shewing to the Earth
> The Idol Virtues of the Natural Heart, & Satans Seat
> Explore in all its Selfish Natural Virtue & put off
> In Self annihilation all that is not of God alone:
> To put off Self & all I have ever & ever Amen.

> (M 38[43]:43–49, E139)

"Natural" here means belonging to the empirical world: the "Idol Virtues" are modes of self-protection fallaciously represented as higher goods. These include Christian norms of behavior, particularly involving sexuality, as well as the four Classical virtues in all their "practical wisdom." These definitions of virtue allow calculation to masquerade as holiness, thereby generating a self-righteousness with no means of regulation. This adducement of self-interested blindness to one's own selfishness summons Satan; he "hear[s]," he comes "in a cloud, with trumpets & flaming fire." He is answering to his name, as it were, the proper definition of what he is. And he responds predictably—with self-assertion, proclaiming his divine power and threatening Milton—"I am God the judge of all, the living & the dead . . . I alone am

God & I alone in Heavn & Earth / Of all that live dare utter this" (M 38[43]:56–57, E139–40). Satan's words echo Urizen's, but this time as farce, and Milton is not to be impressed by this figment of power. He does not even have to reply. The transition has already been made, and in the next instant it manifests itself: the Angels of the Presence surround Milton like "burning" stars, the path in Blake's garden turns to "solid fire," and Milton "silent [comes] down on my path" to rejoin Ololon (M 39[44]:4–5, E140).

Redemption, however, is not complete: Albion awakes on his Couch and strives to walk into the Deep, but his strength fails. If one wishes, one can resolve what happens next into a coherent narrative of transfiguration, although certain difficulties arise that I will address further on in this chapter. In its last movement, the poem portrays the reintegration of Milton and Ololon. Thus one narrative of transfiguration might focus on the correction of Milton's sexual politics. Milton, it turns out, is still struggling with Urizen among the Brooks of Arnon, but he is saved by the intervention of Ololon. They meet in Blake's garden; they stand face to face and he "perceiv[es] the Eternal Form of that mild Vision" (M 40[46]:1–2, E141). She is in part the Divine Voice he had forgotten, and in part a feminine "mildness" he had exiled from his personality. As Milton puts it, his predatory Spectre has been stalking his "Emanation," an intuitive and vulnerable part of himself that Blake represents as female: "He hunts her footsteps thro' the snow & the wintry hail & rain" (M 32[35]:5, E131).

Milton's masculinity, too, was a Covering Cherub. Frye points out that Ololon appears as a "Virgin" because Blake objects to Milton's sexual morality, especially his enthusiasm for the cult of female chastity. When Ololon exorcizes "Rahab Babylon," the wily nature goddess of Natural Religion, her act signifies that Milton is not only renouncing "the False Tongue" but, more deeply, is dissolving his baleful hypostasis of sexual difference. Milton's picture of an angry God and a meek, seductive Eve, his abuse of his wives and daughters, and even the defensive "strength" of his own personality all testify to the malforming effects of sexual ideology. Thus his grand closing monologue ends with a denunciation of "the Sexual Garments, the Abomination of Desolation / Hiding the Human Lineaments as with an Ark & Curtains" (M 41[48]:25–26, E142). At the end of *Milton* the Virgin reiterates the terror of Eternity expressed by the Emanations in Beulah, and then she splits from Ololon and flees "into the depths / Of Miltons Shadow" (M 42[49]:5–6, E143). That is clearly where she belongs—back in the discarded Selfhood from which the fantasy of femininity arose. The clarified Ololon, no longer fearful, descends "Into the Fires of Intellect that rejoic'd in Felphams Vale" (42:9, E143). Now Milton becomes the eighth Angel of the Presence, and all eight consolidate into "One Man Jesus the Savior." The potential fulfilled, he goes to enter Albion's bosom, and the heralds of prophecy prepare for the apocalypse, "the Great Vintage and Harvest of the Nations" (M 43[50]:1, E144).

I have paraphrased the final movements of the poem programmatically, showing how the success of Milton's "redemption" might be inferred by an optimistic apologist. But a closer look reveals wrinkles in the process. Milton's grand peroration, for example, introduces a contradiction. He begins by declaring "All that can be annihilated must be annihilated," and proceeds to identify the Selfhood as that which can: it is a "Negation" to be identified with "the Reasoning Power in Man":

> This is a false Body: an Incrustation over my Immortal
> Spirit; a Selfhood, which must be put off & annihilated alway
> To cleanse the Face of my Spirit by Self-examination.
> To bathe in the Waters of Life; to wash off the Not Human.
>
> (M 40[47]:34–37; 41[48]:1, E142)

The Selfhood seems like the most human, most unique part of one, but it is in fact the "Not Human," the parodic inverse of the "Human Form Divine." Fortunately one can "wash off" this "Incrustation" or (changing the metaphor) shed these "filthy garments"—these grave clothes—and leave them behind in the tomb, along with the science, aesthetics, and religion of the Enlightenment. By discarding the Selfhood and embracing impersonal "Inspiration," Milton himself has recovered his prophetic calling, arriving at a truth good for all, and a redemptive project. Having somewhat peremptorily commanded Ololon to "Obey . . . the Words of the Inspired Man," he describes his mission with boldness and assurance.

> I come in Self-annihilation & the grandeur of Inspiration
> To cast off Rational Demonstration by Faith in the Saviour
> To cast off the rotten rags of Memory by Inspiration
> To cast off Bacon, Locke & Newton from Albions covering
> To take off his filthy garments, & clothe him with Imagination.
>
> (M 41[48]:2–6, E142)

It is a sublime speech—I have not quoted it all—but not without a puzzle. The problem is reflected in the phrase: "I come in Self-annihilation." Who is this "I" that remains after the "I" has been cast off? Clearly Blake would want to distinguish between the confidence of the prophet and the pride of the egoist, as between the rage of Los and the petulance of Satan. Nor should we regard the distinction as rhetorical: identification with impersonal Vision makes it possible, in theory, to experience disinterested anger and unself-involved assurance—that is, to have strength and feel emotion for the Vision's sake rather than one's own. And Vision itself can still be unique. Impersonal does not mean general but detached from Selfhood: so Vision remains partic-ular and distinct. In Blake's heaven, as against Plotinus's, individual minds will not be assimilated into one larger entity; idiosyncrasy and difference will be preserved. The visionaries in Eden engaged in "Mental Fight" are obviously not all thinking the same thing. But no mind will assert itself on behalf of an ego. However unrealistic this psychology may seem, it is at least coherent, and we might be willing to regard the paradox of the "I" that rejects itself as superficial. (The "I" cast off was substantial, where the redeemed "I" is just a figure of speech.) But a deeper quandary remains when we turn from theory to practice. How can the prophet herself tell her indignation from resent-ment, and her surety from self-indulgence? How can Milton know that his as-sumption of authority does not entail the residual nourishment of Selfhood? If this is not a true psychological riddle for Blake, it presents him at least with a problem of language and representation. Can the prophet peremptorily denounce ego without seeming hypocritical?

One detail from a later epic suggests that Blake recognized the problem and decided to circumvent it. In *Jerusalem* he replaces the emphatic Milton with the uncertain Albion who delivers no defiant final speech. Instead, Al-bion implores Jesus to deliver him from his "Selfhood cruel" whose power as a blocking agent he perceives but does not know how to eradicate. Jesus confirms Albion's own intuition that true humanity does not exist "with-out / Mysterious / Offering of Self for Another," and after the Covering Cherub parts them again, Albion, perceiving that he "sleep[s] amidst danger to Friends," throws himself "into the Furnaces of affliction." His self-sacrifice precipitates the magical renovation: "the Furnaces became / Fountains of Living Waters flowing from the Humanity Divine" (J 96:19–20, 34, 35–36, E256). Since *Milton* Blake has changed the terms in an obvious sense by substituting an action for a monologue—a feat of self-sacrifice for a declaration of it—but he has also, more profoundly, refocused his account of "Self-Annihilation." In keeping with the altruistic ethic of *Jerusalem,* Blake now represents "Self-Annihilation" as a possibility to be realized primarily in one's relation to others: that is the test and the proof of psychological progress. Therefore, declarations lose their significance. Thus Blake solves the rhetorical problem of Milton's assertiveness, in part, by having Albion demonstrate his rejection of Selfhood in another way. But he goes well beyond this, redefining the goal so that the puzzle of the "I" that asserts itself by annihilating itself becomes academic: the aim is not self-reformation first, but altruistic behavior first. This objective is more realistic and less paradoxical, although at the same time more conventional.

The puzzle of the "I" is a puzzle about agency: who or what is the agent performing the act of self-annihilation? Questions of agency continue to raise complications throughout the epic prophecies because Blake is working out scenarios of transformation, and such scenarios necessarily involve issues of causality and will. In *Milton* the problem of will can be read in the very structure of the poem: why doesn't it end with Milton's first epiphany? Why is the will to extirpate the Selfhood that he exhibits in that speech insufficient to enact his reformation? In his final peroration, Milton would appear to have incorporated the teaching of the Seven Angels, and to be adopting their language of the Starry Seven, when he speaks of annihilating "All that can be annihilated." But, in fact, he was already using this imagery in his first epiphany when he recognized Satan as his Selfhood: "I will go down to self annihilation and eternal death, / Lest the Last Judgement come & find me unannihilate / And I be seiz'd & giv'n into the hands of my own Selfhood" (M 14[15]:22–24, E108). Why does Milton require the further instruction of the Angels when he has already given the proper diagnosis and the proper prescription for a cure? One might say that the act of "self-annihilation" has not taken place yet and that the intervening episodes show what it entails. But this observation confirms the telling point: insight into the Selfhood does not break its grip.

Knowledge and will are inadequate. Correspondingly, the actual catalysts for some of Milton's changes do not follow from his determinations. Milton himself decides to descend "to Eternal Death," but other pivotal developments in the poem—such as the descent of Ololon—are represented as happening *to* him. They occur without the agency of his consciousness. It could be said

that his decision sets the wheels in motion, or that any decision or act of
Ololon's is on some level his own, yet Blake often shows Milton to be sur-
prised by unfolding events, as if to suggest that he is not precisely the "au-
thor" of his transformation. As Milton labors through his journey, for exam-
ple, "his feet [bleeding] sore," he is suddenly accosted by Urizen: "Urizen
rose, / And met him on the shores of Arnon" (M 19[21]:4–5, E112). It makes
psychological sense that Urizen should act independently because Milton has
disowned him. On the other hand, because he must wrestle Urizen to achieve
his freedom, Milton ought to be hunting *him* down rather than the reverse. It
might be argued in response that Milton naturally meets up with Urizen in
the course of his journey, insofar as he has made progress and, therefore,
brought himself to the next phase in which he can undertake this struggle.
But even that argument would have to confess that he is advancing blindly.
However we interpret the moment, we have to allow for some *unknowingness*
on Milton's part, some inability to foresee or control the process of his trans-
formation. A keen psychologist like Blake is bound to note the element of un-
predictability in psychological change, although this observation interferes
with his design of charting out a course of development. Blake may be think-
ing along the lines of Shelley in *Prometheus Unbound* that moral and psycho-
logical evolution cannot simply be willed.

The subtle tension between Blake's program and his understanding ap-
pears in all the epic prophecies. Even his apocalyptic endings are never so con-
fident as they seem. They generally include a hint of complication or delay.
This is a pronounced issue in *The Four Zoas*, but even *Milton* stutters, ending
on a liminal note. The poem takes us to the verge of apocalypse and stops
there, unwilling to cross the border into Utopia. The Four Zoas blow their
trumpets; Blake's "Soul" returns to its body to await the Judgement; the Lark,
and the Wild Thyme, Los, and Enitharmon arise; and everything mounts to
anticipation of the climax.

> Rintrah and Palamabron view the Human Harvest beneath
> Their Wine-presses & Barns stand open; the Ovens are prepar'd
> The Waggons ready: terrific Lions & Tygers sport & play
> All Animals upon the Earth, are prepard in all their strength
>
> To go forth to the Great Harvest and Vintage of the Nations.
>
> (M 43[50]:1, E144)

Harold Bloom reads this closing passage as wholly exultant.

> Here, in the poem's final vision, Blake comes back to himself, tri-
> umphantly answering the perplexities of the Bard's Song . . . In
> the closing lines, the Mills of Satan have vanished, and the great-
> ness of the Apocalypse is imminent. It is difficult not to hear the
> single line of the final plate as a prophetic battle cry, ringing with
> challenge and with the confidence of the poet-prophet who has
> been tried severely, and has triumphed over his trials.   (E928)

I hear the tone of the line, and the passage, as somewhat less definitive.
Blake's assertion is indeed strong, as any hope can be strong, yet he makes no
promise. Instead he pauses on the threshold, as if to acknowledge that he
cannot go farther in imagination than the moment at which the momentous
change *might* occur. All the Animals are prepared to go forth: the real action is
contained in the infinitive, and it has not begun. There is a tension between
the driving momentum of the rhetoric and the suspended temporality it de-
scribes.

Bloom sees Blake as adopting the oracular assurance of the character Mil-
ton ("I come in the Grandeur of Inspiration") but, interestingly, Blake dissoci-
ates his own voice from that of the poem's last lines. While the final overview
is taking place, he is still lying "outstretched upon the path," his Soul having
just reentered his body, as his wife, his "Sweet Shadow of Delight," stands
"trembling by [his] side" (M 42:28, E143). It probably does not make sense to
think of the poem's last lines as spoken by a new third-person narrator, yet in
their impersonal vigor they do not seem properly to belong to the enervated,
prostrated poet. A rhetorical gap of a kind has been introduced. I believe this
is deliberate; it reflects the fact that the fate of the world is passing out of the
poet's hands. What follows is history, which takes over where the poet has to
leave off. The larger world opens out, still in drastic need of change, after the
individual renovations of Milton and Blake. According to the program, the
great transition will occur when a catalyst like the ideal Milton arises and con-
verts all the Lord's people to prophecy. But how this will happen is not clear.
Even Los, the prophet who stands for them all, appears at the end of the
poem in a suspended posture, passionate but as yet inactive: "Los listens to
the Cry of the Poor Man: his Cloud / Over London in volume terrific, low

bended in anger" (M 42[49]:34–35, E144). What Los hears—the continuance of injustice—reminds us that the reformation of the prophet is not the final goal, and that this goal may remain unachieved for all the prophet's personal "triumph." Blake inserts a lingering pause here between the achieved reformation of Milton and the anticipated reformation of the world.

We do not associate Blake with tentativeness, but I believe this kind of aporia demonstrates caution and sophistication. His epic prophecies, where he creates scenarios of transformation, often include arbitrary, unexplained, or incomplete developments. Such gaps call forth objection from those who expect systematicity. Frye, for example, faults the unmotivated transition to apocalypse in "Night the Ninth" of *The Four Zoas*. He finds an aporia in the action between "Night the Eighth" and "Night the Ninth." But there is also an anomaly at the very end of the poem: two verse paragraphs from the end, Men are still "bound to sullen contemplations in the night / Restless they turn on beds of sorrow" (FZ 138:12–13, E406), yet the next paragraph abruptly announces, "The Sun has left his blackness and has found a fresher morning." Such spontaneous transitions might be taken for lapses on Blake's part. They might also be understood as meaningful: in other words, they look like moments when the narrative sequence breaks down, but perhaps Blake wishes to make a point. He may be introducing the unpredictability of the psyche into his scenario so that transformation takes place punctually, like a sudden jump in evolution. Milton's involuntary changes can be understood in this light. A final possibility is that these aporiae gape as Blake's reminder of how momentous and difficult transformation would be, a reminder for himself as well as for his reader. The retarding motion reflects his vigilance. He thinks as he writes, and preserves the intrusions of skepticism.

5

Jerusalem:
The Will to Solitude

Now we come to the last of Blake's prophecies, *Jerusalem*, begun in 1804. This chapter will be brisk because it approaches *Jerusalem* with a quite particular focus. It deals with what is new and potentially revisionary in the poem's treatment of selfhood. I will not attempt the (formidable) task of working through *Jerusalem*'s account of self-remaking, but I will concentrate instead on mapping out the critical challenge it mounts to Blake's earlier views. *Jerusalem* returns to the millenarian themes of *The Four Zoas:* the prophet's persistence, the redemption of England, and the salvation of humanity. It also—perforce—includes accounts of error, resistance, and "opacity." In fact the bulk of *Jerusalem*, like *The Four Zoas,* consists of describing the obstacles to enlightenment. But there is a major shift of emphasis. In *Jerusalem* the fall is epitomized by every person's entrenchment in his or her own Selfhood and consequent hostility to others. As the prophetess Erin puts it, the Satan in us has made "A World where Man is by Nature the enemy of Man" (J 49:69, E199). Like the earlier prophecies, *Jerusalem* outlines the ways in which various pernicious ideologies or "false religions" have conspired to displace "the Eternal Great Humanity Divine," but it now stresses the idea that this displacement of the Divine Vision within each person isolates him or her. Conversely, it argues that the revival of the Divine Vision inspires friendship and brotherhood, and vice versa. The idea is not new in Blake, but the stress is: he shifts from focusing on solitude *within* the self to alienation *from* others.

This shift follows from the ethical focus of *Jerusalem,* the announced theme of which is the necessity of "Forgiveness." Envy and self-righteousness represent consolidations of the Selfhood, while the "Forgiveness of Sins . . . is Self Annihilation." "Self Annihilation" now means not only suppression of the Selfhood but also active self-sacrifice on behalf of others (J 98:23, E257). Thus Blake dispenses with the residual self-emphasis of the prophet Milton. In the final pages of *Jerusalem,* Albion, like Milton, annihilates his Selfhood, but unlike Milton, he does so to help his "Friends" rather than to redeem himself. This self-sacrifice revives the Divine Vision within Albion, and the heaven that springs into being is a heaven of "conversation." Rather than dwelling apart, each immured in his own blind subjectivity, the inhabitants of Eden are intertranspicuous: "they walked / To & fro in Eternity as One Man reflecting each in each & clearly seen / And seeing" (J 98:38–40, E258).

Blake and his reader earn this communal paradise by struggling their way through *Jerusalem.* The poem thematizes such lonely labor in the struggles of Los, seen hammering at his forge, repeatedly, throughout the four chapters. He sometimes entertains despair because he is forced to confront the same principles of resistance over and over and over, a loop Blake impresses on the reader in the form of the poem's nonnarrative structure, or pattern of "synchronous" repetitions (Paley, *The Continuing City* 294–314). If *The Four Zoas* steeped us in the darkness of night (and its nightmares), *Jerusalem* makes us wander in a labyrinth. As Stuart Curran puts it, the reader is "fated to return again and again to the same landmarks without discovering an egress" ("The Structures of *Jerusalem*" 340). Curran points out that this structure is meant to have a mimetic force, recalling wider failure to progress.

I have noted some of the obstacles to improvement that Blake presented in earlier works. In *Jerusalem* he discovers a new principle of resistance, making an important addition to his psychology: alienation from others is *willed.* We deploy Og and Anak to stand guard at our own gates. We police our borders in defense of the Selfhood. Sex is a parody of love. Memory is a means of isolation. We keep other beings, including the beings of the natural world, at a distance, yet they seem to impinge on us. To the paranoid empiricist subject, who feels himself to be "Shrunk to a narrow doleful form in the dark land of Cabul" (J 79:63, E235), everything seems "remote and separate." Even so, we have no real autonomy; we are entangled in a web of mutual antagonism, "by Invisible Hatreds adjoind." For there is no escaping others, and "He who will not commingle in Love, must be adjoind by Hate" (J 66:56, E219).

The Human Footstep Is a Terror to Me

In an 1801 letter to Thomas Butts, Blake apologizes for failing to execute a commission—failing to attend to the "world of Duty & Reality . . . my Abstract folly hurries me often away while I am at work, carrying me over Mountains & Valleys which are not Real in a land of Abstraction where Spectres of the Dead wander" (E716). This complaint sounds gloomy enough, although it turns out to contain something of a boast or a celebration: try as he may to "chain [his] feet to the world of Duty & Reality . . . the faster I bind the better is the Ballast, for I so far from being bound down take the world with me in my flights & often it seems lighter than a ball of wool rolled by the wind Bacon & Newton would prescribe ways of making the world heavier to me" (E716). That dreary land in which he wanders, although hardly a realm of gold, is a making of the imagination preferable to actuality conceived as a leaden chain. It sounds very like Urizen's night world, populated by the wretched specters, that he tours in Nights 6–8 of *The Four Zoas*. Blake was probably writing the *Zoas* at the time he composed this letter to Butts, so perhaps what he means is that he finds his mind occupied with images of the fallen world. Or he might mean—as at least one critic has thought (Riede 274)—that, like Urizen, he is *experiencing* his mind as a haunted landscape in which he wanders up and down. But why oppose these interpretations? The mind in a fallen world will suffer the alienation it diagnoses, "becoming what it beholds," to use one of Blake's key phrases. Blake in his own mind partakes of the bewilderment, estrangement, and hauntedness of the empirical subject. For this dark realm represents more than Urizen's fallen Creation. It is at once a metaphor and *not* a metaphor—a figure for the benighted world but also simply a description of the outer and inner world as the empiricist subject experiences them everyday. All things are dreadful, yet nothing is real; presences are at once oppressive and remote and those who might be companionable are empty "specters." One is alone in the worst way, encompassed by fearful, tantalizing otherness.

Jerusalem adds to the story by meditating further on the phenomenon of mutual hostility. Of course there is enough mutual hostility in *The Four Zoas* to make this project seem superfluous. In the *Zoas* mutual antagonism explodes in the dramatic interaction of Zoas and Emanations. In *Jerusalem* the cast of characters undergoes a radical simplification. Now there are just three main characters, one of whom, Albion or the Giant Man, frequently figures as a representative consciousness, divided between the competing claims of Vala (false philosophy) and Jerusalem (true vision). The Zoas and Emanations have been relegated to the margins. One of Blake's chief motives in making these changes is to refocus attention on individual subjective experience. *The Four Zoas* represents the mind in a way that recalls David Hume's "theater": fragment after fragment crosses its empty stage. But as Hume had to ask himself, What is the stage in this metaphor? so Blake decides it is necessary to return, in *Jerusalem,* to the ground of the Zoas' shuttling, the "I" that feels itself to be divided.

Blake wants to restore the potential for agency to the individual, who may have lost it for the present but will have to regain it if any progress is to occur. An empty stage has no potential for agency. For this reason Blake replaces the anonymous, helpless masses of "the spectrous dead," wholly dominated by the acts of the Zoas and Emanations, with the single figure of Albion, who may be drastically self-divided and driven by false consciousness but at least provides a single site of contestation and thus of catalysis. Although *Jerusalem* is still a drama—Paley compares it to an oratorio, an arrangement of rival voices (*The Continuing City* 293)—and the chief characters still quarrel, the convergence on Albion has the effect of making individual experience a constant theme. We see to some extent from one point of view, which allows Blake to show that, for Albion, mutual hostility not only characterizes the relationships between different parts of the self but also has infected relationships with other people and with the external world. This antipathy toward others then rebounds, as error always does in Blake, to exacerbate the loneliness of selfhood.

The antipathy not only fastens on others, but on otherness itself. The "dead" object world of the empiricists, which was once either menacing or inert, is now invested—or at least more emphatically invested—with the pathos of estrangement and withdrawal. Blake had said before that when the human "eye & ear" contract, the world that they perceive contracts. Now he seems to extend sympathy to the features of the diminished world, as if they suffered from their reduction in the human mind. Everything flies apart, dwindling and fading into the distance, enlarging the abyssal gulfs:

> the Sun is shrunk: the Heavens are shurnk
> Away into the far remote: and the Trees & Mountains witherd
> Into indefinite cloudy shadows in darkness & separation.
>
> (J 66:50–52, E219)

It has become a sad world. This is pathetic fallacy, and Blake knows it: he intends to render the projection of the empiricist subject, whose sense of "darkness and separation" spreads out to cover everything. Yet nature has truly undergone a loss because it is as it is perceived. Much time in which it might have been engaged more vitally has been wasted. The empiricist subject has looked out, and still looks out, on a world governed by the essential antipathy of being in which every singularity is a citadel, but not a free one because it remains bound to others in its difference from them.

> By Invisible Hatreds adjoind, they seem remote and separate
> From each other; and yet are a Mighty Polypus in the Deep!
>
> (J 66:53–54, E219)

The "Mighty Polypus" brings us back to the vegetative universe, the mechanical system of materialist nature, in which the very alienation of the elements combines to form a whole. That the empiricist subject can see this not only as a menacing world but also (sometimes) as a sad one, shows unacknowledged awareness that it might be otherwise. Mourning for nature is the other side of transcendental remorse. Antipathy brings its opposite to the fore; it arouses longing for communication under cover of its disappointment. (Luvah's love for Vala—for the Goddess Nature—expresses this longing in a mistaken form.) The fallen human being "yearns toward" reconciliation with material nature and its linear temporality, but he or she cannot be reconciled to nature under this aspect. Still, nature is felt to be lost and missed. After all, "Rivers & Mountains / Are also Men" (34:47–8, E180).

Blake portrays this thwarting of Eros in a radical troping of the Noah story. In his retelling, it is a tragedy that the envoy does not return. Its defection spells failure for the attempt to achieve a reconciliation with nature.

> The inhabitants are sick to death: they labour to divide into Days
> And Nights, the uncertain Periods: and into Weeks & Months. In vain
> They send the Dove & Raven: & in vain the Serpent over
>   the mountains
> And in vain the Eagle & Lion over the four-fold wilderness.
> They return not: but generate in rocky places desolate.
> They return not; but build a habitation separate from Man.
>
> (J 66:68–73, E219)

We cannot overcome the dread aroused in us by the linear temporality of the natural world. We send out our ambassadors, the other creatures, in hope of negotiating new terms, or finding a safe harbor. But they desert us and make their own place in the world. Thus our species dwells alone in its sunderance.

The standard eros fares no better. In earlier works, Blake portrays sexual love as a fragile forerunner of deeper spiritual union, but in *Jerusalem* it appears as a very poor substitute. Albion beholds his Sons "bound in the bonds / Of spiritual Hate, from which springs Sexual Love as iron chains" (J 54:11–12 E203). In this anti-Platonic view, sex does not descend from—or ascend toward—love, but really masks hate, ill-disguised. This is specifically "Spiritual" hate, from which it follows that there is a form of spiritual love, not to be confused with sexual love. In fact, by a chiasmatic reversal, spiritual hate begets sexual love, where spiritual love begets the opposition that is true friendship. (Compare "Corporeal Friends are Spiritual Enemies.") What is spiritual hate? It is not personal antagonism, not merely an affect. It is one of the two stances a person can have toward otherness: "He who will not commingle in Love, must be adjoined by Hate." The system is binary: there is no neutral position, as we might be tempted to postulate, no state of solipsism or egotistical sublimity indifferent to otherness. There is either "commingling" with spiritual love—love that has transcended Selfhood—or there is the usual (mere) confrontation of Selfhoods. For Selfhoods cannot commingle; they protect their own integrity at all costs, and each by definition "hates" the others. Thus sexual love, undertaken with whatever conscious hope and happiness, will fail of its promises.

Los indicates what commingling in love is like: "in Eternity Man converses with Man they enter / Into each others Bosom (which are universes of delight) / In mutual interchange" (J 88:3–5, E246). Lest we imagine that the Utopian ideal is wholly intellectual and masculine, Blake also gives us a picture of redeemed sexual love, polymorphous and entire: "Embraces are Comminglings: from the Head even to the Feet / And not a pompous High Priest entering by a Secret Place" (J 69:43–44, E223). As it is now, in place of angelic sexuality, we have genital sex, which Blake treats as distorted and disappointing. Fallen sexuality entails defeat of the union it seems to promise because it isolates consciousness, accentuating divergence and separation. Heterosexual genital coupling is asymmetrical; the partners have different, and in a certain sense, opposite experiences. Its very anatomical nature seems designed to provoke ambivalence. The Spectre of Los maliciously determines to damage sexuality by focusing on the genitals: "I will make their places of joy & love, excrementitious" (J 88:39, E247). (Yeats derives his famous bitter lines from Blake: "But Love has pitched his mansion in/The place of excrement" ("Crazy Jane Talks with the Bishop," *Variorum Edition* 513). In fact, for Blake the physical reality is not definitive; it is the entire cultural context that has perverted relations between men and women in such a way as to vex sexual expression. Patriarchal society introduces a certain power dynamic and a damaging exaggeration of sex roles; under their influence, sex turns into "a pompous High Priest entering by a Secret Place." But the underlying problem is the competition and defensiveness of Selfhoods.

Jerusalem decries the baleful influence that the Selfhood's attachment to Moral Law exerts over sexual politics. In his most provocative treatment of this theme, Blake retells the Nativity story: Joseph forgives Mary for getting pregnant by another man. Forgiveness is spiritual love, the exact inverse of the spiritual hate and sexual love that is all the Selfhood has to offer. Los analyzes the Selfhood's corruption of love when he ironically describes fallen sexuality as "Sexual Death living on accusation of Sin & Judgement." More darkly, he adds: "Without Forgiveness of Sin Love is Itself Eternal Death" (J 64:22, 24, E215). Moral suspicion and self-righteousness—bulwarks of the Selfhood—set one person against another. In a love relationship that confronts two Selfhoods, each will find not comfort but only its own isolation, or Eternal Death. When sexuality has turned into "Sexual Death," or a stimulus to despair, then people have indeed become one another's enemies "by nature."

In *Jerusalem* Blake gives several vivid portraits of this species of isolation. Beyond his misogynist animus against the "Female Will," and his more judicious Wollstonecraftian appraisal of the noxiousness of sex roles, Blake seems to have shared the Neoplatonic intuition that sexual difference is a catastrophe. In Neoplatonic cosmology, the separation of the sexes is the first event in the Fall. By the time Blake wrote *Jerusalem,* he has apparently come to believe, too, that the unfallen human being is sexless. (Compare Hayes.) He has Jerusalem sadly reproach Vala, the incarnation of the Female Will: "O Vala Humanity is far above / Sexual organization . . . Wherefore then do you realize these nets of beauty & delusion" (J 79:73–78, E236). Bear in mind that the Female Will develops in a dialectic with patriarchy; Blake's argument is not that Eve or woman started it all, but that sexual difference gives rise—at least in a misguided culture—to a pernicious dynamic in which masculine tyranny incites "Female Secresy" and seductive wiles. Blake's analysis of skewed sexual dynamics is concentrated in chapter 3, "To the Deists," where he not only demonstrates the connection between the worship of "the God of this world" and the passivating awe of a treacherous Nature but also links both to the desperate effort of appeasement motivating war and sacrifice, and then to the development of selfish prudential morality, which in turn produces sexual repression and distorted sex roles. It is a complicated story of which I wish to highlight only a few elements. After the Antichrist, or Selfhood, is consolidated, "The Feminine separates from the Masculine & both from Man, / Ceasing to be His Emanations, Life to Themselves assuming!" They circumscribe the organs of the Masculine, and as they do so "a Veil & Net / Of Veins of red Blood grows around him like a scarlet robe / Covering them from the sight of Man like the woven Veil of Sleep." Moving from sinister to sorrowful, Blake compares this veil to the "Funeral Mantles" of the "Flowers of Beulah," but specifies, more grimly, that the veil is

> . . . dark! opake! tender to the touch, & painful! & agonizing
> To the embrace of love, & to the mingling of soft fibres
> Of tender affection. that no more the Masculine mingles
> With the Feminine. but the Sublime is shut out from the Pathos
> In howling torment, to build stone walls of separation, compelling
> The Pathos, to weave curtains of hiding secresy from the torment.
>
> (J 90:1–13, E249)

The passage changes in tone as it goes on: it begins by describing the ominous emergence of the Female Will but ends with the tragic estrangement of Masculine and Feminine principles. In large part Blake is analyzing divisions taking place within a single mind—that disassociation of affects or capacities he has often investigated—but the passage at the same time draws on the pathos of ordinary sexual alienation. The strange scarlet robe of blood seems to grow spontaneously from Man, but instead of concealing him from the Emanations—as the metaphor might suggest—it "cover[s] them from the sight of Man." It is a mutual barrier, an obstacle between them that makes a torture of erotic life, "tender to the touch, & painful, & agonizing / To the embrace of love." This obstacle is sufficiently rebarbative to stifle any effort at "commingling." And in place of the veil, Masculine and Feminine each create new barriers of their own—"stone walls of separation" and "curtains of hiding secresy"—in an attempt to ward off the torment that these barriers actually increase. The Sublime and the Pathos lend a hand in securing their own "World[s] of Loneness."

Like all worlds of loneness in Blake, their separate spheres are not truly havens but rather dungeons of restlessness and perturbation. In the midst of their victory song, celebrating the ascendancy of the bloodthirsty goddess Rahab / Tirzah, her "Warriors" inchoately lament their own degradation.

> Once Man was occupied in intellectual pleasures & energies
> But now my soul is harrowd with grief & fear & love & desire
> And now I hate & now I love & Intellect is no more:
> There is no time for any thing but the torments of love & desire
> The Feminine & Masculine Shadows soft, mild & ever varying
> In beauty; are Shadows now no more, but Rocks in Horeb.

> (J 68:65–70, E222)

In this life of erotic dismay, no mind preserves enough clarity for Mental Fight. Blake is not suggesting that everyone grieves all the time from love-suffering. He *is* suggesting that the insecurities of the Selfhood remain all-absorbing. It lives in a perpetual miasma of "grief & fear & love & desire" because it subsists in a restless state of anxiety and self-contradiction. This state expresses itself in a chronic syndrome of attraction-repulsion to others and to everything in the world. Sex roles petrify under these conditions. Thus the Selfhood suffers from ceaselessly thwarted Eros. As a result, there is only the sense of being constantly overwhelmed, and "no time for anything but [these] torments"—no chance of consolidating any ontological confidence and creativity, or ascending into the real vocation of the mind. This is the view from inside of what Urizen saw from outside when he questioned the spectrous dead: "no one answered every one wrapd up / In his own sorrow howld regardless of his words" (FZ 70:42–43, E347).

"Sexual Organization" turns out, in fact, to be bound up with ontological insecurity. When Deism, with its frightening sterile Nature, took over (back at the beginning of history), "The Cities & Villages of Albion became Rock & Sand Unhumanized / The Druid Sons of Albion & the Heavens a Void around unfathomable" (J 63:18–19, E214). Humanity was lost, and its place assumed by merely natural beings for whom anatomy is destiny. Sexual difference defines you; to recognize this is to perceive in turn how helpless, how small a creature you are. Look in the mirror and you can see this for yourself. Now multiply this experience by the number of individuals there are in the world. Blake compresses this whole psychological drama into the extraordinary lines: "No Human Form but Sexual & a little weeping Infant pale reflected / Multitudinous in the Looking Glass of Enitharmon" (J 63:20–21, E214). Sexual difference is linked to materialism, but Blake claims that "Humanity is far above / Sexual Organization," or as Los puts it, "Sexes must vanish & cease / To be, when Albion arises from his dread repose" (J 92: 13–14, E252).

Yet the body in itself is not to blame. And even the barrier or "woven Veil" of sexual disaffection is only symptomatic. The basic obstacle arises from the Selfhood's *aversion* to "commingling." I emphasize the word aversion here because in *Jerusalem* Blake presents the drive to autonomy as a force of its own. Earlier he had thought that suspicion of otherness follows from the Selfhood's defensive nature as a secondary result. But now he regards rejection and disconnection as fundamental instincts of Selfhood, constitutive of it rather than arising from it. The Selfhood has a will to solitude. Chapter 2 opens with Albion's Urizenic repudiation of "Every ornament of perfection, and every labour of love, / In all the Garden of Eden." He associates love, or commingling, with sinfulness, evincing a pathological mistrust of human contact.

> All these ornaments are crimes, they are made by the labours
> Of loves: of unnatural consanguinities and friendships
> Horrid to think of when enquired deeply into; and all

> These hills & valleys are accursed witnesses of Sin
> I therefore condense them into solid rocks, steadfast!
> A foundation and certainty and demonstrative truth:
> That Man be separate from Man.   (28: 6–12, E174)

Blake deliberately uses ambiguous syntax: it is not clear whether the last phrase functions as a definition of the "demonstrative truth" or as the apodosis of a purpose clause. Does Albion wish to establish the fact that man is separate from man, or stipulate that man *should* be separate from man? For a defensive consciousness these are really the same, the desideratum backed up by an assertion of necessity: man ought to be separate from man, and that is because it already is and has to be that way! But why does Albion insist on this? His thoughts about self and other have gotten entangled with the punitive righteousness of the Moral Law, true enough, but the structure of this passage, as it rises to the climax of separation, suggests that the will to solitude is primary. The Moral Law acts out the instinctive aversion to others. As Peter Otto writes, "The Perturbed Man wants to remain within the world of the self" (16). He wants, says Otto, to hunker down "in the middle of [Locke's closet]" so as to savor his secrets and the pleasure of possessing them because he is jealous, like his God (63–64). I argue instead that, as Blake sees it, aversion is radical, the origin not the product of secrecy's attraction. Aversion is a constitutive component of the Selfhood, bound up with its representation of itself as unique, integral, and singular.

One *clings* to solitary subjectivity, as the last refuge of one's reality and substance. The Selfhood seeks isolation, retrenching itself in solitude whenever it can. To engage with otherness is to be dissolved. Before long we will see Albion fleeing from the Divine Family, "lest any should enter his bosom & embrace / His hidden heart" (J 34[38]:8–9, E179). But the result is hardly satisfying. Flight of this kind causes much unneeded suffering, as Blake indicates in drawing the connection to everyday psychological experience. Albion's "cold" rages "against the warmth of Eden" in "loud / Thunders of deadly war." These tumults are "the fever of the human soul," resisting the displacement of Selfhood (J 34[38]:8–9, E179).

Strangely, dread and loneliness prompt greater aversion to otherness. When Albion adduces the terrifying prospect of Eternal Death, he adds a thought unarticulated in the earlier prophetic poems: that Eternal Death is a lonely death. "The shades of death" surround him "Like rocky clouds . . . build[ing him] a gloomy monument of woe" (J 35:16, 18, E181). Fear of death isolates him; and this effect redoubles when he recalls that he must die alone: "Will none accompany me in my death?" The misery of these feelings feeds on itself until it converts loneliness into downright paranoia.

> I have girded round my cloak, and on my feet
> Bound these black shoes of death, & on my hands, death's
>   iron gloves:
> God hath forsaken me, & my friends are become a burden
> A weariness to me, & the human footstep is a terror to me.
>
> (J 35[39]:21–23, E181)

Blake locates Albion's salvation in the dissolution of this dread, and of resistance to the incursions of otherness. "Petrific" Albion turns away "from Universal Love," but the Savior follows him,

> Displaying the Eternal Vision! The Divine Similitude!
> In loves and tears of brothers, sisters, sons, fathers and friends
> Which if Man ceases to behold, he ceases to exist.
>
> (34[38]:11–14, E180)

The Selfhood imagines that it will "die" if it surrenders its integrity to love. And it is right; its self-preservation depends on insularity. But Humanity itself will cease to exist unless it admits love. Overcoming the resistance to others entails removing the Covering Cherub, the dark "opake" obstacle of the Selfhood. Opacity *is* hate; Vision *is* Love. Blake has made the synthesis before, in appositional clusters that equate "the Eternal Great Humanity Divine," the "Divine Vision," Jesus the Savior, and Universal Love. But here Love moves to the forefront. New is the Levinasian idea that the Divine Vision appears in the "loves and tears" of family and friends. This idea supplements the Plotinian model in which the divine impersonal soul is discovered through an "inward turn."[1] I say supplements rather than supplants because Blake still believes that the Divine Vision lives within, "behind" the heart gates, but he now asserts that it also appears "outside"—as it were—in the love of others, rightly beheld and rightly felt. In *Milton* Blake adumbrates this idea in the reunion of Milton with Ololon, who represents not only Milton the prophet's notional "Emanation" but also the actual wives and daughters of the poet. Yet by Love, Blake does not mean sentiment (as Wittgenstein has it, "Love is not a feeling," #504, *Zettel* 66) because of sentiment's manifest connection to fantasy and self-involvement. When the Savior addresses Albion, he declares that love means Mental Fight: "Our wars are wars of life, & wounds of love / With intellectual spears, & long winged arrows of thought" (J 34[38]:14–15, E180). This is the naked encounter–confrontation without the ulterior motives and the delusions of the Selfhood, with its Moral Law. To behold the "Divine Similitude" in the "loves and tears" of others is to *behold* others.

The Barrier between Man and Man

This altruistic ethic explains why Blake intensifies his animus against memory in *Jerusalem*. Blake had always criticized the idea of "memory" foregrounded in the vocabulary of empiricist aesthetics and epistemology. In his antiempiricist polemic at the end of *Milton*, he went so far as to use the phrase "the rotten rags of memory"—associating memory with grave clothes that will be stripped off and abandoned when we are born anew. In that passage Blake represents memory as the antithesis of "Inspiration" and "Imagination," thus culminating a line of thought he had pursued since his early tracts. This relatively transparent handling of memory contrasts with the strange, atmospheric treatment he gives it in *Jerusalem*.

> In Great Eternity, every particular Form gives forth or Emanates
> Its own peculiar Light, & the Form is the Divine Vision
> And the Light is his Garment This is Jerusalem in every Man
> A Tent & Tabernacle of Mutual Forgiveness Male & Female Clothings
> And Jerusalem is called Liberty among the Children of Albion
> But Albion fell down a Rocky fragment from Eternity hurld
> By his own Spectre, who is the Reasoning Power in every Man
> Into his own Chaos, which is the Memory between Man & Man.
>
> (J 54:1–8, E203)

Like Urizen, precipitated out of Eternity when he creates "the soul-shuddering vacuum" of his individuality, Albion falls from the commonality of the shared "Divine Vision" into his own private Chaos, which Blake also defines as "the Memory" separating person from person. This is a fascinating new definition of memory. It takes on a rich psychological meaning in which it undergirds the solitary sense of self.

How did Blake progress from the antiempiricist to the psychological critique of memory? He did not change his mind, but rather he developed his original intuitions. In his marginalia *to The Works of Sir Joshua Reynolds* (1798), Blake was already arguing that the reduction of knowledge to memory displaces Divine Vision. Reynolds is an expositor of empiricist aesthetics, one who believes with Locke that all knowledge is acquired and that, therefore, achievement in art can arise only from instruction and experience—in Blake's scornful paraphrase—"Genius May Be Taught & . . . all Pretence to Inspiration is a Lie" (E642). Blake counters with the Platonic view: "Reynolds Thinks that Man Learns all that he Knows I say on the Contrary That Man Brings All that he has or Can have Into the World with him. Man is Born Like a Garden ready Planted & Sown" (E656). Blake later refers to this inborn knowledge by its philosophical name, "innate ideas." (By contrast, the first section of Locke's *Essay Concerning Human Understanding* argues that there are no innate ideas). And he places artistic intuition in this category: "Knowledge of Ideal Beauty. Is Not to be Acquired It is Born with us Innate Ideas are in Every Man born with him. They are (truly) Himself. The Man who says that we have No Innate Ideas must be a Fool & a Knave" (E648). So far Blake is restating his programmatic attack on empiricism, but he makes a perspicuous leap when he adds that the demystification of genius goes far back: "This Opinion originates in the Greeks Caling the Muses Daughters of Memory" (E642). The myth suggests that artists copy rather than create. In this polemical context, Blake defines "memory" reductively or pejoratively as an acquisition of the merely empirical self. It is pointedly *not* related to the other Greek idea of remembering—Platonic anagnorisis, or the recollection of innate ideas, and hence of the soul's transcendent origin. Blake's "memory" is the antithesis of Platonic recollection; it dodges or even masks "innate ideas," replacing them with the accretions of experience.

Blake takes this definition of memory straight from empiricism. In Locke's epistemology, "impressions" (merely) leave traces on the mind that are then processed into knowledge, so that all knowledge begins in a species of memory. The chapter of Locke's *Essay* on "Identity and Diversity" specifies that personal identity or the self consists of present consciousness and its memories, no more. Blake responds in "There Is No Natural Religion b" by arguing the Lockean subject is locked in the prison of memory or the "ratio" of all we have already known. The "ratio" is the identity of this subject—the "I," the Reason, the self established by the continuity of memory. Thus this "I" binds itself to the egoism of memory, treasuring its stock of testimonies to its own uniqueness. This is identity formation as narcissistic self-confinement: "He who sees the Ratio only sees himself only" (TNNR b, E3). The empiricist subject, whose sense of self includes only the "I" and its memories, sinks back into the meager empirical self, with no access to other people, to living nature, or to her or his own "Immortal Spirit."

This idea of self-enclosure is the key to Blake's psychology of memory. Obviously we require memory to function cognitively at all; what Blake anathematizes under the name "Memory" is the memory that goes into identity formation. Urizen, embodiment of the Ratio, exemplifies the self-enclosure of the empiricist subject; consider the images of him as blind, or locked in a stony sleep, or curled up in a fetal clutch. In "Night the Eighth" of *The Four Zoas,* Urizen is transformed into the statue of a serpent, nightmarishly pent in his own being: "His wisdom still remaind & all his memory stord with woe / And still his stony form remaind in the Abyss immense . . . memory strives to augment his ruthfulness" (FZ 106:34–35; 107:10, E382). Within him the accumulation of memories has gradually consolidated his identity at the cost of self-confinement. His form is impassive but his inner life is tormenting: he is like Dante's Satan, frozen solid but still shedding tears. The cloud cannot be dispelled because Urizen has (he believes) no power of spontaneous creative refreshment. He is backward looking, trapped in the "dull round" of yesterday.

Thus memory passivates; it underscores finitude and helplessness. Good or bad, memories are by definition recollections of what is gone. They serve to remind us that we are powerless in relation to time, which is rapidly converting everything into memory. As the ninetieth Psalm says: "we spend our years as a tale that is told." But under Utopian conditions, the momentum of time will not be allied with finitude. In the great scene of reconciliation at the end of *Jerusalem,* Heaven and the Four Faces of Humanity will go "forward forward irresistable from Eternity to Eternity" (J 98:27, E257). But the temporality of memory is the antithesis of the Eternal Now: The Eternal Now expands infinitely in this moment while memory stops here, feebly reaching backward.

Memory assures the empirical self of its weakness and mortality. It ratifies the self's conception of itself as singular and unique at the expense of assuring it that it is finite and solitary. It also concentrates the isolation of consciousness and deepens the obscurity of selfhood. In *Jerusalem* Albion's Spectre tells him he is "a fortuitous concourse of memorys accumulated & lost" (J 29:8, E175). One finally feels oneself to be no integral self but rather a bundle of disconnected material. "Memory, which the empiricists saw as defining the self, is in Blake's view the symptom of a fragmented consciousness that interprets reality as a collection of discrete phenomena instead of as a single Form" (Damrosch 27). The reality that memory interprets as mosaicized in this way is not only exterior but interior. The inner world of Natural Man is a world of obscure impulses and dark memories, material that can barely be owned by the central consciousness. The self has been reduced to what Melanie Klein terms "inner chaos," provoking that anxiety of interiority from which many Blake characters suffer. This corrosive effect of memory contrasts with the recuperative power attributed to it in the Wordsworthian tradition. But Blake would argue that Wordsworth is debilitatingly "haunted" by his memories in just the way he, Blake, would predict.

Memory blockades each consciousness in a drift of half lights, one's own necessarily absorbing "Chaos." It plays this role because it consolidates the sense of identity, the idea that this particular self, this "I," is unique. Memory individuates and by individuating it isolates. It sets one's own interests against those of others. Frye's description of memory in Blake stresses its role in creating antagonism toward what is "outside": "For in the state of 'memory' or reflection we withdraw into ourselves and are locked up there with our own keys in a dark spiritual solitude in which we are unable to conceive activity except in terms of hindrance and restraint" (57). Memory promotes separation and, hence, antagonism. Thus in *Jerusalem* Blake names it as the means by which consciousness succeeds in barricading itself. The Selfhood willfully erects this barrier "between Man & Man."

What is the solution? It is not as if we can do away with memory. At its end, *Jerusalem* images Memory in its redeemed form. Even empiricism is redeemed, or at least its creators are: "Bacon & Newton & Locke" arrive in triumph, accompanying the Chariots of the Almighty Humanity Divine "at the

clangor of the Arrows of Intellect" (J 98:7, E257). The apocalypse reached in
Jerusalem represents mental transformation: the intellect is remade, all its
debased forms rotated into Edenic ones. The four Zoas who attend the Char-
iots "converse together in Visionary forms dramatic." In this new world of
provocative interchange, memory will assume a creative nature. The Zoas
are building "exemplars of Memory and of Intellect . . . according to the
wonders Divine / Of Human Imagination" (J 98:30–32, E258). Memory will
become an aid to imagination rather than displacing it. The Intellect itself
will cease to be identified as Reason, and the Symbolic order will lose its
power to alienate and oppress: "every Word and Every Character" will grow
"Human." Forgiveness will replace Moral Law. And it is perhaps in this trans-
formation that memory will be most fully redeemed if we recall that "For-
giveness of Sins . . . is Self Annihilation." The memories to which the Self-
hood clings, and by which it maintains its identity, will give way to neutral
memories, surviving without their power and their sting. For that is what
forgiveness does: it surrenders the past.[2]

And yet there is a hitch. Blake's praise of love and forgiveness should be
contrasted with his chilling couplet (from the verse prologue to Chapter 2 of
Jerusalem): "A man's worst enemies are those / Of his own house & family"
(J 27:81–82, E173). These lines surely represent a burst of antagonism on
Blake's part. In context Blake is denouncing "soft Family-Love," "cruel Patri-
archal pride," and "the "Religion of Generation" (J 41[46]:26–27, E189). In
other words, he criticizes the species of the insularity, greed, and tyranny
that can afflict the nuclear family. Familial self-absorption derails one's voca-
tion as a human being and a prophet. In *The Four Zoas* the Children of Man
have visions; they call out each to each, "What are we terrors to one an-
other. Come O brethren," but their cries fall on deaf ears; some say they see
no visions, while "many stood silent & busied in their families" (FZ 28:16,
E318). This is a very sharp indictment of domesticity. Blake implies that the
closeness of families may be, not the type of love, but rather a travesty of it.
Thus Los at one point denounces the destructive false intimacy that has re-
placed spiritual love.

> But here the affectionate touch of the tongue is closd
>   in by deadly teeth
> And the soft smile of friendship & the open dawn of benevolence

> Become a net & a trap, & every energy renderd cruel,
> Till the existence of friendship & benevolence is denied.
>
> (J 38[43]:24–27, E185)

False or "Corporeal" friendship—the friendship of those in one's own house and family—is so ambivalent and so *unfriendly* that one despairs of human contact. What is the nature of this discouragement? Perhaps we should think of what the Swiss educator Johann Heinrich Pestalozzi remarked, as quoted by Ralph Waldo Emerson at the end of "The American Scholar": "I learned that no man in God's wide earth is either willing or able to help any other man" (70). That dark thought is liable to come to anyone. Blake himself seems to conclude in some moments that forms of real friendship have been universally diverted into their opposites: coldness, selfishness, and hostility.

> And the two Sources of Life in Eternity, Hunting and War,
> Are become the Sources of dark & bitter Death & of
>   corroding Hell:
> The open heart is shut up in integuments of frozen silence.
>
> (J 38[43]:31–33, E185)

It is enough to make each person give up and resign herself to solitude—to "frozen silence"—even the prophet.

But regarding one's family as one's "worst enemies" raises the prospect of an awful isolation. As Bloom comments, Los's speech provides "a palpable indication of Blake's spiritual loneliness" (E937), although Blake did not, of course, resign himself to "frozen silence." In an autobiographical parenthesis just a few plates prior, Blake thanks the English language for giving Los the tools to act "against / Albion's melancholy, who must else have been a Dumb despair." Blake is grateful because in poetry he is able to break the vicious cycle of remaining mute and hopeless. But clearly Blake also desired more Spiritual Friendship—as Los does, so often lonely as he forges in the darkness. Apparently, then, there are two forms of solitude, that of the prophet and that of the Selfhood. Blake makes a perspicuous theoretical distinction between them, but emotionally they are not so easy to tell apart, and this will pose a dilemma for the prophet. In Los's speech, the loneliness of the Selfhood and the loneliness of the prophet converge. Willed aversion and balked initiative come to the same thing. Even the *open* heart is shut up in integuments of frozen silence.

In the wars of Eternity, contention is vital contact; in our world, the effort fails, leaving greater loneliness in its wake.

> For the Soldier who fights for Truth, calls his enemy his brother:
> They fight & contend for life, & not for eternal death!
> But here the Soldier strikes, & a dead corse falls at his feet.
> Nor Daughter nor Sister nor Mother come forth to
>   embosom the Slain!
> But Death! Eternal Death remains in the Valleys of Peor.

(J 38[43]:41–45, E185)

In a better world, Mental Fight is cerebral and invigorating and does not lead to death. In the unredeemed world—"here"—war takes a bodily and, therefore, truly mortal form. But here the war of the spirit is also fatal. For in this passage Blake writes less of physical battle than of the prophet's attempt to wage Mental Fight in an unaccommodating world, where he who tries to befriend inadvertently "kills" what he touches, meeting only inertness, and where no mother or sister offers tenderness or care. The prophet seeking Spiritual Friendship is repulsed, plunged back into Albion's solitary body of this death. In *Milton* Beth-Peor, the burial place of Moses, provides the ground where Milton wrestles with Urizen. In *Jerusalem* Beth-Peor becomes the site of defeated intimacy. Despondent, Los concludes that the sons of Albion "accumulate / A World in which Man is by Nature the Enemy of Man."

The last and subtlest obstruction is the very rectitude of the prophet, which in part causes his loneliness and the fatality of his touch. *Jerusalem* highlights this lingering problem despite its apocalyptic conclusion. From time to time Los is seen "becoming what he beholds." *Jerusalem* repeats this formulation as one character or redemptive possibility after another becomes the disaster it witnesses. With this image of contagion, Blake acknowledges our vulnerability to despair. Los experiences it too, but as we would anticipate, he comes back to battle it vigorously. Yet we see him resisting the love or "comminging" that entails the dissolution of the Selfhood. In Chapter 4 of *Jerusalem*, there is a final confrontation among Los, Enitharmon, and the Spectre of Urthona in which Los tries to make Enitharmon subservient, she re-exerts her own will, and the Spectre is pleased with the rift he has brought about. The prophetic spirit has to regather and concenter itself, overcoming the self-divisions created by worldliness. In its struggle with the Female Will, it is combating temptations to the ego or Selfhood—the lure of pleasures and rewards that can come from the world "outside," and that are, therefore, subject to vain "love & jealousy." These seductions emanate from "Sussex shore," or Felpham, where Blake himself had been subject to them, as he self-reprovingly shows in *Milton*. In an earlier scene, the Spectre cries, weary of Los's demand for unrewarded labor and sacrifice. Now he delights to find the prophetic will divided and disabled because that gives free rein to his cravings and ambitions.

> Thus joyd the Spectre in the dusky fires of Los's Forge, eyeing
> Enitharmon who at her shining Looms sings lulling cadences
> While Los stood at his Anvil in wrath the victim of their love
> And hate; dividing the Space of Love with brazen Compasses.

> (J 88:44–47, E247)

The sadomasochistic engagement of Enitharmon with the Spectre of Urthona leaves Los "the victim of their love / And hate"; he is paralyzed, torn between the competing claims of transcendent intuition and worldly desire. He reacts by disassociating himself, standing apart from "the Space of Love" and "dividing" it.

How surprising to find Los in the posture of Urizen, the Ancient of Days, measuring his subject world with compasses! Some final resistance is being roused in Los, some Urizenic impulse to solitary dominion that requires the rejection of love and of otherness. Perhaps, like Milton's last monologue, this moment dramatizes the subtle tenacity of self-assertion. The prophet's sense of integrity may be hard to distinguish from the obstinacy of the Selfhood. Certainly, if the Selfhood is as hostile as Blake seems more and more to think, it will exercise its antagonism in the prophet in a form peculiar to prophecy. Blake is only being honest when he acknowledges in his own avatar this persisting node of Selfhood, this last obstacle to self-recreation. But it is poignant that the hindrance to freedom in the individual mind should come down to this: wariness of "the Space of Love."

The fulfillment of love and the fulfillment of self-reformation seem subtly to clash at the end of *Jerusalem*. The sexes are reconciled in the poem's concluding Utopian vision, but the fate of the "Real Man" is more complicated. As in a Shakespearean comedy, all the characters in the story—Albion, the Zoas, the empiricists, the Human Body, and so forth—come together on the stage in a glow of transformation. Male and Female are united by "Mercy

& Loving-kindness laying / Open the hidden Heart" (J 97:12–13, E256). Beyond sexual difference, human and human are united by "Forgiveness of Sins which is Self-Annihilation" (J 98:23, E257). Forgiveness exacts self-sacrifice insofar as it requires suppression of the ego's demands, and Blake had intimated as much before. But now he goes farther, suggesting that benevolence is a zero-sum economy: to be good to another (say, in the form of forgiveness) is to subtract from the goodness remaining to oneself.

Socrates contends that "care of the self," which brings understanding, ultimately leads one to behave altruistically.[3] Against Socrates, Blake now emphatically argues that one cannot care for oneself—or, at least, for one's "Selfhood"—and care for another at the same time; "every kindness to another is a little Death" (J 96:27, E256). We grasp the psychology: denial of the ego is painful, and irreal if it is not experienced as such. But is virtue then its own reward? For Blake, the mortification of the ego is to be desired—if it spurs one on to annihilate the Selfhood. And such annihilation brings with it a reward— the attainment of Divine Vision—but this reward may not be ready and immediate. Thus at this juncture in his thought, Blake seems to be suggesting that altruism and care of the self cannot be synchronous. He inverts the priorities of both Socrates's ethics and what had been his own. Although self-annihilation can be construed as healthy in the end—it counts as "care of the self" in the deep sense of self-remaking—self-remaking is no longer the primary goal. It becomes the side effect not the source of altruism.

Blake may be reorienting his ethics at the end of *Jerusalem*. His prescription no longer starts with self-transformation but with Love, a turning away from the inner life toward the other. In *Milton* "Self-Annihilation" was required for spiritual reformation, and that reformation allowed for the perfection of the prophet's mission, his altruistic work in the world. But *Jerusalem* apparently cuts out the inward turning to remake the self. Self-annihilation skips straight to "Love." In fact, it defines love. Thus Blake's Jesus identifies "Man" in his full sense—when he rises into his true divinity—with his capacity for self-sacrifice.

> And if God dieth not for Man & giveth not himself
> Eternally for Man Man could not exist. for Man is Love:
> As God is Love: every kindness to another is a little Death
> In the Divine Image nor can Man exist but by Brotherhood.
>
> (J 96:25–28, E256)

This is a radical ontological redefinition of *agape* or Charity in which "Man," or the full and divine potential of humanity, remains unrealized until the self is annihilated on another's behalf. Albion asks rhetorically, "Cannot man exist without Mysterious / Offering of Self for Another" (J 96:20–21, E256). The answer is no: true humanity does not come into being until self-sacrifice is done. When Blake's Jesus says that the true "Man" exists only "by Brotherhood," he means the Brotherhood established by self-sacrifice. But this definition of "Man"—the Eternal Great Humanity Divine—as the *product* of self-sacrifice is new for Blake, who usually represents the "Real Man" as an internal capacity to be accessed by means of self-discovery. On his deathbed in 1827, he again called "The Real Man . . . The Imagination which Liveth for Ever" (E783), but here in *Jerusalem* he seems to open up a gap between "Man," "Brotherhood," and "Love," on the one hand, and "Vision," "Imagination," and "Prophecy," on the other. At this point, there is a significant difference, even if the concepts are related, between "Love" and "Imagination," since Love has to come first.

In *Milton* self-reformation, and thus self-annihilation, were ends in themselves. With the dissolution of the Selfhood, one rose by one's own power into possession of one's divinity. One could secure the end of transformation by means of self-examination and self-correction. The journey could be solitary. *Jerusalem* revises this view. The first act in the new era of the self no longer follows Plotinus's "Withdraw into yourself and look." The ancient *convertere ad se* is reversed. Now it is: empty yourself and turn outside. You cannot "exist" in a new form except "by Brotherhood." The avenue to self-remaking opens by way of attention to the other. Thus the turning point in *Jerusalem* occurs not with a crisis of self-recognition or a healing of self-division, as it does in *Milton,* but with a gesture of true self-abandonment, when Albion throws himself willingly "into the Furnaces of affliction."

If I am reading the poem aright, and Blake did change his mind, why did he do so? Is there is an element of redaction in this new view? The preoccupations of *Jerusalem* suggest that he may have been recalibrating the tenacity of the Selfhood and the efficacy of self-reformation. Perhaps Blake was losing faith in the project of solitary self-remaking, as he recognized the obstacles inhering in the nature of the self. Can the self ever become translucent to itself? Can it pass through itself in intertranspicuous orbs? *Jerusalem* shows more dubiety on this score than Blake's earlier poems; it may have seemed to

Blake less likely that the self could transform itself of its own volition and by its own powers. In *Jerusalem*, the stubborn Selfhood remains; the potential for self-trickery, and the will to solitude. Even Los the prophet is capable of self-deceit and aversion to Love. One must beware one's own Brazen Compasses. If the prophet himself chooses to dodge the "Space of Love" by mimicking Urizen, then perhaps the self can neither perfectly right itself nor set itself free from the essential claustrophobia of subjectivity.

Notes

Introduction

1. More recent historians of religion have challenged the notion that there was any such thing as a "Gnostic religion," that is, a unified body of Gnostic thinking or practice. That may be, but for our purposes the term *Gnosticism* remains useful insofar as it designates a complex of ideas Blake would have known under that term and which he would have valued. I continue to quote from Jonas because, of all the scholars of Gnosticism, he is most attentive to its existential purchase. Readers who wish to learn more about the scholarly controversy surrounding the term Gnosticism should consult Michael A. Williams, *Rethinking "Gnosticism": An Argument for Dismantling a Dubious Category* (Princeton, N.J.: Princeton Univ. Press, 1996) and Karen L. King, *What Is Gnosticism?* (Cambridge, Mass.: Harvard Univ. Press, 2003).

2. I borrow this phrase from the title of Martin and Barresi's earlier book, *Naturalization of the Soul: Self and Personal Identity in the Eighteenth Century* (London: Routledge, 2000).

3. This is a literary-critical commonplace. For an example, see Roy Porter's Introduction to *Rewriting the Self.*

1. Empiricism and Despair

1. Hall's stimulating book *Materialism and the Myths of Blake* studies the evolution of Blake's thoughts about materialism with some attention to the despair of Natural Man. As she says, she wishes to emphasize "metaphysics not psychology."

2. But compare with Steve Clark, "'Labouring at the Resolute Anvil': Blake's Response to Locke," for a refreshing account of Blake's secret sympathies with Locke.

3. See, for example, E. P. Thompson, "Blake's 'London.'"
4. See David Riede, "Blake's *Milton*," for a reading of Blake as a critic of St. Paul.
5. Compare with Thomas Frosch, *The Awakening of Albion,* for a compelling counterargument.
6. Blake's invocation of this term has a distinctly misogynistic character, although I believe that insofar as it has any empirical purchase, it refers to effects of socialization, not to any essentially "female" trait. The issue of Blake's attitude toward women is a very vexed one. For a recent summary of the debate, see Tom Hayes, "William Blake's Androgynous Ego-Ideal." The most helpful discussion of the subject I know is Alicia Ostriker, "Desire Gratified and Ungratified," which argues that Blake held several different views, compatible somehow to him although they do not seem so to us.
7. For comparisons of Urizen to the Demiurge, see Andrew Lincoln, *Spiritual History,* p. 51; Henry Summerfield, *A Guide to the Books of William Blake for Innocent and Experienced Readers,* p. 123; and Morton D. Paley, *Energy and Imagination,* p. 67.
8. Peter J. Sorenson, among others, treats Blake as a recapitulator of Gnostic symbols; see *William Blake's Gnostic Myth* (Lewiston, N.Y.: Edwin Mellen Press, 1995).
9. See Keri Davies, "William Blake's Mother."
10. See Frank B. Evans, "Platonic Scholarship in Eighteenth-Century England" and "Thomas Taylor, Platonist of the Romantic Period." For a recent account of what Blake knew about Gnosticism, and how much of it came to him through popular sources, see A. D. Nuttall, *The Alternative Trinity,* pp. 200-25. Also compare Stuart Peterfreund's chapter on "Blake, Priestly and the 'Gnostic Moment,'" pp. 85-104, in *William Blake in a Newtonian World.*

2. Wordsworth, Plato, and Blake

1. Unless otherwise specified, quotations come from the 1805 version of *The Prelude.* I give book and line numbers followed by a page reference to the Norton Critical edition of *The Prelude.*
2. But compare with Raymond Martin, "Locke's Psychology of Personal Identity."
3. For recent subtle articulations of Wordsworth and empiricism, see Keith Thomas, *Wordsworth and Philosophy,* and Cathy Caruth, *Empirical Truths and Critical Fictions.*
4. Indeed, Klein's description of the psyche as a repository for "innumerable inner objects" in an ever-mutating configuration recalls Hume's notorious view of the mind as "a bundle or collection of different perceptions, which succeed each other with an inconceivable rapidity and are in a perpetual flux and movement" (252). A perception and an inner object are two very different creatures. Nonetheless, I would argue that there is a meaningful parallel between these two representations of interiority, and that they are in fact historically related, the ground for psychoanalysis having been laid by the psychological translation of Locke that Wordsworth and others of his time performed.

5. Blake excelled in detecting bad faith. Doctor Johnson declared that the Bible cannot be "understood at all by the *unlearned*," evincing an elitism Blake was bound to reject, but he also perceives that Johnson's esoteric argument is self-belying: "The Beauty of the Bible is that the most Ignorant & Simple Minds Understand it Best— Was Johnson hired to Pretend to Religious Terrors while he was an Infidel or how was it" (E667). This virtual interchange appears in Blake's annotations to Thornton's *The Lord's Prayer, Newly Translated* (London, 1827). Blake is responding to Johnson as quoted by Thornton.

6. I have given detailed readings of Wordsworth's major autobiographical poems along these lines in an earlier book, and it seemed superfluous to repeat them here. The curious reader can find them in the Wordsworth chapter of *The Poetics of Disappointment*.

3. The Four Zoas

1. David Fuller thinks so too: "it is in many ways his most exciting and successful work" (88).

4. Milton

1. A. D. Nuttall's Gnosticism is an inversion of the trinity in which Son becomes superior to Father. In a compelling discussion of Milton, to which most of *The Alternative Trinity* is devoted, he suggests that *Paradise Lost* shared this form of Blake's Gnosticism.

2. When the devils explore Hell in Book II, they find "Rocks, caves, lakes, fens, bogs, dens, and shades of death, / A Universe of death" (*Paradise Lost* II.621–22).

5. Jerusalem

1. Compare Phillip Cary's account of the "inward turn" in Plotinus. He contrasts the Plotinian image of the inner life with Locke's "picture of a dark room where there is nothing to see but images projected within" (5).

2. Herbert Tucker pointed this out to me in a Q&A at the annual meeting of the North American Society for the Study of Romanticism, September 3, 2006.

3. See Michel Foucault's seminars of January 6 and 13, 1982, *Hermeneutics*, pp. 25–79.

Bibliography

Ackroyd, Peter. *Blake: A Biography.* New York: Knopf, 1996.

Altizer, Thomas, J. *The New Apocalypse: The Radical Christian Vision of William Blake.* East Lansing: Michigan State Univ. Press, 1967.

Augustine, Saint. *Confessions.* Translated by F. H. Sheed. Indianapolis: Hackett, 1993.

Barnstone, Willis, and Marvin Meyer, eds. *The Gnostic Bible.* Boston: New Seeds Books, 2006.

Belsey, Catherine. "Literature, History, Politics." In *Contexts for Criticism.* 4th ed. Edited by Donald Keesey, 427–36. New York: McGraw-Hill, 2003.

Bentley, G. E., Jr., ed. *Blake Records.* Oxford: Clarendon, 1969.

Blake, William. *The Complete Poems.* Edited by Alicia Ostriker. London: Penguin, 1978.

———. *The Complete Poetry and Prose of William Blake.* 2nd ed. Edited by David Erdman with commentary by Harold Bloom. Berkeley: Univ. of California Press, 1982.

———. *Milton: A poem.* The Illuminated Books, vol. 5. Edited by Robert N. Essick and Joseph Viscomi. Princeton, N.J.: Princeton Univ. Press, 1993.

———. *Songs of Innocence and of Experience.* The Illuminated Books, vol. 2. Edited by Andrew Lincoln. Princeton, N.J.: Princeton Univ. Press, 1991.

———. *The Urizen Books.* The Illuminated Books, vol 6. Edited by David Worrall. Princeton, N.J.: Princeton Univ. Press, 1995.

Caruth, Cathy. *Empirical Truths and Critical Fictions: Locke, Wordsworth, Kant, Freud.* Baltimore: Johns Hopkins Univ. Press, 1991.

Cary, Phillip. *Augustine's Invention of the Inner Self: The Legacy of a Christian Platonist.* Oxford: Oxford Univ. Press, 2000.

Castle, Terry. *The Female Thermometer: Eighteenth-Century Culture and the Invention of the Uncanny.* New York: Oxford, 1995.

Clark, Steve. "'Labouring at the Resolute Anvil': Blake's Response to Locke." In *Blake in the Nineties,* edited by Steve Clark and David Worrall, 133–52. New York: St. Martin's Press, 1999.

Coleridge, Samuel Taylor. *Biographia Literaria.* Princeton, N.J.: Princeton Univ. Press, 1985.

Curran, Stuart. "Blake and the Gnostic Hyle: A Double Negative." *Blake Studies* 4, no. 2 (1972): 117–33.

———. "The Structures of *Jerusalem.*" In *Blake's Sublime Allegory: Essays on "The Four Zoas," "Milton," and "Jerusalem,"* edited by Stuart Curran and Joseph Anthony Wittreich Jr., 329–46. Madison: Univ. of Wisconsin Press, 1973.

Damon, S. Foster. *A Blake Dictionary: The Ideas and Symbols of William Blake.* 1965. Reprint, 3rd ed. Hanover, N.H.: Univ. Press of New England, 1988.

Damrosch, Leopold. *Symbol and Truth in Blake's Myth.* Princeton, N.J.: Princeton Univ. Press, 1982.

Davies, Keri. "William Blake's Mother: A New Identification." *Blake: An Illustrated Quarterly* 33, no. 2 (1999): 36–50.

Emerson, Ralph Waldo. *Essays and Lectures.* New York: The Library of America, 1983.

Evans, Frank B. "Platonic Scholarship in Eighteenth-Century England." *Modern Philology* 41, no. 2 (1943): 103–10.

———. "Thomas Taylor, Platonist of the Romantic Period." *PMLA* 55, no. 4 (1940): 1060–79.

Foucault, Michel. *The Care of the Self.* Vol. 3 of *The History of Sexuality.* Translated by Robert Hurley. New York: Random House, 1986.

———. *The Hermeneutics of the Subject.* Translated by Graham Burchell. New York: Picador, 2005.

Frosch, Thomas. *The Awakening of Albion: The Renovation of the Body in the Poetry of William Blake.* Ithaca, N.Y.: Cornell Univ. Press, 1974.

Frye, Northrop. *Fearful Symmetry.* 1949. Reprint. Princeton, N.J.: Princeton Univ. Press, 1968.

Fuller, David. *Blake's Heroic Argument.* London: Croom Helm, 1988.

Goslee, Nancy Moore. "'Soul-shudd'ring Vacuum': Space for Subjects in Later Blake." *European Romantic Review* 15, no. 3 (2004): 391–407.

Grob, Alan. *The Philosophic Mind: A Study of Wordsworth's Poetry and Thought, 1797–1805.* Columbus: Ohio State Univ. Press, 1973.

Hall, Mary. *Materialism and the Myths of Blake.* New York: Garland, 1988.

Harper, George Mills. *The Neoplatonism of William Blake.* Chapel Hill: Univ. of North Carolina Press, 1961.

Hartman, Geoffrey. *Wordsworth's Poetry, 1787–1814.* New Haven, Conn.: Yale Univ. Press, 1964.

Hayes, Tom. "William Blake's Androgynous Ego-Ideal." *ELH* 71 (2004): 141–65.

Hume, David. *A Treatise of Human Nature.* London: Penguin, 1985.

James, William. *The Varieties of Religious Experience.* London: Longman's, 1905.

John, Donald. "They Became What They Beheld: Theodicy and Regeneration in Milton, Law and Blake." In *Radicalism in British Literary Culture: 1650–1830.* Edited by

Timothy Mortin and Nigel Smith, 86–100. Cambridge: Cambridge Univ. Press, 2002.

Jonas, Hans. *The Gnostic Religion*. 2nd ed. Boston: Beacon, 1963.

———. "The Soul in Gnosticism and Plotinus." In *Philosophical Essays*, 324–35. Englewood Cliffs, N.J.: Prentice-Hall, 1974.

Kant, Immanuel. *The Critique of Judgement*. Translated by James Creed Meredith. Oxford: Clarendon Press, 1973.

Kierkegaard, Søren. *Concluding Unscientific Postscript*. Edited by Howard V. Hong and Edna H. Hong. Princeton, N.J.: Princeton Univ. Press, 1992.

King, Karen L. *What Is Gnosticism?* Cambridge, Mass.: Harvard Univ. Press, 2003.

Klein, Melanie. "On the Sense of Loneliness." In *Envy and Gratitude and Other Works: 1946–63*, 300–14. London: Hogarth, 1975.

Krell, David Farrell. "General Introduction: The Question of Being." In Martin Heidegger, *Basic Writings*, edited by David Farrell Krell. New York: Harper Collins, 1977.

Lacan, Jacques. *The Four Fundamental Concepts of Psychoanalysis*. The Seminar of Jacques Lacan, Book 11. Edited by Jacques-Alain Miller, translated by Alan Sheridan. New York: Norton, 1981.

Lincoln, Andrew. *Spiritual History: A Reading of William Blake's* Vala *or* The Four Zoas. Oxford: Oxford University Press, 1996.

Locke, John. *An Essay Concerning Human Understanding*. Edited by Peter H. Nidditch. Oxford: Clarendon, 1975.

Martin, Raymond. "Locke's Psychology of Personal Identity." *Journal of the History of Philosophy* 38 (2000): 41–61.

———, and John Barresi. *Naturalization of the Soul: Self and Personal Identity in the Eighteenth Century*. London: Routledge, 2000.

———, and John Barresi. *The Rise and Fall of Self and Soul; An Intellectual History of Personal Identity*. New York: Columbia, 2006.

Milton, John. *Paradise Lost*. Edited by Gordon Teskey. New York: Norton, 2005.

Nuttall, A. D. *The Alternative Trinity: Gnostic Heresy in Marlowe, Milton and Blake*. Oxford: Oxford Univ. Press, 1998.

———. *A Common Sky: Philosophy and the Literary Imagination*. Berkeley: Univ. of California Press, 1974.

Ostriker, Alicia. "Desire Gratified and Ungratified: William Blake and Sexuality." *Critical Essays on William Blake*. Edited by Hazard Adams, 90–110. Boston: G. K. Hall & Co., 1991.

Otto, Peter. *Constructive Vision and Visionary Deconstruction: Los, Eternity, and the Productions of Time in the Later Poetry of William Blake*. Oxford: Clarendon, 1991.

Paley, Morton D. *The Continuing City: William Blake's Jerusalem*. Oxford: Clarendon, 1983.

———. *Energy and Imagination: A Study of the Development of Blake's Thought*. Oxford: Clarendon, 1970.

———. *The Traveler in the Evening: The Last Works of William Blake*. Oxford: Oxford Univ. Press, 2003.

Pelikan, Jaroslav. *The Emergence of the Catholic Tradition (100–600)*. Vol. 1 of *The Christian Tradition: A History of the Development of Doctrine*. Chicago: Univ. of Chicago Press, 1971.

Peterfreund, Stuart. *William Blake in a Newtonian World*. Norman: Univ. of Oklahoma Press, 1998.

Plato. *Complete Works*. Edited by By John M. Cooper. Indianapolis: Hackett, 1997.

——. *Republic*. Translated by Robin Waterfield. Oxford: Oxford Univ. Press, 1993.

Plotinus. *The Enneads*. Translated by Stephen MacKenna. Reprint. New York: Penguin, 1991.

——. *Five Books of Plotinus*. Translated by Thomas Taylor. London: E. Jeffrey, 1794.

Porter, Roy, ed. *Rewriting the Self: Histories from the Renaissance to the Present*. London: Routledge, 1997.

Quinney, Laura. *The Poetics of Disappointment: Wordsworth to Ashbery*. Charlottesville: Univ. of Virginia Press, 1999.

Raine, Kathleen. *Blake and the New Age*. London: George Allen and Unwin, 1979.

——. *Blake and Tradition*. 2 vols. Princeton, N.J.: Princeton Univ. Press, 1968.

Reed, Edward S. *From Soul to Mind: The Emergence of Psychology from Erasmus Darwin to William James*. New Haven, Conn.: Yale Univ. Press, 1997.

Riede, David. "Blake's *Milton:* On Membership in the Church Paul." In *Re-Membering Milton: Essays on the Texts and Tradition*. Edited by Mary Nyquist and Margaret W. Ferguson, 257–77. New York: Methuen, 1988.

Rousseau, Jean-Jacques. *Confessions*. Translated by Angela Scholar. Oxford: Oxford Univ. Press, 2000.

Shelley, Percy. *Shelley's Poetry and Prose*. Edited by Donald Reiman and Neil Fraistat. New York: Norton, 2002.

Siegel, Jerrold. *The Idea of the Self: Thought and Experience in Western Europe since the Seventeenth Century*. Cambridge: Cambridge University Press, 2005.

Sorenson, Peter J. *William Blake's Gnostic Myth*. Lewiston, N.Y.: Edwin Mellen Press, 1995.

Spector, Sheila. *"Glorious Incomprehensible": The Development of Blake's Kabbalistic Language*. Lewisburg, Pa.: Bucknell University Press, 2001.

Stevens, Wallace. *The Collected Poems*. New York: Random House, 1982.

Stevenson, Robert Louis. *The Complete Stories of Robert Louis Stevenson*. New York: Modern Library, 2002.

Summerfield, Henry. *A Guide to the Books of William Blake for Innocent and Experienced Readers*. Gerrards Cross, Bucks, UK: Colin Smythe, 1998.

Taylor, Charles. *Sources of the Self*. Cambridge, Mass.: Harvard Univ. Press, 1992.

Taylor, Thomas. *Thomas Taylor the Platonist: Selected Writings*. Edited by Kathleen Raine and George Mills Harper. Princeton, N.J.: Princeton Univ. Press, 1969.

Thomas, Keith. *Wordsworth and Philosophy: Empiricism and Transcendentalism in the Poetry*. Ann Arbor, Mich.: UMI Research Press, 1989.

Thompson, E. P. "Blake's 'London.'" In *Interpreting Blake*, edited by Michael Phillips. Cambridge: Cambridge Univ. Press, 1978.

————. *Witness against the Beast: William Blake and the Moral Law.* New York: The New Press, 1993.

Tuveson, Ernest. *The Imagination as a Means of Grace: Locke and the Aesthetics of Romanticism.* Berkeley: Univ. of California Press, 1960.

Wilkie, Brian, and Mary Lynn Johnson. *Blake's* Four Zoas: *The Design of a Dream.* Cambridge, Mass.: Harvard Univ. Press, 1978.

Williams, Michael A. *Rethinking "Gnosticism": An Argument for Dismantling a Dubious Category.* Princeton, N.J.: Princeton Univ. Press, 1996.

Wittgenstein, Ludwig. *Zettel.* Edited by G. E. M. Anscombe and G. H. von Wright. Translated by G. E. M. Anscombe. Berkeley: Univ. of California Press, 1970.

Wordsworth, William. *Poetical Works.* Edited by Thomas Hutchinson and E. D. Selincourt. Oxford: Oxford Univ. Press, 1969.

————. *Poetical Works.* 5 vols. Edited by E. D. Selincourt and Helen Darbyshire. Oxford: Oxford University Press, 1940–49.

————. *The Prelude: 1799, 1805, 1850.* Edited by Jonathan Wordsworth, M. H. Abrams, and Stephen Gill. London: Norton, 1979.

Yates, Frances. *Giordano Bruno and the Hermetic Tradition.* Chicago: Univ. of Chicago Press, 1964.

————. *The Occult Philosophy in the Elizabethan Age.* London: Routledge, 1979.

Yeats, W. B. *The Variorum Edition of the Poems of W. B. Yeats.* Edited by Peter Allt and Russell K. Alspach. New York: Macmillan, 1940.

Yousef, Nancy. *Isolated Cases: The Anxieties of Autonomy in Enlightenment Philosophy and Romantic Literature.* Ithaca, N.Y.: Cornell Univ. Press, 2004.

Index

Ackroyd, Peter, 23

Agency: restoration of, 22, 158; resignation of, 92, 99–100; transcendental, 98–99; loss of, 102–107, 143; in self-annihilation, 150–151. *See also* Empiricism, Lockean: as promoting passivity

Ahania, 64, 93, 106–107, 130

Albion: and Selfhood, 63, 126; in *Vala*, 93–94; in *The Four Zoas*, 94–95; and self-annihilation, 150–151, 156; as focus of *Jerusalem*, 158; and death, 165–166

Altizer, Thomas, 56

Ammons, A. R., 86, 146

Ashbery, John, 86, 102

Atomism, sensory, 8, 25

Augustine, Saint, 3, 17, 18, 96

Averroës, 19

Barresi, John. *See* Martin, Raymond

Behmenism, 55, 56

Belsey, Catherine, 6

Blake, William: agreement with Averroës, 19; and care of the self, 23–26; agreement with Kant, 98

—antagonism to nuclear family, 171; concept of soul, 19–20; on egoism, 20–21, 50, 149–151; concept of transcendence, 20–22; concept of afterlife, 21, 145, 150, 156; on dualism, 22, 34–38; as dualist, 22, 38; on Stoicism, 23, 51; as atheist, 26, 59; on temporality, 29–30, 52; on women's oppression, 40–41; as Moravian, 55; on innate ideas, 83–84, 168; pathos in, 87–89; as Platonic idealist, 99; on necessity, 106–107; on art, 118–119, 138–145; as character in *Milton*, 134, 146–147, 174; on sexual difference, 160–164

—and Christianity, orthodox: on theology, 15, 30, 56, 68; and Western history, 39; on concept of soul, 56; redefinition of "resurrection," 95; redefinition of "sin," 105

—and Christianity, radical, 55–56

—and empiricism: critique of empiricist psychology, 12–14, 29–30; on empiricist concept of human nature, 27–28; on empiricist epistemology, 29, 34–36; on empiricist concept of

Blake, William *(continued)*
  nature, 29–30, 39–43; on empiricism
    and the senses, 34–36, 46; on passiv-
    ity of the mind in Locke, 44–46, 52;
    on empiricism and memory, 48,
    167–169; on Locke's view of per-
    sonal identity, 48, 168–169
—and Gnosticism, 54–56; and transcen-
    dental intuition, 15, 17; and divinity
    of soul, 19, 20, 54; on Gnostic dual-
    ism, 38; on Gnostic Demiurge, 54,
    56–57, 100; acquaintance with
    Gnosticism, 54, 180; rejects Gnostic
    mythology, 55, 56–57; self-
    identification as Gnostic, 56; rejects
    Gnostic God, 57; rejects equation
    of knowledge with salvation, 114;
    and Gnostic "sleep," 127; on Gnos-
    tic accreted soul, 132–134
—and Neoplatonism: and transcenden-
    tal intuition, 15, 17; and divinity
    of soul, 19, 20; corrects Plotinus's
    definition of soul, 20, 125–127,
    150; scholarship on Blake's Neopla-
    tonism, 55; and Plotinus on individ-
    uation, 57–60; and Plotinus on
    impersonal soul, 85, 120
—self-reproach, 134; skepticism, 153–154
—Self-revision: reworks *Urizen* in *The
    Four Zoas,* 91–93, 96–97, 108–109;
    newly characterizes Urizen, 92;
    newly characterizes Enitharmon,
    93; newly allegorizes descent of
    human beings, 111; adds sorrow of
    reason, 113; radicalizes view of Self-
    hood, 133–134, 136–138, 143; newly
    characterizes Orc, 142–143; rede-
    fines "self-annihilation," 150, 156;
    introduces willed solitude in
    Jerusalem, 155–157, 164–165; shifts
    from Zoas to Albion, 158; revises
    definition of memory, 167–168; re-
    vises ethics in *Jerusalem,* 175–177

—and Wordsworth: similarity, 17; sym-
    pathy for, 66; on the Intimations
    Ode, 67, 82–84; on Wordsworth
    and empiricism, 67–69; on
    Wordsworth and Nature, 82–83;
    difference on exile of the soul,
    84–86; difference on childhood, 98;
    critique of memory in Words-
    worth, 170
—Works: *The Four Zoas,* 12–13, 34, 41, 61,
    68–69, 87, 90–124, 126, 128, 134–135,
    138, 141, 152, 154, 171; *Milton,* 19, 22,
    39, 50, 61, 62, 69, 87, 128–154, 175;
    Annotations to Lavater's *Aphorisms
    on Man,* 21; *Songs of Innocence and
    Experience,* 22, 31, 41, 90, 92, 98; *The
    Marriage of Heaven and Hell,* 22, 32,
    35, 36–38, 145; *The Book of Thel,* 27,
    28, 30–36, 46, 90, 91; *Tiriel,* 27–28,
    39; "An Island in the Moon," 28;
    Visions of the Daughters of Albion,
    28, 46–51, 90; "There is No Natural
    Religion b," 29, 169; *Jerusalem,* 34,
    51, 59, 69, 87, 126, 135, 150, 155–177;
    "London," 37; "The Angel," 37, 104;
    "To Tirzah," 37–38, 39, 142; Annota-
    tions to *The Works of Sir Joshua
    Reynolds,* 38, 168; *America a Prophecy,*
    39, 42, 90; *Europe a Prophecy,* 39–42,
    90, 91; *The Book of Urizen,* 46, 50,
    52–63, 90–92, 96–97, 136; *The
    Book of Los,* 63–65; *The Book of
    Ahania,* 63–65, 130; Annotations to
    Wordsworth's *Poems* (1815), 68;
    Annotations to Wordsworth's
    Preface to *The Excursion,* 68; "The
    Smile," 87–89; *Vala,* 93–94; "To
    the God who is the Accuser of this
    World," 145–146; letters, 157, 176;
    Annotations to Thornton's *The
    Lord's Prayer, Newly Translated,* 181
Bloom, Harold, 153, 172
Butts, Thomas, 157

Caruth, Cathy, 180

Cary, Philip, 181

Castle, Terry, 78

Catharism, 55

Chastity, cult of, 40–41, 50, 148

Christianity: and sacrificial religion, 30, 162; concept of afterlife, 49, 61–62; and egoism, 61–62. *See also* Blake, William: and Christianity, orthodox

Clark, Steve, 179

Coleridge, Samuel Taylor, 7, 9, 89

Consciousness, isolation of: in Romanticism, 9–10; Blake's understanding of, 11–12; and materialism, 30–36; and identity, 52–54; and empiricism, 69, 81; in Wordsworth, 79; cure for, 125; and memory, 170. *See also* Loneliness

Curran, Stuart, 57, 156

Damon, S. Foster, 141

Damrosch, Leopold, 38, 82, 170

Davies, Keri, 180

Deism ("Natural Religion"): and Selfhood, 20; materialist ontology of, 29, 164; god of, 49, 57; and reason, 51; religion of, 59

Derrida, Jacques, 6

Descartes, 3, 9, 13; "Cartesian moment," 23, 25

Dualism: soul-body, 9, 11, 15; Blake and, 22, 34–38; empiricist, 34–37; vs. mind-body, 37; Christian, 37–38; Gnostic, 38

Empiricism, Lockean: on introspection, 5; and identity, 12–14; as promoting passivity, 12–14, 35–36, 41–43; materialist ontology, 28–30; and linear temporality, 29, 43; on the senses, 34–36; as promoting self-alienation, 35–36, 47–51, 77–78; as promoting self-division, 43–46, 78–79; and memory, 48, 78,

168–169; and soul, 60. *See also* Blake, William: and empiricism; Locke, John

Enion: as prophet, 92–93; in *The Four Zoas,* 101–107; and Urizen, 108; as desperate hope, 123; lost splendor of soul, 126

Enitharmon: in *Europe,* 39–43; change of character in *The Four Zoas,* 93; redemption in *The Four Zoas,* 118–124

Epictetus, 24

Eternal Death: and egoism, 21, 30, 61; fear of, 34, 118, 139; and loneliness, 165–166. *See also* Mortalism

Eternal Now, 21, 85–86, 125, 169–170

Evans, Frank B., 180

Fatalism, 41–42, 100–101, 113

Foucault, Michel, 6; care of the self, 23–26, 181

Freud, Sigmund, 3, 17, 26, 53, 79, 96. *See also* Psychoanalysis

Frosch, Thomas, 89, 180

Frye, Northrop, 29, 41, 43, 91, 148, 154, 170

Fuller, David, 181

Gnosticism: concept of soul, 3; Mandaean hymn, 16; exile of the soul, 16, 18, 26, 67–68; and intuition of transcendence, 17; and care of the self, 25; Sophia, 30, 46; "sleep," 32, 94; dualism, 38; and individuation, 53, 58; Blake's use of, 54–60; on accreted soul, 131–132; on Creator God, 145. *See also* Blake, William: and Gnosticism

God, Christian, 30, 56, 127, 145

God, of *Genesis,* 30, 31, 49, 57, 137, 145

Goslee, Nancy Moore, 107

Grob, Alan, 70–73

Hall, Mary, 27, 28, 179

Harper, George Mills, 55

Hartley, David, 5
Hartman, Geoffrey, 66–67
Hayes, Tom, 162, 180
Hegel, G. W. F., 11, 28
Heidegger, Martin, 17–18, 25
Homer, *Odyssey*, 4, 7
Hume, David, 5, 11, 74, 158, 180

Iamblichus, 132
Identity: and empiricism, 12–13; and tyranny, 50; destructiveness of, 53–54, 60–63; and egoism, 62–63; Blake's redefinition of, 136, 146; and memory, 168–170
Individuation, 53–45, 58–61
Isidorus, 132

James, William, 5–7, 26
Jesus, 31, 175–176
John, Donald, 125
Johnson, Samuel, 61, 181
Jonas, Hans: concept of "existential alienation," 16, 68; on Heidegger, 18–19; contrasts soul in Gnosticism and Plotinus, 58; on Gnostic awakening, 60, 123; on Gnostic accreted soul, 131–132; and contemporary scholarship, 179

Kant, Immanuel: faculty psychology, 3; on the sublime, 42, 98–99; and Wordsworth, 68, 70
Kierkegaard, Soren, 26
King, Karen L., 179
Klein, Melanie: on "inner chaos," 3, 97, 170; on self-division, 75; on loneliness, 79–80; and Hume, 180
Krell, David Farrell, 17–18

Lacan, Jacques, 2–3, 6, 17, 18, 79
Lateran Council, 19

Lincoln, Andrew, 180
Locke, John: and isolation of consciousness, 26; "dark room," 26, 35, 85, 181; Blake's paranomasia, 28; on personal identity, 43, 48, 60, 77–78, 168–169; on mental operations, 44–46; Wordsworth and metaphors of mental life, 66–80; on innate ideas, 81, 83–84, 168. *See also* Blake, William: and empiricism; Empiricism, Lockean
Loneliness: of Blake 28, 157, 172; of Thel, 34; of Theotormon and Bromion, 47; of empiricist subject, 49, 157; of Urizen, 52–54; of the soul, 54; as a consequence of individuation, 58–59, 62; contrast of Lockean and Platonic, 60; Blake and Wordsworth on sources of, 67–68; Wordsworth and Klein on, 79–80; Blake and Wordsworth differ on, 84–85; of human beings, 92, 108–110; art as therapy for, 142; of Los, 156, 172; and sexual difference, 163; of death, 166; of the prophet, 172–173. *See also* Consciousness, isolation of
Los, 39, 41; fall of, 63–64; in *The Four Zoas*, 94, 105, 118–124; as compromised prophet, 135, 140; and art, 139; at the end of *Milton*, 153; lonely labor, 172; resistance to love, 173–175

Marcion, 38
Martin, Raymond, 179; and John Barresi, 1–2, 6, 10
Marx, Karl, 116
Materialism: Romantic reaction, 9–10; and empiricism, 29–30; and consciousness, 29–36, 53–54; and mortalism, 61; and sexual difference, 164
Memory: Blake's psychology of, 169–167; redemption of, 170–171. *See also* Empiricism, Lockean; Identity; Subjectivity, anxiety of

Milton, John: *Paradise Lost*, 64, 112, 141;
    Miltonic language, 101, 135; Blake's
    criticism of, 128; 141, 142–144
Moravian, 55
Mortalism, 61, 101. *See also* Eternal
    Death
Muggletonian, 55

Natural Man. *See* Subject, empiricist
Nature: Blake's ambivalence toward, 38;
    "Mother Nature," 39–43; Blake's cri-
    tique of Milton's Nature, 142–144;
    subject pines for Nature, 158–160.
    See also Empiricism, Lockean;
    Materialism
Neoplatonism: and care of the self, 25; and
    metaphor of the body as a prison-
    house, 26, 84; Blake as Neoplatonist,
    55; on sexual difference, 162. *See also*
    Blake, William: and Neoplatonism;
    Plotinus
Newton, 14, 39, 157; in phrase, "Bacon,
    Newton and Locke," 11, 65, 149, 170;
    Newtonian physics, 52, 59, 101
Noah, Blake's revision of *Genesis* story, 160
Nuttall, A. D., 85, 180, 181

Orc, 39, 41–42, 94, 142–143
Orphic, 15, 84, 132
Ostriker, Alicia, 180
Otto, Peter, 14, 165

Paley, Morton, 56, 158, 180
Pascal, 59
Paul, Saint, 38
Pelikan, Jaroslav, 38
Pestalozzi, Johann Heinrich, 172
Peterfreund, Stuart, 180
Plato: tripartite division of soul, 3, 26,
    51; immortality of the soul, 4;

self-division, 4; soul-body dualism,
    9, 15; exile of the soul, 15–16, 26;
    self-alienation, 17, 23, 175; care of
    the self, 23, 175; distraction of phe-
    nomenality, 84; love, 144; anagno-
    risis, 168
Plotinus: impersonal soul, 20; individua-
    tion, 57–59; against the Gnostics, 84;
    "inward turn," 125–127, 166, 176; and
    afterlife, 150
Porter, Roy, 179
Prophecy, 105; female prophets, 50, 105–107;
    compromised, 115, 118, 122, 134–135,
    143; and worldly ambition, 117; and
    orthodox religion, 121; and egoism
    (self-assertion), 149–151, 156, 174; and
    loneliness, 172; and will to solitude,
    173–175
Psychoanalysis: and care of the self, 25; and
    loneliness, 75, 79–80; and Romanti-
    cism, 78–79, 86. *See also* Freud, Sig-
    mund; Klein, Melanie
Psychology, scientific, 5–9
Psychotopography, 24–25; Blake's, 25,
    135–138
Pythagorean, 16, 23, 84, 132

Raine, Kathleen, 55–56
Reason, 37, 51–52, 62–64, 92, 99, 113–114, 169
Reed, E. S., 5–8
Riede, David, 157, 180
Robinson, Henry Crabb, 56, 82, 127
Rousseau, Jean-Jacques, 11, 20, 22

Satan: "religion of," 14; and Christianity,
    61, 145, 147; Moment he cannot find,
    87; as Selfhood, 129, 143, 146; his inte-
    rior world, 135–138
Saussure, Ferdinand de, 6
Self, integral, 1–2, 7; as obsolete concept,
    1–2, 6–8; self-doubt of, 2–3; intuition

Self, integral *(continued)*
   of, 2–8, 11; and memory, 170. *See also*
   Subjectivity, experience of
Self-division: and intuition of self, 2–3,
   4; models of, 3, 24–25; as self-
   fragmentation, 3–4, 43; and catachre-
   sis, 26; Blake's models of, 26, 121, 126,
   135–138; and will to solitude, 158. *See
   also* Psychotopography
Self-estrangement or alienation: in
   Wordsworth, 16, 74–81; and existen-
   tial alienation, 17–18; and empiricism,
   28, 47–51; and Selfhood, 52; and indi-
   viduation, 53–54; in Augustine, 96; in
   The Four Zoas, 96, 102–105. *See also*
   Subjectivity, anxiety of
Selfhood: definition of, 19–20, 62–63; and
   self-reformation, 85–87, 125–128, 147;
   and passivation, 92; as "false Body,"
   126; and masculinity, 129, 148; com-
   parison with Gnostic accreted soul,
   132–134; inner topography, 136; and
   Milton, 145; and will to solitude,
   160–161; and sexual difference,
   160–164. *See also* Satan; Urizen
Self-reformation: Blake's concept of, 22–23,
   125–128; in care of the self, 23–25; obsta-
   cles to self-reformation, 127–128; inner
   life as obstacle to self-reformation,
   127–135; willed, 151–153; vs. love, 174–177
Shelley, Percy: "Mont Blanc," 9; Works:
   Adonais, 10; *Alastor*, 10; "A Defense of
   Poetry," 119; *Prometheus Unbound*, 139
Siegel, Jerrold, 1
Sorenson, Peter, 180
Soul: as an obsolete concept, 1, 8; immor-
   tality of, 4, 19; and materialism, 8–9;
   exile of, 15–16, 18, 26, 67–68; apostasy
   of, 57–59. *See also* Gnosticism; Neopla-
   tonism; Plato; Plotinus
Spector, Sheila, 31–32
Stevens, Wallace, 39, 83, 86, 114
Stevenson, Robert Louis, 8–9

Stoicism, 23, 26, 51
Subject, empiricist: and identity, 12–14;
   despair of, 27–29, 34–36, 51, 139;
   Oothoon's repudiation of, 46–47;
   relation to nature, 52, 158–159; selfish-
   ness of, 105; pining for nature,
   144–145; alienation of, 156–157; and
   memory, 169
Subjectivity, anxiety of: Blake and, 11–14; in
   Theotormon, 47–81; in *The Four Zoas*,
   92, 95–105; and memory, 170. *See also*
   Self-estrangement or alienation
Subjectivity, experience of, 1–3; and self-
   division, 2–8, 11
Summerfield, Henry, 180
Swedenborg, Emmanuel, 56

Taylor, Charles, 1
Taylor, Thomas, 57–59
Temporality, linear ("clock time"): dread
   of, 21, 29–30, 52, 160; and nature, 43;
   and memory, 170
Tharmas; and identity, 12–13, 60, 63; and
   passivity, 51, 94–101; new in *The Four
   Zoas*, 92; contrast with Urizen, 100;
   comparison with "spectrous dead," 111
Thel: in *The Book of Thel*, 30–36; and fear of
   nature, 40, 42, 83; and isolation of con-
   sciousness, 46, and land of death, 135
Thomas, Keith, 180
Thompson, E. P., 55–56, 180
Transcendence: intuition of, 10–17, 41,
   86–87, 93, 102–107; recovery of, 118–124
Transcendental remorse: defined, 93; in
   Enitharmon, 122–124; and nature, 159
Tucker, Herbert, 181
Tuveson, Ernest, 78

Urizen: sleep of, 29; first named, 49; and
   tyranny, 50; and Selfhood, 51; and in-
   dividuation, 52–59; compared with

Gnostic Demiurge, 54, 56–57; identification with Reason, 63; possible redemption of, 64–65; change of character, 92; religion, 108, 114–115; remorse, 109, 112–114; as internal obstacle, 129–130; as Satan, 137; compared with Albion, 167; and Dante's Satan, 169; and memory, 169

Williams, Michael A., 179
Wittgenstein, Ludwig, 167
Wordsworth, William: on loneliness, 67–68; and Kant, 68, 70, 82; and empiricism, 70–79; and Locke's metaphors of mental life, 71–73; and Lockean "impressions," 73–77; and self-division, 76–80; and self-estrangement, 76–80, 81; and Locke on personal identity, 77–78; and isolation of consciousness, 79, 81; Gnosticism and Neoplatonism in, 82–84; legacy, 86; and Enion, 102; and memory, 170
—Works: the Intimations Ode, 10, 16, 67, 68, 70, 82–84, 122; The Prelude, 66–80; Tintern Abbey, 68, 70, 72, 79, 81 83; "Expostulation and Reply," 69; 1799 Prelude, 71; fragments, 73, 75–76; "Elegiac Stanzas," 98

Yates, Frances, 55
Yeats, W. B., 161
Yousef, Nancy, 34–35